Centre for Educational Research and Innovation (CERI)

Ministry of Education, Ontario
Information Centre, 13th Floor,
Mowat Block, Queen's Park,
Toronto, Ont.   M7A 1L2

IMMIGRANTS' CHILDREN AT SCHOOL

ORGANISATION FOR ECONOMIC CO-OPERATION AND DEVELOPMENT

Pursuant to article 1 of the Convention signed in Paris on 14th December, 1960, and which came into force on 30th September, 1961, the Organisation for Economic Co-operation and Development (OECD) shall promote policies designed:

- to achieve the highest sustainable economic growth and employment and a rising standard of living in Member countries, while maintaining financial stability, and thus to contribute to the development of the world economy;
- to contribute to sound economic expansion in Member as well as non-member countries in the process of economic development; and
- to contribute to the expansion of world trade on a multilateral, non-discriminatory basis in accordance with international obligations.

The original Member countries of the OECD are Austria, Belgium, Canada, Denmark, France, the Federal Republic of Germany, Greece, Iceland, Ireland, Italy, Luxembourg, the Netherlands, Norway, Portugal, Spain, Sweden, Switzerland, Turkey, the United Kingdom and the United States. The following countries became Members subsequently through accession at the dates indicated hereafter: Japan (28th April, 1964), Finland (28th January, 1969), Australia (7th June, 1971) and New Zealand (29th May, 1973).

The Socialist Federal Republic of Yugoslavia takes part in some of the work of the OECD (agreement of 28th October, 1961).

The Centre for Educational Research and Innovation was created in June 1968 by the Council of the Organisation for Economic Co-operation and Development for an initial period of three years, with the help of grants from the Ford Foundation and the Royal Dutch Shell Group of Companies. In May 1971, the Council decided that the Centre should continue its work for a period of five years as from 1st January, 1972. In July 1976, and in July 1981, it extended this mandate for further five year periods, 1977-1981 and 1982-86.

The main objectives of the Centre are as follows:

- *to promote and support the development of research activities in education and undertake such research activities where appropriate;*
- *to promote and support pilot experiments with a view to introducing and testing innovations in the educational system;*
- *to promote the development of co-operation between Member countries in the field of educational research and innovation.*

The Centre functions within the Organisation for Economic Co-operation and Development in accordance with the decisions of the Council of the Organisation, under the authority of the Secretary-General. It is supervised by a Governing Board composed of one national expert in its field of competence from each of the countries participating in its programme of work.

Publié en français sous le titre :

LES ENFANTS
DE MIGRANTS A L'ÉCOLE

© OECD, 1987
Application for permission to reproduce or translate
all or part of this publication should be made to:
Head of Publications Service, OECD
2, rue André-Pascal, 75775 PARIS CEDEX 16, France.

It is over ten years now since a number of OECD Member countries started to introduce special measures and programmes designed to improve the education of immigrants' children. Recently, however, immigration flows have come to acquire different characteristics and this is posing serious problems for the host countries. The purpose of this publication is to consider how policies for the education of immigrants' children have been working and whether today there is a case for some new directions and emphases.

To evaluate educational programmes for the children of immigrants has been the raison d'être of the CERI project "Education and Cultural and Linguistic Pluralism" launched in 1982, which, in response to the desire of participating Member countries, has collected objective data with a view to providing a firmer knowledge base for informing policy decisions.

The first three parts of this study arising from the project deal exclusively with data submitted by the National Statistics Offices of seven European countries which are among the main recipients of immigrants -- Belgium, France, Germany, Luxembourg, the Netherlands, Sweden, Switzerland -- and of two non-European countries, Australia and Canada. These data cover a ten-year span and are subjected to comparative analysis. Thus, this constitutes the first comprehensive assessment of the outcomes of policies for improving the education of immigrants' children over a significant period of time. Parts Four and Five of the study analyse quantitative evidence, weighting socio-economic background against cultural factors. The analysis draws upon certain indicators yielded by special enquiries little known in the international field.

No doubt we could benefit from still more detailed knowledge of the processes involved and in the outcomes of educating the children of immigrants. Meanwhile, the statistical evidence produced by this four-year study clearly shows that such children are disadvantaged under the present arrangements.

The study has been conducted throughout by Norberto Bottani, Head of the CERI Project on Education and Cultural and Linguistic Pluralism, Daniel Blot, of the OECD Education Division, Catherine Duchêne, Statistical Assistant in CERI, and Sophia Mappa, Research Assistant. On the organisational side, the Project owes much to André Lebon, the Secretariat consultant, who is also the author of the French case study, the chapter on family characteristics and educational careers of schoolchildren in France, and the overview of their social and cultural handicaps.

This volume is published on the responsibility of the Secretary-General of the OECD.

J.R. Gass
Director of the Centre for Educational
Research and Innovation

Also available

THE FUTURE OF MIGRATION (May 1987)
(81 87 01 1) ISBN 92-64-12949-9 320 pages
£10.00   US$20.00   F100.00   DM44.00

EDUCATION AND TRAINING AFTER BASIC SCHOOLING (August 1985)
(91 85 03 1) ISBN 92-64-12742-9 132 pages
£8.00   US$16.00   F80.00   DM35.00

EDUCATION IN MODERN SOCIETY (July 1985)
(91 85 02 1) ISBN 92-64-12739-9 108 pages
£7.00   US$14.00   F70.00   DM31.00

MIGRANTS' CHILDREN AND EMPLOYMENT. The European Experience (May 1983)
(81 83 02 1) ISBN 92-64-12434-9 64 pages
£4.00   US$8.00   F40.00   DM16.00

Forthcoming

MULTICULTURAL EDUCATION

Prices charged at the OECD Bookshop.

THE OECD CATALOGUE OF PUBLICATIONS and supplements will be sent free of charge on request addressed either to OECD Publications Service, Sales and Distribution Division, 2, rue André-Pascal, 75775 PARIS CEDEX 16, or to the OECD Sales Agent in your country.

TABLE OF CONTENTS

Part One

FOREIGN CHILDREN IN SCHOOLS: THE ANALYSIS

I.	Introduction	8
II.	Background to the study	10
III.	What the figures reveal	12
IV.	Salient features of foreign enrolment	21
V.	Conclusions and implications	31

Part Two

COUNTRY ANALYSES

ENROLMENT OF FOREIGN CHILDREN IN SEVEN COUNTRIES:

I.	Belgium	40
II.	France	56
III.	Germany	74
IV.	Luxembourg	87
V.	The Netherlands	100
VI.	Sweden	113
VII.	Switzerland	132

Part Three

OTHER CONTINENTS, OTHER PROBLEMS

I.	Overseas-born children and children of immigrant descent in Australian schools	154
II.	Canada's growing cultural diversity: Some preliminary observations	167

Part Four

FACTORS OF INEQUALITY: A CAUSAL ANALYSIS

I. Social and cultural inequalities: An overview.......	178
II. Comparison of family characteristics and educational careers of schoolchildren from indigenous populations in France.............................	186
III. Passport or social position? Some facts and figures on the success and educational careers of Swiss and foreign children in the light of their families' social class......................	220
IV. West Indian and Asian children in England and Wales..	249

Part Five

EDUCATIONAL STRUCTURES FOR IMMIGRANTS' CHILDREN

I. Background..	260
II. Change but continuity: The European model..........	262
III. Outside Europe: Similarities and differences........	278
IV. Conclusion..	283

Annexes

1. Graphs on comparative development of nationals and foreigners in schooling.........................	287
2. General data on foreign populations.................	295
3. Analysis of the data derived from the three samples of pupils used in the foregoing study in France..	300

Part One

FOREIGN CHILDREN IN SCHOOLS:

THE ANALYSIS

I. INTRODUCTION

The extension of migratory movements over the past three decades has been a process fraught with social problems in most OECD countries. Changes in migratory flows and the gradual slowdown of labour migration, which has in many instances been replaced by family migration encouraged by family reunification policies, has generated new social problems difficult to overcome. And now the whole picture is changing because of structural transformations in production and marketing systems, so that the arrangements that had gradually been set up to receive and integrate the immigrant population are wrong footed.

Schools, in common with other social institutions, have been unable to escape the consequences of these events, and the arrival of pupils from different cultures, speaking different languages and often practising different religions, has faced all education systems with the difficulties of integrating them.

The purpose of the CERI study was neither to set down the history of the installation of special arrangements for immigrants' children in schools (though such a history still remains to be written), nor to describe or compare the initiatives taken and the innovations introduced in order to facilitate these children's schooling. The aim was rather to assess, as objectively as possible, the results obtained. Using empirical data provided from official statistical services only, an attempt was made to evaluate the educational situation of immigrants' children and, by so doing, to provide an objective basis for interpretation of the measures applied and for analysis of future trends.

So, after assessing the school performance of immigrants' children as revealed by educational statistical yearbooks (which in fact meant looking at all foreign children in schools, since the statistics used make no distinction between foreign pupils as a whole and those whose parents are immigrants), a closer look was taken at the correlations between educational achievement, nationality, socio-economic and socio-cultural variables. The results of this work are presented in Part Four.

Parts One and Two are concerned most largely with the European scene, comprising seven country studies analysing the educational situation of foreign children in Belgium, France, Germany, Luxembourg, the Netherlands, Sweden and Switzerland). Additionally, however, it has been possible to add a (much shorter) part dealing with two non-European countries (Australia and Canada). Although the surveys there could not be conducted in such depth as was the case in Europe (the same statistics not being available) the two studies nevertheless throw light in an interesting manner on the problems faced by schools in a context where migratory flows have often been on a much larger scale than in Europe.

Findings for Europe show, first, that the proportion of foreigners is higher in the lowest age groups (0-14) than in the population as a whole. The proportion of young foreigners is higher among children in the 0-4 age group than among older children, except in Germany and Switzerland; presumably, therefore, in the absence of unforeseen factors, the proportion of foreign children attending pre-primary and primary schools will continue to increase over the next ten years. Neither must it be forgotten that this age structure is also determined by the number of births in the foreign population, which account for a significant proportion of the total number of births in most of the countries reviewed. Although it is falling, the fertility rate among foreigners is still higher than among nationals, so that there is now a "second generation". In the mid-80s over 2 1/2 million foreign pupils in all were attending schools in the seven countries reviewed.

Broadly speaking, the school career of the vast majority of young immigrants is difficult and, compared with that of nationals, rarely follows a normal course. Looking at this in greater detail, it can be seen that:

-- Immigrants' children are over-represented in special education (on average, 6 per cent of foreign pupils against 2.8 per cent of nationals in special primary education in four comparable countries);

-- In relative terms, there are more young foreigners than nationals in short streams or in the less difficult cycles of secondary education. A high percentage of foreign pupils fails to acquire a solid general school grounding;

-- Differences in educational performance by nationals and foreigners are not so great where the foreign children's families have been resident in the host country for a long time.

After considering these findings, the CERI Governing Board asked for a further study to discover the reasons behind them. The Secretariat was asked, in particular, to check whether underachievement by foreign children was due, above all, to the fact that most of them belonged to disadvantaged social classes or to other factors such as nationality or culture of origin. These questions are examined in Part IV of the study, "Factors of inequality: A causal analysis", which looks at data from three sources that lent themselves to interpretation and analysis of the mechanisms of underachievement, comparing the school careers of foreign pupils with those of nationals:

-- Three French surveys that had covered about 78 200 French and foreign pupils attending primary and secondary schools (Chapter II);

-- A survey that had covered the 55 700 children in public and private-sector schools in the Canton of Geneva (about 20 000 of whom were foreign) (Chapter III);

-- The Swann Report on the reasons for underachievement or achievement by children from ethnic minorities, published in 1985 by the United Kingdom Government (Chapter IV).

The conclusions of these surveys correspond and can be summed up as follows:

-- Social background is a major explanatory factor in underachievement;

-- Children who belong to a disadvantaged social class, whether they are foreigners or not, whether they belong to an ethnic minority group or to the majority, tend to be low achievers or failures at school and obtain results that are on average lower than those of children belonging to the middle or upper classes;

-- Social background is a more determinant factor in underachievement than nationality;

-- Being of foreign origin or belonging to an ethnic minority group are factors that can accentuate educational inequality, although it is still difficult at this stage to assess exactly the effect of these factors on underachievement.

It must also be remembered that the performance patterns of pupils belonging to ethnic minority or migrant groups are not all the same; average achievement by different nationalities or different ethnic groups varies widely.

The analytical section is rounded off by a description of the steps taken to help immigrants' children achieve better results at school (Part Five).

In order to give a sufficiently detailed picture of the questions analysed, it was necessary to sift through a mass of statistical information and draw up a number of tables which may deter some readers. Those who have little time or are put off by figures can, however, refer to the summaries at the beginning of each of the two constituent parts of the report for a quick rundown of its main points.

Similarly, to keep the report down to manageable size, two explanatory notes have been omitted, one on the methodology used in compiling factor analysis of correspondence diagrams, the other on the significance of the differences in French and foreign school children's levels of achievement, giving details of the data drawn from the French surveys used in Annex 3.

II. BACKGROUND TO THE STUDY

Although each country has its own way of organising its school system, the arrangements for the education of foreign children and their school careers have enough in common for it to be possible to attempt to summarise and compare the information derived from the case studies carried out.

Before reaching this stage, however, a lengthy process had to be completed, involving seven countries with a significant proportion of foreigners in their schools: Germany (7.5 per cent), Belgium (9 per cent), France (6.8 per cent), Luxembourg (26 per cent), the Netherlands (4 per cent), Switzerland (14.5 per cent) and Sweden (5 per cent) (1). This process involved:

-- Compiling statistical series for total and foreign enrolment in the various levels, types and stages of education over a period long enough to show up any trends that may have emerged, and

-- Comparing the position of foreign school-children with that of the total school population comprising both nationals and foreigners.

Subsequently, the requirements of more detailed analysis led to the category "foreigners" (a handy term covering a multitude of individual situations) being broken down so as to reveal the enrolment pattern for each of the main nationalities.

Thorough as this analysis was, it does suffer from a number of limitations due to the quality of the statistical material available, and certain of these need to be pointed out before going any further:

-- Using the criterion of "nationality" (the only one available) to identify foreign children means leaving out of account a quite substantial number of children who, although of foreign origin, have acquired the nationality of the host country either, for example, as the result of a change in the laws regarding the hereditary right of citizenship or as a result of their parents' acquiring the said nationality;

-- It has not always been possible to eradicate completely the effects of the "age" variable, which exercises a decisive influence on the breakdown by level of education, firstly, between nationals and foreigners and secondly, amongst foreign children, between those who form part of the long-established, traditional migratory flows and those who are more recent arrivals;

-- Lastly, the statistics (compiled at national level) which were analysed do not provide any information on the socio-economic category of the parents, whether they be nationals or foreigners; yet it is certain that a number of characteristics stem both from the type of social background from which the children come, and from whether they have or do not have nationality of the host country.

This report, which is essentially statistical in nature, does not attempt to seek the causes of the situations it describes. Its intention is quite different: to go beyond the merely descriptive level to which most previous studies in this field have restricted themselves in order to emphasize and to measure, with supporting figures, the disparities which are emerging, and tending to persist, between the school careers of children from immigrant backgrounds and those of their native-born counterparts. It marks the first stage in a project that needs to be continued in a number of directions:

-- A study of the position of foreign children (or, whenever possible, those belonging to ethnic or linguistic minorities) within the education system of other host countries, both European and non-European, using the same analytical framework so as to highlight similarities and differences;

-- Investigation on a more detailed level than a nationwide survey, using a number of monographs on towns or small geographical areas in order, particularly, to analyse the effects of geographic concentration;

-- Monitoring of pupils (native-born and foreign) by age group in order to gain a clearer idea of various data on which the general statistics provide no information: the average age of the children at a given level, repeat rates, an increased tendency to fall behind as pupils move up the grades, and so on; and possibly,

-- A comparison of the school careers of children returning to schools in their countries of origin after the return of their parents, with those of native-born children of the same age who have never emigrated.

As it stands, this summary, based on data extracted from the seven accompanying reports, is designed to create awareness of and stimulate discussion on:

-- The growing numbers (in absolute and relative terms) of foreigners in schools in several host countries;

-- Some of the problems encountered by certain immigrant children during their school careers;

-- The relationship between their school career profiles (in terms of the type of education received and the number of years spent in school) and the process of access and entry to the labour market.

At this stage in the research, this summary has certainly not attained its final form. There is a need for broadening the field of investigation, and for a better understanding of the inter-relation of different variables (e.g., how long the family has been established in the country of residence, or the economic and social status of the parents) with the type of education in which the majority are enrolled. Nonetheless, it is probably already sufficiently well documented for it to be possible to draw some conclusions from the more important facts highlighted.

III. WHAT THE FIGURES REVEAL

The figures for the six countries -- with the addition, whenever possible, of Sweden -- show trends in foreign enrolment in three levels of education (whatever terms may be used to describe these): pre-school, primary and first and second-cycle secondary. However, higher education -- where the children of migrants still constitute only a minority of the foreigners enrolled -- is not dealt with.

Discussion of these figures will be preceded by a brief introductory overview, presenting various more general demographic and economic data related to various aspects of foreign enrolment in the educational system of the countries studied.

Introductory Overview

Although a detailed exposition of the structural features of the immigrant populations (total and labour force) resident in each of the host countries considered has no place in this study, it may nonetheless be of value to summarise some characteristic features in order to throw light on the subject treated. We shall single out three of these.

Firstly, the proportion of foreigners appears always to be higher in the lower age group (in this case 0-14 years) than in the total population combining all ages (Table 1).

Table 1

Proportion of Foreigners by Age Groups
(as percentages)

Country	All Ages	0-14	0-4	5-9	10-14
Belgium	8.9	14.2	15.8	14.4	12.3
France	6.8	8.4	9.0	8.9	7.6
Germany (1)	7.5	10.1	11.5	12.5	7.8
Luxembourg	26.3	37.3	40.3	40.6	32.0
Netherlands	3.8	5.9	7.7	6.1	4.4
Sweden	4.9	6.5	6.8	6.5	6.1
Switzerland	15.5	16.2	15.9	17.4	15.5

(Detail of 0-14 years age group shown in columns 0-4, 5-9, 10-14)

1. Under 6 years old (and not 0-4 years old); 6 to under 10 years old (and not 5-9 years old); 10 to under 15 years old (and not 10-14 years old).

Source: Annex 2.

The difference between the two rates, less than one percentage point in Switzerland (16.2-15.5), ranges from 1.5 to 2.5 per cent in Sweden, France, the Netherlands and Germany, attains 5 per cent and more in Belgium and as much as 11 per cent in Luxembourg.

A breakdown of the 0-14 age group into three sub-groups confirms that there are only a few exceptions to this general rule (e.g. Germany and Switzerland, where the proportion of young foreigners is relatively higher among children in the 5-9 age group than among those aged from 0-4).

Consequently, assuming the same rate of school attendance, this more favourable age structure should have its counterpart in higher enrolment in nursery schools and primary education.

Table 2

Proportion of Foreign Births
(as percentages)

Year	Belgium	France (2)	Germany	Luxembourg	Netherlands	Sweden	Switzerland
1975	14.5 (1)	9.5	16.0	41.5	4.6	8.5	29.5
1978	15.2	10.1	13.0	38.7	6.3	9.3	19.1
1982	15.4	10.8	11.8	38.8	7.7	6.2	16.6

1. 1976 and not 1975.

2. Births where both parents are foreigners.

Source: Country analyses.

A factor which, along with family reunification, contributes to this situation, is that foreign births (or, in France, of births to parents both of whom are foreigners) constitute a significant and/or increasing proportion of the total number of births recorded in most of the seven countries under review (Table 2).

A closer study, for which the reader is referred to the country analyses, shows that the drops in numbers noted in three countries are, in part, "artificial". They are in fact the result either of a change in the laws regarding transmission of nationality in Germany (1975) and Switzerland (1978), or of a liberal policy on the naturalisation of adults (in Sweden), the consequence being that a proportion of the births previously recorded as foreign are now included in the national birth rate.

Lastly, the distribution by main economic sectors of the immigrant labour force, that is, of the parents of pupils whose schooling we are to go on to study, differs from that of the total labour force (nationals + foreigners). The foreign labour force continues to be concentrated in the primary and secondary sectors, and particularly in the latter (see Table 3). This breakdown by sector of activity permits an indirect study of distribution by socio-economic category, known to affect the school careers of all children, of whatever nationality.

A few examples of school populations of various ages (Tables 4, 5, 6 and 7), at different academic levels, and comprising all pupils (nationals and foreigners), will illustrate the inequalities between socio-economic groups in the sphere of education (2).

Table 3

Breakdown of the Foreign Labour Force by Sector of Activity
(as percentages)

Economic Sector	Belgium (1977) Total	Foreign	France (1982) Total	Foreign	Germany (1982) Total	Foreign	Luxembourg (1981) Total	Foreign	Netherlands (1981) Total	Foreign	Sweden (1980) Total	Foreign	Switzerland (1981) Total	Foreign
Primary and secondary sectors	39.3	48.8	42.4	60.4	51.0	69.2	36.4	42.6	36.5	59.0	37.9	46.9	45.7	60.0
Tertiary sector	60.7	51.2	57.6	39.6	49.0	30.8	63.6	57.4	63.5	41.0	62.1	53.1	54.3	40.0

Total: Total labour force
Foreign: Foreign labour force

Source: Country analyses.

Table 4

France: Academic Levels by Socio-economic Groups (1980)

	Professional, Senior Managerial, Business Heads	Middle Managerial	White-collar Workers	Manual Workers, Agricultural Workers, Service Personnel	Farmers
Per 100 pupils enrolled in 4e (eighth year)	22.2	14.4	9.6	40.2	5.5
Per 100 pupils enrolled in CPPN	6.3	2.6	5.2	62.5	4.4

Notes: Statistics on state education only.
For each line, a heading Other, not reproduced here, brings the total to 100.
CPPN: Classes pré-professionnelles de niveau: see the analysis on France.

Table 5

Germany: Academic Levels by Socio-economic Groups (1976)

	Self-employed	Civil Servants	White-collar Workers	Manual Workers	Other
Per 100 Pupils at Gymnasium	19.1	16.5	38.0	19.7	6.6
Per 100 Pupils in vocational schools	14.6	5.5	20.5	44.3	11.9

Even if it proves impossible to distinguish, within the school populations studied, those who are native-born and those who are not, what is known about the socio-economic and socio-cultural level of the vast majority of migrants should be seen in terms of a _combination_ of handicaps, i.e. the fact of belonging, in most cases, to a particular social category (a characteristic shared by a fraction of native-born school children) _plus_ being of a foreign nationality.

Table 6

Netherlands: School Orientation of Males After Primary Education at School Performance Level 3 (1977)

	Senior Managerial	Middle Managerial	White-collar Workers	Self-employed Workers	Manual Workers
Per 100 boys, percentage opting for:					
General secondary (Long)	32	24	19	15	11
General secondary (Short)	57	56	56	53	52
Vocational training	7	15	17	23	33

Notes: There are 5 levels, level 1 being the lowest.
In each column, a heading "Other", not reproduced here, brings the total to 100.

Table 7

Sweden: Proportion of Male Pupils Completing Compulsory Schooling in 1971 Who Went on to Second Cycle of Secondary School

	University Graduates	Other Senior Managerial	Middle Management Employees	Skilled Workers, Farmers	Unskilled Workers
Percentage of boys leaving compulsory education to go on to upper secondary	86	82	68	63	55
of which:					
3- and 4-year lines	75	49	29	19	12
2-year vocational courses	2	15	19	30	27

Notes: In each column, the 2-year theoretical lines and the specialised upper school course, not reproduced here, bring the total to 100.
On the precise significance of the headings, see the analysis on Sweden.

The Current Situation

The figures in Table 8 reveal two dominant features:

-- First, that circumstances differ very greatly from country to country, with average enrolment levels varying from 3.7 per cent in the Netherlands to 15.5 per cent in Switzerland and 30 per cent in Luxembourg (3); this reflects, albeit to a rather more marked degree, the total proportion of foreigners living in these countries;

-- Second, that everywhere there is a higher level of foreign enrolment in the pre-primary and primary age groups, which gives an initial indication of the likely future trend.

In total, more than 2.5 million foreign pupils (or, in the case of Sweden, pupils speaking a language other than Swedish) were enrolled in schools in these seven host countries in 1981/82 or 1982/83.

Table 8

Foreign Enrolment Rates in Schools in Selected Host Countries
(Latest Available Figures)

Country and date	All Levels of Education nb.	%	Pre-primary	Primary	Secondary
Belgium					
All languages (1981/82)	247 200	11.9	13.0	13.5	9.9
France (1982/83)	1 021 982	8.4	9.8	10.1	6.4
Germany (1) (1981/82)	827 438	7.2	17.5	11.9	3.8
Luxembourg (1982/83)	17 802	30.0	37.0	38.0	19.3
Netherlands (1982/83)	120 398	3.7	5.9	4.8	2.3
Switzerland (1981/82)	193 322	15.5	20.1	18.0	12.8
Sweden (2) (1982/83)	120 697	7.9	7.9	8.7	5.0

1. Partial data only (see the analysis on Germany).
2. Children speaking a language other than Swedish (and not foreign children).

Notes: Pre-primary (France) or nursery (Belgium) or pre-school (Germany, Netherlands, Switzerland) or pre-primary (Luxembourg, Sweden).
Primary (Belgium, France, Netherlands, Switzerland) or primary and upper primary (Germany) or primary and supplementary (Luxembourg), or compulsory (Sweden).
Secondary (Belgium, France, Germany, Netherlands, Switzerland) or post-primary (Luxembourg).

Source: Country analyses.

Historical Trend

The trend over the past eight years (between 1974-75 and 1982-83) shows clearly that the proportion of foreign children in all levels of education in the six countries concerned (except for Sweden, where the relevant information was not available) -- increased sharply in the pre-elementary and elementary levels and less sharply in the secondary. Switzerland is the only exception to this -- the figures indicating a levelling-off at elementary level and a slight fall at pre-school level (see Table 9).

The steady growth in the proportion of immigrant children in the school population in each country is the result of the following two trends and their cumulative effects:

-- Pre-primary and primary: a rise in the number of foreign children, combined with a decline -- sometimes sharp as in Germany -- in the number of native-born children;

-- Secondary: an increase in both groups (foreign and native-born children), but more sustained in the case of the former.

Table 9

Recent Trends in Foreign School Enrolment Rates in Selected Host Countries
(As percentages)

Level of Education	Belgium	France	Germany	Luxembourg	Netherlands	Switzerland
Pre-primary						
1974/75	10.1	7.2	6.2	28.7	..	..
1977/78	11.8	8.3	9.6	35.9	2.8	21.5
1982/83	13.0 (1)	9.8	17.5 (1)	37.0	5.9	20.1 (1)
Primary						
1974/75	10.2	7.5	4.7	26.2	1.4	..
1977/78	11.4	8.5	6.0	30.3	2.2	18.1
1982/83	13.5 (1)	10.1	11.9 (1)	38.0	4.8	18.0 (1)
Secondary						
1974/75	7.6 (3)	..	2.0	13.5	..	..
1977/78	8.1	5.5 (2)	2.0	15.0	1.1 (2)	11.7
1982/83	9.9 (1)	6.4	3.8 (1)	19.3	2.3	12.8 (1)

1. 1981/82.

2. 1978/79.

3. Estimates.

Source: Country analyses.

Table 10 and the graphs in Annex 1 highlight these contradictory trends (or, as in the case of secondary level, similar trends but of differing intensity) which, it should be remembered, do not apply to Switzerland. For reasons explained in the analysis on Switzerland (in particular, the measures introduced since 1970 regulating migratory flows and a change in the law on transmission of nationality, introduced in 1978), this country has in common with the remainder only the second of these two trends (i.e. a differential growth rate at secondary level), whereas at pre-primary and primary levels the number of native-born _and_ foreign children is decreasing.

Because the figures in Table 10 are expressed in overall percentages (i.e. all levels combined) and because the scale used for the diagrams tends to "reduce" the magnitude of these trends, it is sometimes difficult to grasp the extent of the profound changes which have taken place in the composition of the school population. In this connection, a few simple figures may be more meaningful:

-- Between 1974/75 and 1981/82, the number of pupils in German schools (excluding the pre-primary level) fell by 700 000, being the net result of a loss of 1.1 million German children and a gain of 400 000 foreign children;

Table 10

Trends in the Proportion of Immigrants' Children in School Populations
(as percentages)

Country	Period Covered	Overall Changes	Of which Nationals	Foreigners
Belgium	(1974/75-1981/82)	-06.8	-09.6	20.2
France	(1978/79-1982/83)	-01.9	-03.1	13.5
Germany	(1974/75-1981/82) (a)	-05.8	-09.4	95.3
Luxembourg	(1974/75-1982/83)	-08.8	-17.7	22.2
Netherlands	(1978/79-1982/83)	-04.3	-05.9	67.5
Switzerland	(1976/77-1981/82)	-03.1	-03.6	-00.4

a) Pre-primary education (Schulkindergarten) has not been included in these figures.

-- Over the same period, the total school population in all Belgian schools fell by more than 150 000, the net result of a loss of 190 000 native-born children, and a gain of 40 000 foreign children;

-- Between 1974/75 and 1982/83, the number of children enrolled in first level education in France (i.e. nursery and elementary combined) fell by 560 000, i.e. a loss of 690 000 native-born children against a gain of 130 000 foreign children;

-- Lastly, over the same eight-year period, the number of pupils receiving primary education in the Netherlands fell overall by around 250 000 children, i.e. a loss of 285 000 Dutch children and a gain of 35 000 foreign-born children.

Many more such examples could be given, since this trend is a general one (4). Its causes are well known: on the one hand the decline in host country birthrates and, on the other, the increase in the foreign population's birthrate and the continuance of family immigration.

From this description of recent trends and the present situation, a number of conclusions can already be drawn and the exercise is all the more necessary in that this trend is far from over.

For instance, a report prepared at the request of OECD (<u>Migrants' children and employment -- The European Experience</u>, 1983), shows that for the seven countries reviewed here and over the period 1978-2000, the number of children in the 0-14 age group is likely to fall by about six million (half of that figure in Germany, and one-fifth in France). What is more, these population forecasts do not give separate figures for the changes occurring within each sub-group (i.e. native-born on the one hand and foreigners on the other), although the two trends are becoming increasingly divergent.

It can therefore be considered as certain that, if migration policies remain the same and unless there are radical transformations in reproductive behaviour (of which there are no signs at present), the process of fundamental change in the composition of the school population will continue over the years to come.

IV. <u>SALIENT FEATURES OF FOREIGN ENROLMENT</u>

Despite the individual differences in school systems as regards the pattern of primary and secondary education, an attempt has been made -- by constructing a series of indicators described briefly below -- to present on a comparable basis some of the characteristics of foreign enrolment commonly encountered in the different countries. In this connection, two main features stand out: firstly, a noticeably high proportion of foreigners in special education (a term which will need to be defined later) and secondly, the direction imparted to (or imposed on) their educational careers when they reach the stage in secondary level where a choice has to be made between the different streams.

The Methodology Used

At the level adopted for this initial investigation (i.e. national level), the difficulties were, firstly, to extract the relevant information from a vast array of statistics without, however, going into excessive detail, whilst at the same time retaining sufficiently large categories for the percentages calculated in subsequent, more specific, breakdowns to be of significance.

As far as the two factors explored by this study are concerned (i.e. enrolment in special education and in certain streams at secondary level), the purpose of the ratios calculated was to provide first of all a means of defining, first, the position of "foreigners" (all nationalities combined) in relation to the total school population (made up of nationals + foreigners) and, secondly, a means of comparing the distribution of one hundred native-born school children with that of one hundred school children of each individual foreign nationality in terms of their enrolment in a particular type of education at a given level, or in a particular stream within a given cycle. The following two indicators were constructed:

a) In the case of special education:

$$\% \; \frac{\text{foreign pupils}}{\text{total school population}} \quad \text{and} \quad \% \; \frac{\text{pupils of a particular nationality}}{\text{total number of pupils of the same nationality}}$$

enrolled in this particular type of education, compared with the same ratios for all types of education (normal + special) at that same level (pre-school, primary or secondary, depending on the structure of each country's education system -- see Table 11).

b) In the case of streaming:

$$\% \; \frac{\text{foreign pupils}}{\text{total school population}} \quad \text{and} \quad \% \; \frac{\text{pupils of a particular nationality}}{\text{total number of pupils of the same nationality}}$$

enrolled in the short stream (or, less specifically, the stream that does not dispense general education), compared with the same ratios for all streams (short and long) within the same cycle (see Table 12).

What is more, by comparing the ratios for several years, it is possible to see what changes have taken place in the breakdown between those enrolled in special education and the remainder, or between those enrolled in short cycles and the remainder, and thereby assess whether or not there has been any improvement over the period. Not all of the detailed information contained in the individual country analyses is reproduced in this summary, which is confined to comments on the trends observed.

Table 11

Foreign Enrolment by Type of Education
(latest available figures)

Country	Level	Year	Special Education	All Types of Education (Normal + Special) at the Same Level
Belgium (French-speaking areas)	Nursery	1981/82	30.7	23.8
	Primary	1981/82	24.6	23.1
	Secondary	1981/82	26.1	18.5
France	Primary	1980/81	15.2	9.3
	Secondary	1982/83	15.2	6.4
Luxembourg	Primary	1981/82 (a)	40.9	35.8
Switzerland	Primary	1981/82	26.4	18.0

a) Figures for special classes after deduction of those pupils attending induction classes.

Source: Country analyses.

The Position of "foreigners" as a whole

Tables 11 and 12, showing the situation for the latest year for which all the necessary statistics are available, illustrate the two main, and globaly measurable,(5) characteristics of foreign enrolment:

-- A relatively higher rate of enrolment in special education (or in the various special education courses where there is one at each level) than in education as a whole at that particular level;

-- A higher rate of enrolment in streams (or cycles), either of the short-course variety or those with less stringent requirements, than in education as a whole at that particular level.

Although it appears impossible to provide a definition of special education that is valid for all the systems of education under review, it can be said that, leaving aside the children attending induction classes who are sometimes included under this heading (as in Luxembourg), it comprises children either suffering from personality disturbances or with certain mental or physical deficiencies. These handicaps make it difficult for them to follow a normal course of education and cause them to be more backward than the average. It seems however, that this original purpose has been steadily (and unduly) broadened to such an extent that special education has come increasingly, and by the mere fact of its existence, to accept children having difficulty in attending normal schools for a variety of other reasons -- because of language problems in particular (6).

Table 12

RELATIVE LEVEL OF FOREIGN ENROLMENT BY TYPE OF EDUCATION
(as percentages)

(Percentages)

Country	Year	Comparative foreign enrolment rates by level and type of education
Belgium (French-speaking-system)	1980/81	10.9 per cent in general education as a whole but 16.7 per cent in lower general education
	Secondary (type 2)	21 per cent in technical education as a whole but 25.7 per cent in lower technical education
		30.1 per cent in vocational education as a whole but 55.5 per cent in lower vocational education
France	1982/83	1st cycle: 6.45 per cent in the cycle as a whole but 11.35 per cent in CPPN/CPA (prepatory vocational and apprenticeship training)
	Secondary	2nd cycle: 5.65 per cent in the cycle as a whole but 8.75 per cent in the short second cycle and 3.45 per cent in the long second cycle
Germany	1981/82 Secondary (except vocational)	2.5 per cent in the three types of education as a whole (Realschulen, Gesamtschulen, Gymnasium) but 3.1 per cent in short-course secondary (Realschulen + Gesamtschulen)
	Secondary + vocational education	3.7 per cent but 5.25 per cent in vocational education alone

24

Luxembourg	1981/82	Post-primary (normal + special)	40.3 per cent in supplementary education but 17.9 per cent in secondary (post-primary)
			17.9 per cent in post-primary education as a whole but 22 per cent in technical secondary education
Netherlands	1982/83		General secondary + vocational training: 2.3 per cent but 2.8 per cent in vocational training alone
			Vocational training: 4.4 per cent in the lower level (LBO) and 0.9 per cent in the intermediate and higher levels taken together (MBO + HBO)
Switzerland	1981/82	Secondary I	14.2 per cent in the cycle as a whole but 11.3 per cent in the "stricter qualifications" stream, 17.5 per cent in the "basic qualifications" stream and 25.9 per cent in the "no selection process" stream

Note: The country analyses should be consulted for details regarding the exact position of individual types of education within the particular level referred to.

What is more, the trend as regards the relationship between the two percentages which have been worked out every year since such figures were available (i.e. the ratio of the percentage of foreigners in special education to the percentage of foreigners in all types of education of the same level) does not reveal any radical change in the situation and, at best, only a slight improvement. This is true, with reference to primary education, in the case of Luxembourg, (down from 1.19 in 1974/75 to 1.14 in 1981/82, figures recalculated by deducting those pupils attending induction classes), in France (down from 1.7 in 1975/76 to 1.6 in 1980/81)and in Belgium (French-speaking system) where, admittedly, it has always been at a very low level.

By contrast, the same ratio is increasing in Switzerland (from 1.25 in 1976/77 to 1.5 in 1981/82) where the number of immigrants' children in special education has remained practically unchanged over five years (9 176 and 9 331 respectively), whereas the number in normal primary education has dropped substantially, falling from 89 455 to 75 264, or 15 per cent, over the same period.

With regard to the streaming which occurs during secondary education, Table 12 gives several examples of the different education children receive depending on whether they are nationals or foreigners.

Before analysing the findings arrived at on a more general basis for all the countries under review, the approach adopted should first be explained by taking one particular case chosen from amongst a number of similar ones. At a given level of education (in this case, second-cycle secondary education in France), children belonging to the same age group (with the exception of those who have progressively dropped behind in their previous grades) can find themselves in either a long or a short cycle. At this point, what is found is that there are relatively more immigrant children in the short second cycle than in the second cycle as a whole (long + short), the figures being respectively 8.75 and 5.65 per cent; and that, conversely, their enrolment rate is lower in the long second cycle (3.45 per cent) (7).

Although, as has been said, this is only one example, the figures for the other countries show that this situation is widespread. In short, it is a fact that levels of foreign enrolment are always higher whenever:

-- The type of education followed does not include a selection process or requires only basic qualifications (for example, in Switzerland the level of foreign enrolment in Secondary I as a whole amounts to 14.2 per cent, as opposed to 25.9 per cent in what is designated as the "no selection process" stream);

-- The education provided involves applied training (i.e. vocational or technical) and not general education; Belgium, for instance, provides a perfect example of this "tiered" effect: in 1980-81 the level of foreign enrolment in type 2 (or "traditional") secondary education was roughly 18 per cent, but was as high as 30 per cent in the "vocational training" stream (compared with 11 per cent in general education) and 35.5 per cent in what is termed "lower vocational training" compared with 25.5 per cent in "higher vocational training";

-- The length of the course is shorter (which is the case in France, as mentioned above).

What is more, the ratios worked out in order to illustrate the trend over the past few years show that this situation is persisting; that is to say, the growing influx of foreign children in secondary education (simply as they grow older) has not changed the way this population group is distributed between the various types of education (i.e. short or long course, vocational or general) that are (theoretically) available to them.

Although the same system of analysis cannot strictly be applied to Sweden, it does seem relevant to compare the observations made for the other countries with those on the future academic prospects of pupils leaving basic (or compulsory) schooling. Admittedly, for those entering upper secondary, there appears to be no difference in the distribution by level attended (from the ones with the greatest prestige, the "three and four-year lines", to the least advanced, the "specialised upper secondary" courses) between nationals and those speaking a language other than Swedish. However, it can be seen that selection takes place upstream at the time of leaving compulsory schooling. In fact, according to statistics dating from 1978/79, 80 per cent of young Swedes succeed in passing through the double filter of application and admission procedures to continue their studies in upper secondary schools, whereas only 69 per cent of those speaking a foreign language are successful.

The Position as Regards Particular Nationalities

So far, the situation has been analysed using aggregate figures for the total foreign school populations, thereby giving the impression that the different nationalities making up this population encounter the same problems and follow an identical path through the system. This, however, is far from being the case, and the figures in Tables 13 and 14 show how the situations in which immigrant children find themselves differ widely depending on what nationality they are.

The next step therefore is to take the analysis a stage further, using the same two parameters (i.e. the differential level of enrolment in special education and in certain other standard types of education), but going into greater detail nationality by nationality (8). This approach yields two main findings:

-- Firstly, that behind the aggregate figures, which supposedly depict the situation of "foreigners" as a whole within a particular segment of a country's education system, there lies what amounts to a hierarchy of nationalities, as is demonstrated by the dispersion of the figures for each one;

-- Secondly, that children of a given nationality living in various different host countries can find themselves in a vastly different position within each of these hierarchies, as is illustrated by the individual "scores" in relation to the average for all nationalities combined.

We shall now go on to examine these two aspects in more detail, starting with the second, which will be dealt with briefly and mainly in order to suggest a number of possible avenues for research.

Table 13

Enrolment of Foreigners and Nationals in Special Education at
the Primary Level, by Nationality
(percentages)

Nationality	Belgium (1980/81) (a)	France (1980/81)	Luxembourg (1981/82) (c)	Switzerland (1981/82) (a)
Total school population	4.0	2.5	3.6	7.5
Of which:				
Nationals	4.0	2.4	3.2	6.8
Foreigners	4.1	4.1	4.2	11.0
Total foreigners (as above)	4.1	4.1	4.2	11.0
Of which:				
Italians	3.7	3.5	4.4	11.0
Spaniards	4.7	3.8	5.2	11.9
Portuguese	4.3	4.0	4.9	..
Greeks	4.5	..	..	8.1
Yugoslavs	..	2.2	..	7.9
Turks	2.5	3.9	..	19.4
Algerians	..	5.1	..	..
Moroccons	..	4.3	..	..
Tunisians	..	4.7	..	..
Maghrebis	5.2	..	..	..
Germans (or other EEC)	2.4	0.9 (b)	2.6	6.1

Common indicator used:

Enrolment in special education

Total enrolment in primary education (normal + special)

a) French-speaking system.
b) In France, EEC nationals excluding Italians.
c) Proportions recalculated after deducting figures for those attending induction classes.

Source: AFC tables.

The figures given in Tables 13 and 14 (which show only a few examples selected from the country analyses) show clearly that the school career of

Table 14

Enrolment of Foreigners and Nationals by Type of Education and by Nationality
(percentages)

Nationality	Belgium (a) (1980/81)	France (1980/81)	Germany (1981/82)	Luxembourg (1981/82)	Netherlands (1982/83)	Switzerland (1981/82)
Total school population Of which:	48.3	19.1	42.4	75.9	47.9	37.5
Nationals	43.8	18.5	42.1	74.9	47.6	36.1
Foreigners	68.6	29.4	51.8	79.4	57.8	46.3
Total foreigners (as above) Of which:	68.6	29.4	51.8	79.4	57.8	46.3
Italians	74.0	30.1	63.0	83.2	36.2	54.7
Spaniards	65.6	27.0	57.3	78.9	46.5	55.6
Portuguese	59.9	30.9	63.6	92.0	53.1	..
Greeks	59.2	..	44.9	..	..	47.2
Yugoslavs	..	23.4	57.1	..	45.4	39.9
Turks	80.8	37.6	67.8	..	70.8	70.4
Algerians	..	33.7	..	..	..	..
Moroccons	..	32.0	..	..	76.2	..
Tunisians	..	29.6	..	..	..	..
Maghrebis	74.9	..	..	..	..	..
Germans (or other EEC)	28.1	8.7 (b)	40.2 (c)	72.6	38.5(d)	20.5

Indicators used:

Belgium: Enrolment in vocational and technical education / Total enrolment in secondary education (Type 2)

France: Enrolment in CPPN-CPA and short second cycle / Total enrolment in secondary education (1st and 2nd cycles)

Germany: Numbers in Realschulen + Gesamtschulen / Numbers in Gymnasien + Realschulen + Gesamtschulen

Luxembourg: Enrolment in technical, vocational and agricultural education / Total enrolment in post-primary education

Netherlands: Numbers in vocational training (LBO,MBO,HBO) / Total general secondary + vocational training

Switzerland: Enrolment in secondary I requirement only basic qualification / Total enrolment in secondary I

a) Frensh-speaking system.
b) In France, EEC nationals (excluding Italians).
c) In Germany, Dutch children.
d) 1981/82 figures.

Source: AFC tables.

Italian children in Switzerland is not the same as that of their compatriots living in France, where only 3.5 per cent of Italian children in primary education are enrolled in special education (as against 4.1 per cent for foreigners as a whole), whereas in Switzerland the figure is 11 per cent for Italians and for foreigners as a whole. Furthermore, in France their level of enrolment in a less demanding type of education does not differ greatly from the average for all foreigners (30 per cent and 29 per cent respectively), whereas in Switzerland it is substantially higher (almost 55 per cent, against 46 per cent, i.e. a difference of around 9 points). The contrast is revealed still more clearly by the situation of young Italians living in the Netherlands, who achieve the best "score" of all immigrants for enrolment in general secondary education (64 per cent enrolled in the secondary system, against 42 per cent for "foreigners" as a whole).

This comparative analysis needs to be done in greater detail and extended to other nationalities that are found in a sufficient number of countries to make such an exercise meaningful, such as the Spanish or the Turkish. What is more, in a country where several languages are spoken (e.g. Switzerland, Belgium), an analysis of this kind, conducted language system by language system, could provide a wealth of interesting data.

At the moment, however, the information contained in Tables 13 and 14 shows clearly how necessary it is to disaggregate the "foreigners" category in order to get a true picture of the particular problems facing individual immigrant communities and subsequently decide what should be done to remedy them. The percentage breakdowns for native-born children and for each of the nationalities surveyed reveal vast differences in the case of special education at primary level (Table 13), as well as in the case of the particular type of secondary education chosen as an example (Table 14).

As regards _special education_, whereas in France 4 per cent of all foreign children in primary education are assigned to special education (compared with just over 2 per cent of French children), the figure is as high as 5 per cent in the case of Algerian children. A similar observation, involving identical orders of magnitude, may be made for the French-speaking system in Belgium, where Maghrebis as a whole rather than Algerians alone are the category affected. Similarly, in Switzerland, whereas 11 per cent of foreigners are enrolled in special education at primary level (compared with less than 7 per cent of Swiss children), more than 19 per cent of Turkish children are in this type of education.

Lastly, although the Netherlands do not figure in Table 13 -- since the special education provided for children and adolescents suffering from physical, sensory or locomotor handicaps covers all age groups between 3 and 18 and, consequently, equates to all levels of education -- it can nevertheless be noted that in the Netherlands the percentage of pupils involved ranges from 6 per cent, the average for all nationalities together, to 9 per cent for Turks and almost 13 per cent for Moroccans, i.e. more than double the average.

As regards the _type of education received_ (Table 14), deviations from the mean are even more marked. In Belgium, for example, whereas of all foreign children enrolled in "traditional" secondary education 69 per cent attend vocational or technical schools (as opposed to 44 per cent of nationals), the figure for Turkish children is 81 per cent. In France, whereas more than 29 per cent of foreign adolescents in secondary education (first and second cycles) are enrolled in short streams, the figure for Algerians is almost 34 per cent. In Luxembourg, whereas of all foreign children in post-primary education 79 per cent are enrolled in technical schools (as against 61 per cent of Luxembourg children), the figure for Portuguese children is 92 per cent. To take another example, in Switzerland, whereas 36 per cent of nationals enrolled in secondary I attend classes requiring only basic qualifications, the figure for foreigners is 46 per cent, and 55 per cent for Italians and Spaniards.

Table 14 gives a fuller picture of the situation. Included therein, and in Table 13, for the purposes of comparison and to emphasize the contrast, are figures for the German immigrant population (or, in the case of Germany itself, the figures for Dutch children and, in the case of France, the figures for EEC nationals excluding Italians), all of which nationalities are included in the average figures for "foreigners" as a whole and, in this particular case, have the effect of lowering them.

There remains the situation in Sweden. We have previously shown that, in the course of 1979, 69 per cent of children speaking a language other than Swedish who had finished their compulsory schooling were admitted to upper secondary education (against 80 per cent of young Swedes). The average percentage reaches 76 for those speaking Estonian, and 87 per cent for French-speakers, but is only 52 per cent for Turkish-speakers and 43 per cent for Spanish-speakers.

At the conclusion of this analysis dealing with several host countries which, in certain respects, each offer their own specific features, it may seem an over simplification to put forward one guiding principle by which to assess the numerous observations that have been made (see Table 14).

It does, however, emerge from the figures obtained from this series of indicators, that the least favourable positions are occupied by children belonging to one or the other of the following two categories, and particularly if they fall into both categories. On the one hand are those from the more recent inflows of migrants, on the other hand, those from societies whose cultural norms and individual and collective values are the furthest removed from those of the host country, i.e. from the norms which its schools transmit and inculcate.

V. CONCLUSIONS AND IMPLICATIONS

A number of conclusions can at this point be drawn from the two-stage analysis during which we have examined, in turn, the number of foreign children enrolled in the six national school systems (and of children speaking a language other than the national language in a seventh system), and certain of the broad features which characterise their school careers. The full significance of these conclusions becomes apparent if, leaving aside the world of education, they are seen in the context of these children's access to and advancement in the world of work.

Before turning to these conclusions, it should rapidly and parenthetically be stated that the extension of the field of investigation to include Sweden, where children are no longer identified on the basis of their nationality, but of the language spoken at home, had added a supplementary dimension to this study yielding valuable information, since it has shown that the changing of a discriminatory variable does not prevent situations arising similar to those encountered elsewhere. And it is, in fact, often the case that the situation of certain children speaking a language other than Swedish strongly resembles that of foreign children in other countries.

The Educational Situation of Foreign Children

The nature of these conclusions is both quantitative (the scale of foreign enrolment) and qualitative (the pattern of the school career) -- which, in this latter case, does not imply that no exact measurement has been made.

Firstly, at the pre-school and primary levels in the countries surveyed a twofold trend can be seen at work in the shape of an increase in the number of foreigners and at the same time a decrease in the number of nationals; at secondary level both groups continue to expand, although more rapidly in the case of foreigners. The diagrams appended hereto give a clear picture of these trends as well as their scale, which is more pronounced in the case of Germany and Luxembourg and more gradual in the case of Belgium, France or the Netherlands. Moreover, the magnitude of these trends is somewhat understated by virtue of the fact that a number of children of foreign origin are included in the "nationals" category. Some of these children, however, who acquired citizenship at birth or subsequently, retain their "non-national" cultural and social traits and have to contend with the same problems at school as those who are officially classed as foreigners.

Although for the country as a whole it is not yet, strictly speaking, possible to say that nationals are being supplanted by foreigners within these age groups, but rather that there has been a change in the proportion which they represent within each freshly enrolled generation of school children, this stage has however already been reached in some areas and in certain schools. It would therefore seem essential that education should adapt (in terms of structures, teaching methods, teacher training) to a change in the composition of its clientele, which is by no means at an end.

Turning from the quantitative to the qualitative aspects of the type of education received, one of the first anomalies to appear is the percentage of foreign children in special education, which is invariably higher than the overall rate of foreign enrolment in all types of education at that particular level. This situation, which persists over the years without any apparent significant improvement, affects primarily certain of the nationalities that are more recent arrivals and/or whose cultural values are further removed from those of the host country.

This primarily reflects the failure or at least the inadequacy of specific arrangements for facilitating the admission into the education system of those foreign children who need such help. Due to a shortage of places and due to the fact that they do not receive sufficient remedial training (in the language in particular), some of these children find themselves relegated to special classes, not because their condition warrants this but because they are for the moment unable to follow a normal course of education. This approach, which over the short term provides an easy solution to the problem but which over the longer term seriously jeopardises the school careers of the children concerned, needs to be strenuously opposed by the authorities of the host countries. With its original function restored, special education would then cater for foreign children in the same proportion as for native-born children.

The second aspect highlighted by the qualitative analysis of the pattern of education concerns the streaming process that takes place more particularly at the various stages in secondary education. The figures show that when there are a number of alternative streams available, the enrolment rate of foreign children is always higher than that of nationals in those streams or cycles which either require only minimal qualifications or provide only a short course of instruction. It is clear that this type of streaming, which affects certain nationalities in particular, is the result not of a choice made by the children themselves (or their parents), but of a "weeding out" process which, by degrees, cuts off their access to the "prestigious streams" -- that is to say those that provide a sound general education.

Unfortunately, the entry into the labour market of youngsters with nothing or very little in the way of qualifications -- due to the fact that they have either left school early or with no real skills, or both -- is happening at a time when, in the industrial sector in particular, the number of unskilled jobs is diminishing, and also at a time when a prerequisite for the necessary future matching of the labour force to the new working conditions created by the technological revolution is that a worker should at the outset of his working career have received an adequate general education. It would probably be no exaggeration to say that those young foreigners leaving school without these basic qualifications are in a worse situation at the outset of their working lives than were the first generation of immigrants at the moment of their arrival; there are fewer of the types of job in industry which would suit them than there were 20 or 30 years ago and the number of run-of-the-mill jobs in the service sector is unlikely to go on expanding indefinitely.

One can therefore gauge the consequences of a system of educational streaming that relegates to the fringes of advanced industrial societies an increasing number of young people (owing to the steady growth in the number in secondary education) and the need to reverse this process of exclusion.

Consequences as Regards Employment

It is not the intention here to deal in detail with a subject as complex as this but simply to highlight, with the help of a number of specific examples, the relationship between the situation of school-leavers and a particular aspect of their entry (successful or otherwise) into the world of work. In the current economic climate, we shall pay special attention to unemployment, which has reached particularly disturbing proportions among young people.

Table 15

Germany: Breakdown of Unemployed Youth by Level of Education

	Year (September)			
	1976	1978	1980	1982
Per 100 unemployed aged 15-19:				
Had failed to complete vocational training	62.6	71.0	74.2	65.2
Had completed vocational training	37.4	29.0	25.8	34.8

A survey carried out in Germany in 1980 on a sample of 2 500 young foreigners of both sexes revealed that 70 per cent of those without a job had no (German) school leaving certificate (9).

Furthermore, when they were asked why they had not enrolled for vocational training, close on one-third (30 per cent) said it was because the final diploma was inadequate; what is more, the younger those interviewed, the higher the percentage quoting this as their reason: below 30 per cent for the 21-26 age group; 32.7 per cent for 19-20 age group; 34.2 per cent for the 17-18 age group; and 35.6 per cent for 15-16 age group. The second reason given (i.e. a lack of information) came some way behind, being mentioned in only 17 per cent of the replies. The comment of CEDEFOP (the European Centre for the Development of Vocational Training) on these findings is that comparison with their elders shows that "the importance of a school-leaving certificate for vocational training has apparently increased in the past few years as a result of the scarcity of places for trainees".

A recent report by the OECD (10) quoting statistics for Germany gives a breakdown by level of education for unemployed youth (nationals and foreigners) in the under-20 age group for the period 1974-1982. We shall quote the figures for just four years; these reveal the profound differences in the employment situation of those who completed their vocational training and those who failed to complete it (Table 15).

Lastly, a survey carried out in 1982 by the French Agence Nationale pour l'Emploi (11) shows very clearly that the vast majority of the young long-term unemployed, i.e. those who have been looking for a job for a year or more, have only minimal educational qualifications and that in this category there is a relatively higher proportion of foreigners (Table 16).

These figures are sufficiently eloquent in themselves and require little comment: it is the levels of education with the relatively highest proportion of foreigners (see the figures for France in Table 12) that produce the "hard core" unemployed, made up of individuals who, right from the start of their working life, find it impossible to secure permanent, stable employment.

In the final analysis, it is clear that exclusion from the education system constitutes the first stage in a process of marginalisation, culminating in exclusion from the system of production and -- since social integration depends on integration within the labour force -- in exclusion from society itself.

The fact of having left school early, very often without obtaining any diploma, and of having acquired no adequate initial training, can lead only to an unfavourable position on the labour market, whether in terms of types of employment accessible, of conditions of work, or of vulnerability to unemployment. This relation is likely to create handicaps in any case, but all the more so for those whose best chance of social integration resides in access to the most highly qualified employment available.

Identifying and then eradicating the causes of the situations described herein does not only mean tackling the problem of "educational achievement", but also taking the first step towards genuine integration of children of foreign origin in the society of the countries in which they live, and in which, increasingly, they have been born.

Table 16

France: Educational Level of the Long-term Unemployed in the Under-30 Age Group
(percentages)

Level	French	Foreigners	Total
Higher education	2.6	2.1	2.6
Final grade (terminale) of secondary education	5.7	2.1	5.5
Penultimate grade (première) of secondary education	37.7	27.1	37.0
End of secondary 1st cycle and 2nd short cycle	14.9	13.8	14.9
Secondary 1st short cycle (CPPN-CPA) and primary level (CEP)	38.9	54.7	40.1
Total	100.0	100.0	100.0

Notes: CPPN-CPA: Preparatory apprenticeship and pre-vocational education.

CEP: Vocational education.

NOTES AND REFERENCES

1. It should be stated at the outset that, in the case of Sweden the available data had to be specially processed, since the division between categories of pupils is not made by nationality but by the language spoken in the home ("home language"). Attention will several times be drawn to this distinctive feature as this report proceeds. However, as a general rule (and although the two concepts are not precisely identical), the report may be read with the assumption that the two concepts of "foreign pupil" and "pupil speaking a language other than Swedish" are closely related.

2. These examples are taken from a recent OECD publication, _Educational Trends in the 1970s: A quantitative analysis_, Paris, 1984.

3. The percentage given for Germany in not entirely meaningful. In fact, the figure of 7.2 per cent is less that the true figure, since not all the foreign school children are included, in particular those in the so-called "international" schools (see analysis on Germany).

4. On this matter see _Educational Trends in the 1970s_, op.cit. However, this publication describes only changes in overall numbers, without distinguishing between changes among nationals and those specific to foreigners.

5. There is, in fact, one other that would be worth detailed analysis, i.e. educational retardation in a given grade and how this evolves (in other words, worsens) as pupils move up through the grades. There are no overall figures for retardation, which has been measured solely on the basis of samples or cohorts of pupils monitored throughout their school careers.

6. The reader is referred to the country analyses, which give more details of the content of each special education programme and of the type of child for whom it is intended. It thus seems that the original, narrower concept of special education has been retained in Germany (in the case of the _Schulkindergarten für Behinderte_ and of the _Sonderschulen_) and in the Netherlands (in the case of _Buitengewoon onderwijs_), making impossible any form of comparison with the other host countries. This is all the more true since there are other special structures for children of immigrants in Germany, for which figures are not available (see analysis on Germany).

    For this reason, although the percentages for these countries have been calculated (see analysis on Germany and on the Netherlands), they have not been included in Table 13.

7. So as not to overload the summary tables, the percentages worked out for the level or stream providing the longer course of education have not been included on a systematic basis. However, they can be found in the tables in the individual country analyses.

8. In addition, it should be mentioned that in order to have sufficient numbers in each of the educational categories to be analysed, even when a particular nationality is not very numerous, a different indicator was used from that adopted previously. This consisted in working out what percentage of school children of a particular nationality -- Belgian, French, Italian, Spanish, etc. -- in primary education were enrolled in special education and similarly, in the case of secondary education, what percentage were enrolled in a short-course stream or in one with less stringent requirements (see above, Methodology).

9. <u>Vocational training of young migrants in the Federal Republic of Germany</u>, CEDEFOP, Berlin, 1982.

10. <u>Youth employment in France -- Recent strategies</u>, OECD, Paris, 1984.

11. <u>Chômeurs de longue durée</u>, ANPE, Paris, October 1982.

Part Two

COUNTRY ANALYSES

ENROLMENT OF FOREIGN CHILDREN IN SEVEN COUNTRIES

I. ENROLMENT OF FOREIGN CHILDREN IN BELGIAN SCHOOLS

BASIC FACTS AND FIGURES ON THE FOREIGN POPULATION

a) The Trend in Recent Years

Belgium, a small country at the cross-roads of important trade routes and international communications, has seen its foreign population more than double in the space of 35 years from a figure of 367 619 in 1947 to 878 577 in the 1981 Census (these figures representing 4.3 and 8.9 respectively of the total population).

Immigration continued at a very rapid pace until 1974 -- the year when recession took hold in most European countries -- and had levelled off by the 1980s.

The figures in Table 1 show the foreign population trend since 1977 in the different regions: Flanders, Wallonia and Brussels, each of which has its own language culture, which explains some of the differences in the enrolment figures.

Table 1

Foreign Population Trend in Belgium, 1977–83
(Figures as at 1st January of each year)

Year	Total Country nb.	% (1)	Brussels Region nb.	% (1)	Flanders nb.	% (1)	Wallonia nb.	% (1)
1977	851 601	8.7	219 459	21.1	220 996	4.0	411 146	12.8
1978	869 696	8.8	224 609	21.8	226 711	4.1	418 376	13.0
1979	876 577	8.9	227 741	22.4	230 595	4.1	418 241	13.0
1980	890 038	9.0	234 275	23.2	234 907	4.2	480 856	14.9
1981	903 736	9.2	239 957	24.0	240 190	4.3	423 589	13.1
1982	885 729	9.0	243 624	24.5	234 923	4.2	407 182	12.7
1983	891 244	9.0	248 002	25.0	238 597	4.2	404 645	12.6

1. Percentage of total population (nationals + foreigners).

Source: Institut national de statistique: Démographie et mouvement de la population.

The larger part of the foreign population lives in regions where coal mines were exploited and where iron manufactures were installed (Wallonia, Limburg) and also in Brussels. Agriculture has called less for immigrant labour, consequently, there are less foreigners in the Flanders and in South Belgium.

b) The Immigrant Birthrate

Taking the country as a whole, the number of births is increasing more rapidly among the foreign population than it is among the native-born population: between 1976 and 1982 the number of children born to Belgian nationals fell by 1 229 (i.e. a fall of 1.2 per cent) whereas foreign births rose by 1 139 (i.e. an increase of 6.5 per cent).

Geographically the differences are even more marked: it is particularly in Brussels -- where almost every other child born is of foreign extraction -- that the proportion of foreign births has risen most sharply, from 37.6 per cent in 1976 to 44.1 per cent in 1982 (See Table 2).

Unfortunately, birthrate statistics are not broken down by nationality.

Table 2

Foreign Birthrate Trend in Belgium, 1976-1982

Year	Total Country nb.	% (1)	Brussels Region nb.	% (1)	Flanders nb.	% (1)	Wallonia nb.	% (1)
1976	17 410	14.5	4 585	37.6	5 558	8.0	7 267	18.5
1977	18 269	15.0	5 089	41.2	5 770	8.2	7 410	19.2
1978	18 480	15.2	4 956	41.4	5 998	8.4	7 526	19.6
1979	19 010	15.4	5 192	42.9	6 271	8.6	7 546	19.5
1980	19 584	15.7	5 355	42.8	6 447	8.9	7 782	19.6
1981	19 373	15.5	5 448	43.9	6 428	8.9	7 497	18.8
1982	18 549	15.4	5 230	44.1	6 161	8.8	7 158	18.5

1. Percentage of total births (nationals + foreigners).

Source: Institut national de statistique: Statistiques démographiques.

c) The Current Situation

   i) Distribution by nationality

The 878 577 foreigners recorded in the 1981 Census comprised 279 700 Italians (31.8 per cent of the total foreign population), 105 133 Moroccans (12 per cent), 103 512 French (11.8 per cent), 66 233 Dutch (7.5 per cent), 63 587 Turks (7.2 per cent), 58 255 Spaniards (6.6 per cent), 26 756 Germans (3.1 per cent), 23 080 British (2.6 per cent) and 21 230 Greeks (2.4 per cent).

Nationals from EEC countries are therefore very numerous, accounting for about 60 per cent of the total -- well ahead of immigrants from African countries (Moroccans in particular), who account for roughly 12 per cent of the total).

The size of the Italian population is due to the fact that this immigration movement is a long-established one, dating back to the 1920s and 30s, which picked up again immediately after World War II. Since the 1960s, however, immigration has been from farther afield and also more from the South with an influx of Greeks, Turks, Spaniards, etc.

   ii) Distribution by age

The age factor has to be taken into account in any analysis of foreign enrolment since this is the explanation for the generally high foreign enrolment in nursery and primary schools (which will be discussed below).

Table 3

Foreign Population by Age and by Region
(Figures from 1st March 1981 census)

Age Group	Total Country nb.	% (1)	Brussels Region nb.	% (1)	Flanders nb.	% (1)	Wallonia nb.	% (1)
0- 4 Years	96 608	15.8	26 292	46.3	31 136	8.8	39 180	19.8
5- 9 Years	92 899	14.4	24 461	43.7	26 740	7.3	41 698	18.7
10-14 Years	88 639	12.3	22 767	37.8	24 397	5.8	41 475	17.7
15-19 Years	80 580	10.1	20 401	30.3	20 656	4.3	39 515	15.7
ALL AGES	878 577	8.9	237 875	23.8	232 544	4.1	408 158	12.7

1. Percentage of total population (nationals + foreigners) in each age group.

Source: Institut national de statistique: Recensement de la population.

The figures in Table 3 show that the proportion of foreigners in the 0-4 age group is virtually double that for all age groups combined (the figures being 15.8 and 8.9 per cent respectively for the country as a whole).

This is true for every region with the exception of Wallonia, where the size of the industrial sector is the reason for the existence of an adult foreign workforce.

In the next age groups (the 5-9 and 10-14 year-olds) the proportion of immigrants is lower but, as a result of family reunification policy, still higher than the average for the population as a whole.

iii) The labour force

With the employment data due to emerge from the 1981 Census still available, processing of the returns being as yet incomplete, the information summarised below is drawn from a socio-economic survey carried out in 1977. Three major sectors (manufacturing, construction and retailing employed no less than two-third of the foreign labour force (66.7 per cent), compared with only half of the native-born labour force (51.5 per cent) (Table 4).

Naturally enough, it is in these three major sectors that the foreign penetration rate is higher than the average of 8 per cent for all sectors combined: namely construction (11 per cent), manufacturing (10.7 per cent) and retailing (8.8 per cent).

Table 4

Labour Force by Sector and Nationality, 1977

Sector	Total Population nb.	Foreign Population nb.	%
Agriculture	129 443	2 172	1.7
Manufacturing	1 088 575	116 573	10.7
Construction	280 488	30 821	11.0
Retailing	642 977	56 862	8.8
Transport	266 243	11 163	4.2
Banking and Insurance	201 840	9 471	4.7
Other Services	882 442	33 895	3.8
Total (Including activities not classified above, the unemployed and members of the armed forces)	3 817 292	306 398	8.0

Source: April 1977 socio-economic survey for the Kingdom of Belgium.

A breakdown by nationality, moreover, reveals the uneven distribution of the foreign labour force by type of activity (Table 5).

There is a clear pattern of nationality concentration: Italians and Moroccans in manufacturing; Italians in construction and retailing; French, Dutch and also Italians in the banking sector.

These background demographic and socio-economic facts will make it easier to understand the pattern of enrolment of foreign children in Belgian schools.

Table 5

Foreign Labour Force by Sector and by Nationality (1977)
(as percentages)

Sector	Total Foreigners	Moroccans	Spaniards	Italians	French	Dutch	Others
Manufacturing	100.0	28.5	8.9	41.2	11.6	7.2	2.6
Construction	100.0	9.1	10.9	39.8	12.5	7.9	19.8
Retailing	100.0	4.5	7.8	28.9	17.4	11.2	30.2
Banking and Insurance	100.0	1.3	4.3	21.1	18.3	17.1	37.9

Source: April 1977 socio-economic survey for the Kingdom of Belgium.

FOREIGN CHILDREN IN BELGIAN SCHOOLS

a) <u>Preliminary Remarks</u>

A number of points need to be made before moving on to the actual analysis of the enrolment of children of immigrants in Belgian schools.

i) <u>The language laws</u>

These are very strict in Belgium: the language of instruction is that of the region, with the exception of Brussels where it can be a matter of choice as long as the individual concerned resides in one of the 19 communes of Brussels.

Belgium's internal structure is relatively complex since the 1980 institutional change which created three communities (French, Flemish and Walloon) which are competent for cultural subjects and three regions (Wallonia, Flanders and Brussels) which are competent for some economic subject. Education is a jurisdiction divided between the Central State and the three communities. There are two Ministers of Education in the National government. The Minister of Dutch-speaking Education has authority over Dutch-speaking schools whereas his French-speaking Education counterpart has authority over French and German-speaking schools. However, school population falls within the responsibilities of those national ministers who hand out statistics. Statistics on job searchers and on the unemployed fall within the authority of various ministers. Lastly, some data come from the "Institut National des Statistiques" which depends of the Ministry of Economic Affairs. Consequently, there are difficulties to establish homogeneous statistics at a national level for the subjects concerned.

ii) Secondary education

Since 1968, "traditional" (or Type 2) secondary education is being gradually replaced by "reformed" (or Type 1) secondary education. In a few years, the transition will be complete: in seven years enrolment in the traditional French-speaking school system has dropped by 64 per cent (from 213 071 in 1974/75 to 76 256 in 1981/82) whereas enrolment in the reformed school system has risen by more than 158 per cent (from 100 296 in 1974/75 to 259 080 in 1981/82).

Amongst the aims of this "reform" of secondary education were the desire to abolish the existing segregation between general education and technical (and vocational) training, the possibility of postponing the moment of "definitive" choice of stream and also the possibility of switching streams. In the traditional system of education, which is divided into two cycles (upper and lower) there are three streams: general education, technical education and vocational training, whereas the reformed system of education is made up of three levels each comprising two years of instruction: the first of "observation" level, the second or "streaming" level and the third of "final choice" level. Thus it is not until the third or even fourth year of instruction in this reformed system of education that a pupil needs to decide. Even then he still has the possibility of switching streams, and in reality his final decision as to choice of stream is not made until he starts attending the third level.

iii) The new Compulsory Education Act

In July 1983, the Belgian Government introduced an Act on compulsory education for children aged 14 to 18. Compulsory education is full-time up to the age of 15, with a maximum of seven years primary school and at least the two first years of secondary education. In no case is compulsory education full time beyond the age of 16. Full-time compulsory schooling is followed by part-time compulsory studies. This new Act modified the structure of secondary education: Royal Decrees in 1984 implemented a short type of education offering vocational education and training.

b) The Overall Position

Table 6 gives the figures for the school year 1980/81 broken down by level and type of education and by language area. The distribution of the school population among schools using the different languages is as follows: 57.5 per cent in Dutch-speaking schools, 42 per cent in French-speaking schools and 0.5 per cent in German-speaking schools.

Table 6

Total Number of Schoolchildren (Belgian + Foreign) in French- and
Dutch-Speaking Areas, 1980/81 School Year

	Total	French- and German-speaking		Dutch-speaking	
	nb.	nb.	%	nb.	%
Pre-primary	384 694	160 721	41.8	223 973	58.2
Primary	857 418	381 192	44.5	476 226	55.5
Secondary, Type 1 (or reformed)					
1st level (Observation)	174 322	113 595	65.2	60 727	34.8
2nd level (Guidance)	143 129	81 408	56.9	61 721	43.1
3rd level (Consolidation)	67 188	30 847	45.9	36 341	54.1
Secondary, Type 2 (or traditional)					
Lower General	96 581	15 257	15.8	81 324	84.2
Higher General	102 586	40 436	39.4	62 150	60.6
Lower Technical and Vocational	164 782	38 104	23.1	126 678	76.9
Higher Technical and Vocational	100 129	27 483	27.4	72 646	72.6
Total	2 090 829	889 043	42.5	1 201 786	57.5

Sources: Ministère de l'Education nationale (régimes francophone et germanophone) ; Ministerie van Nationale Opvoeding (régime neérlandophone).

In addition, it will be noted that, as regards the type of education, enrolment in the "reformed" school system is higher in the French-speaking area than in the Dutch-speaking area. Two reasons can be put forward for this:

-- The "reformed" education system (Type I) has developed faster in the French-speaking than in the Dutch-speaking area;

-- The non-State schools represent 67.5 per cent of all Dutch-speaking schools, but only 42.5 per cent of all French-speaking schools.

c) The French-speaking School System

The figures given in Table 7 show that the enrolment of foreigners in the French-speaking school system as a whole has grown at a steady pace, rising from 18.2 per cent in 1974/75 to 22.3 per cent in 1981/82.

Were it not for the foreigners, enrolment rates would have been more sharply affected by the steep decline in the birthrate among the Belgians. This is shown by the following figures covering the period 1974-1982:

-- School system as a whole

Total schoolchildren	down by 66 982 or 7.9 per cent
of which: Belgian	down by 89 400 or 13.5 per cent
Foreign	up by 22 418 or 11.8 per cent

-- Pre-primary

Total schoolchildren	down by 23 517 or 14.9 per cent
of which: Belgian	down by 25 652 or 21.4 per cent
Foreign	up by 2 135 or 5.7 per cent

-- Primary

Total schoolchildren	down by 35 392 or 9.9 per cent
of which: Belgian	down by 41 052 or 14.9 per cent
Foreign	up by 5 660 or 6.8 per cent

-- Secondary (Types 1 and 2)

Total schoolchildren	up by 21 969 or 6.6 per cent
of which: Belgian	up by 8 083 or 3.0 per cent
Foreign	up by 13 886 or 22.3 per cent

Moreover, these counts (particularly those for preprimary and primary levels) are a very clear reflection of the scale of immigrant family reunification, already described, and thus confirm the importance of the "age" variable in any analysis of the foreign school population.

Over and above the purely quantitative aspect of the growth in the number of schoolchildren of foreign nationality, the next step will be to take a closer look at their position with respect to special education and certain types of secondary education before going on to describe the results of a correspondence analysis of the position of the various foreign nationalities with regard to the different levels and types of education.

i) Special education

This is concerned primarily with children with sensory or mental handicaps -- whether these be mild, moderate or severe -- and is divided into eight types of education, each adapted to a particular mental or physical handicap: mild or severe mental retardation, psychopathic disorders, motor disabilities, illnesses, visual impairments, hearing impairments, dexterity disabilities (Table 8).

Table 7

Trends in Percentage of Foreign Children in the French-speaking School System in Belgium

	1974/75	1975/76	1976/77	1977/78	1978/79	1979/80	1980/81	1981/82
Ordinary nursery	19.5	19.8	19.7	21.2	21.6	22.3	23.4	23.8
Special nursery	28.2	23.2	23.2	14.1	30.5	33.6	31.4	30.7
Total, nursery	19.6	19.8	19.8	21.1	21.6	22.3	23.5	23.8
Ordinary primary	19.6	20.1	20.4	21.1	21.5	22.1	22.6	23.1
Special primary	21.7	19.7	21.7	12.6	21.1	22.8	22.7	24.6
Total, primary	19.7	20.0	20.4	20.7	21.5	22.1	22.6	23.1
Secondary, Type 1 (or reformed)								
Level 1 (Observation)	18.8	19.4	20.2	..	..	..	18.4	..
Level 2 (Guidance)	17.1	18.2	17.7	..	..	..	17.4	..
Level 3 (Consolidation)	11.7	12.4	11.9	..	..	..	14.5	..
Total	17.6	17.9	17.7	16.9	15.7	17.2	17.6	18.8
Secondary, Type 2 (or traditional)								
Lower general	10.0	10.1	9.7	9.5	11.0	13.4	16.7	..
Higher general	7.0	7.2	6.3	7.7	7.7	8.3	8.7	..
Total, general	8.8	9.0	8.4	8.9	9.6	10.6	10.9	11.6
Lower technical	20.1	20.9	19.5	21.4	22.4	23.5	25.7	..
Higher technical	17.0	16.4	15.9	19.3	17.3	15.4	17.7	..
Total, technical	18.4	19.2	18.2	20.7	20.4	19.6	21.0	20.0
Lower vocational	30.1	32.1	30.8	31.7	31.3	32.1	35.5	..
Higher vocational	18.3	19.3	19.8	21.3	20.4	20.5	25.5	..
Supplementary vocational	10.2	11.5	10.9	11.7	..	..	17.4	..
Total, vocational	26.2	27.7	26.9	27.7	27.5	27.5	30.1	28.5
Special secondary	22.5	20.7	19.3	18.9	19.1	21.0	22.1	26.1
Total, secondary	15.6	16.1	15.7	16.0	15.9	17.1	17.9	18.5
Total, School system as a whole	18.2	18.6	18.5	19.0	19.4	20.2	20.9	22.3

Source: Etudes et Documents, Ministère de l'Education nationale.

It is true that a recent ESEPSET/CEE report (1) on special education and the children of foreign workers in EEC countries has pointed out that the number of children with a physical or mental impairment is higher among the immigrant than among the native-born population due to less hygienic living conditions, malnutrition, parents' lack of education. However, it is unlikely that these factors, although far from negligible, are a sufficient explanation for the higher foreign enrolment rates in special education compared with standard education at the same level. A number of immigrant workers' children, studying in ordinary classes, find great difficulty studying in a language which they have little control of. Whatever their intelligence, they accumulate failures.

Table 8

Proportion of Foreign Schoolchildren in the Different
Streams and Levels of Education (1981/82)
(as percentages)

	Ordinary Education	Special Education
Pre-school education	23.8	30.7
Primary education	23.1	24.6
Secondary education	18.5	26.1

ii) <u>Traditional secondary education</u>

Table 9 also shows the over-representation of foreign schoolchildren in the "lower" levels of the different streams within Type 2 secondary education (i.e. general, technical, vocational).

What is more, the figures for the past seven years (see Table 7) show that, for each of these types of education, there has been no significant change in the pattern of distribution of foreign children between the lower and higher levels, except for the steady increase which is apparent at the higher vocational level. Going into the details of individual nationalities, it is apparent that enrolment rates in each of the three types of education and within these, in the higher and lower levels, differ substantially according to nationality. Table 10 shows disparities for 100 pupils (five nationalities) enrolled in "traditional" secondary school education. The disparities are also explained by the passing "in cascade": foreign pupils fail more easily in general education, they then go to technical education and later to professional education.

Table 9

Proportion of Foreign Schoolchildren in the Different Streams and Levels
of Traditional Secondary Education in 1980/81
(as percentages)

	Lower Level	Higher Level
General education	16.7	8.7
Technical education	25.7	17.7
Vocational education	35.5	25.4

Taking each type of education first of all, it will be seen that there is always one nationality with a proportionately higher enrolment than the other foreigners as a whole (all nationalities combined): this is true of Dutch children in the case of general education (40 out of every 100 enrolled in Type 2 secondary education compared with a figure of 31 for all foreign children); of Spanish children in the case of technical education (the figures being respectively 38 and 28); and of French children in the case of vocational education (respectively 47 and 24).

Table 10

Breakdown by Nationality of Foreign Schoolchildren in the Different Streams
and Levels of Traditional Secondary Education
1980/81

	General Education		Technical Education		Vocational Education	
	Higher	Lower	Higher	Lower	Higher	Lower
All nationalities combined	18	13	14	14	13	26
Of which:						
Italians	16	10	13	15	12	30
Spaniards	16	18	19	19	3	17
Moroccons	11	14	12	21	8	32
French	15	10	14	12	26	21
Dutch	16	24	16	10	6	8

Secondly, in terms of the higher and lower levels, the proportion of Moroccan children enrolled in the lower level of each type of education is always higher than the average figure for all foreign nationalities combined; the reverse is true, however, for French children.

iii) Correspondence analysis

By means of correspondence analysis we were able to review the various nationalities most strongly represented in the French-speaking school system for the 1980/81 school year and to group them by type of education (see the Factor Analysis Diagram). However, caution is needed in interpreting these results, the "age" variable having an effect since there is a significant correlation between the level of education and the date of arrival in Belgium.

About 80 per cent of the initial information (aggregated broken down by nationality and type of education) is represented in the Diagram. The sum of the data is given by adding the two axes together: 62.2 per cent and 16.1 per cent.

The horizontal axis could be defined as that of the hierarchic representation of the school level (ranging from secondary down to pre-primary). This "hierarchisation" has a two-fold significance since, for one thing, in any correspondence analysis where one of the variables is time-related, the first axis has a temporal dimension which can be more or less artificial. For another, the various school levels are distributed about the horizontal axis in accordance with a hierarchy of those levels.

The interpretation of the vertical axis is extremely difficult because of the little information plotted around it (only 16.1 per cent of all initial data). It is easier for so-called "random" events to be placed at one place or another on this axis. Here, it would represent an immigration time-scale, because at the lower end of the axis are to be found the Turks and Moroccans -- the "new immigrants" -- whereas higher up the same axis there are the "older" foreigners like the French, Spaniards and Greeks. On the Diagram, the Germans come closer to the Turks and the Moroccans although they have been in Belgium for many years.

As for the Belgians, they are close to the centre of gravity which indicates that they are present in all levels of education.

What the analysis amounts to is that there is an appreciable correlation between immigrants' level of school enrolment and date of arrival. It is not surprising that recent arrivals in Belgium should have more children to put in nursery classes than foreigners who have already been there for some time.

But there is also a correlation between nationality and the varyingly "prestigious" types of education. Turkish and Moroccan children, for example, whose parents are not only part of the new immigration wave but also more disadvantaged than other nationalities, are to be found in larger numbers in the so-called special types of education.

At the other end of the scale, the Dutch, Germans and Luxemburgers, together with people from Zaire and Rwanda-Burundi (former Belgian colonies) are proportionately more numerous in secondary level education: 9.5 per cent of children from Luxembourg, 7.5 per cent of children from Zaire and Rwanda-Burundi, and 6.5 per cent of German children receive "general" secondary education, compared with only 2 per cent of Moroccan and barely 1 per cent of Turkish children.

Lastly, pupils of Italian, Spanish, Portuguese and Greek background are all in roughly the same situation and, in most cases, are satisfied with lower-level technical or vocational training.

d) The Dutch-speaking School System

While the proportion of foreign children remains small and is not changing spectacularly, it is nevertheless increasing steadily in all the education levels considered here (Table 11).

If however the trend in Belgium and foreign enrolment is looked at more closely, it will be seen that over a period of six years (from 1976/77 to 1982/93) the pattern of enrolment for these two categories has been quite different:

-- At the pre-primary level: decreasing of the number of Belgian children (down from 245 425 to 231 621), whereas foreign enrolment increased by 30 per cent (from 11 378 to 14 834);

-- At the primary level: a drop of 17 per cent in the number of Belgian children and a rise of 21 per cent in the number of foreign children.

Table 11

Trend of Foreign Children in the Dutch-speaking School System in Belgium
(in percentage)

	1976/77	1977/78	1978/79	1979/80	1980/81	1981/82	1982/83	1983/84
Pre-primary	4.6	5.0	5.3	5.5	5.5	5.5	6.4	6.8
Primary	4.0	4.4	4.6	4.9	5.2	5.7	6.0	6.1
Special primary	3.2	3.3	3.5	..	..	..	5.3	5.7
Secondary (1)	2.6	2.8	2.9	3.1	3.4	3.7	4.0	4.4

1. All streams combined.

Source: Ministerie van Onderwijs.

Here too, the influx of young foreigners has cushioned the effects of the fall in the birthrate in the Flemish area of Belgium (at least up until the 1980s) and prevented an even greater drop in enrolment.

Where secondary education is concerned, the contrast between trends in Belgian and foreign enrolment is even more marked. Whereas the number of Belgian children in secondary education rose by only some 2 per cent, the number of foreigners increased by 55 per cent (2).

As in most West European countries, compared with total foreigners there are large numbers of Turkish and Moroccan children -- i.e. recent immigrants -- enrolled in pre-primary and primary education, whereas in secondary education there are relatively more Dutch and Italians -- i.e. foreigners resident in the Flemish area for many years.

By way of a summary, Table 12 shows which foreign nationalities are best represented in the Dutch-speaking school system.

Table 12

Percentage of Belgian and Foreign Children in the Dutch-speaking School System Compared with the Belgian School System as a Whole (Dutch-, French- and German-speaking Systems)
1979/80 School Year

	Pre-primary	Primary	Secondary
Total Population	58.2	55.9	59.3
Belgian population	63.0	60.8	63.3
Foreign population	25.3	21.5	18.5
Of which:			
France	12.9	9.1	4.6
Germany	30.0	30.1	40.2
Greece	16.3	14.5	17.4
Italy	10.6	8.7	8.6
Luxembourg	7.3	4.3	4.5
Netherlands	83.4	82.4	84.4
North Africa (Morocco)	35.7	26.7	18.8
Portugal and Spain	13.2	15.2	16.9
Rwanda-Burundi	1.8	4.7	12.1
Turkey	58.2	48.7	54.8
United Kingdom	31.7	37.2	47.6
Zaïre	7.9	4.8	3.8

Sources: Ministère de l'Education et de la Culture française.
Ministère de l'Education et de la Culture néerlandaise.

Amongst the foreign nationalities, therefore, the Dutch are the only ones who have the majority of their children enrolled in the Dutch-speaking system, being far in advance of the Turks, the Moroccans, the English and, to a lesser extent, the Germans. As far as the children of other foreign nationalities are concerned, between 80 and 90 per cent are enrolled in the French-speaking system.

Admittedly, this concentration in one or other of the school systems reflects the geographical distribution of the immigrant population throughout the kingdom, since there is no choice as regards the language of instruction except in Brussels.

It is also possible that the affinity of some mother tongues with the French language (as is the case for the Italians, Spanish, Portuguese, Greeks and, of course Luxemburgers) plays a part in the distribution observed (for example, through the geographical mobility of parents seeking to facilitate their children's school career). However, the statistical information needed to assess the extent of the influence of this factor is not available.

NOTES

1. ESEPSET/CEE: Enseignement spécial, enseignement professionnel et scolarisation des enfants de travailleurs étrangers dans les pays de la Communauté européenne.

2. Unfortunately, it is not possible to make a more detailed analysis within this level of education since the statistical services of the "Ministère de l'Education nationale et de la Culture néerlandaise" makes no distinction between nationals and foreigners as far as the different types of secondary education are concerned (e.g. traditional general, vocational and technical, reformed, special, etc.).

BELGIUM

FACTOR ANALYSIS OF CORRESPONDENCE BETWEEN EDUCATIONAL LEVELS AND NATIONALITIES FOR THE SCHOOL YEAR 1980/81

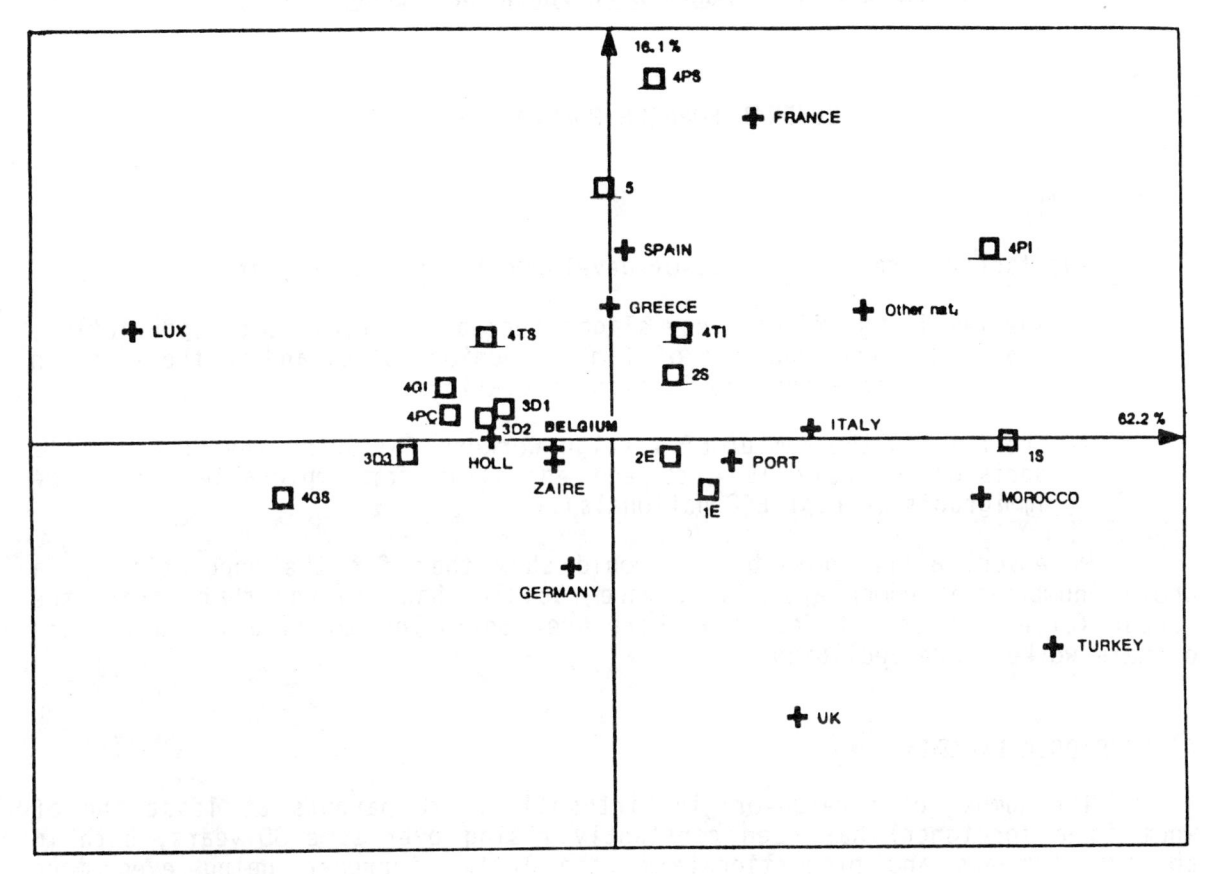

1 E	- Ordinary pre-primary
1 S	- Special pre-primary
2 E	- Ordinary primary
2 S	- Special primary
3 D1	- Secondary 1st cycle, 1st level
3 D2	- Secondary 1st cycle, 2nd level
3 D3	- Secondary 1st cycle, 3rd level
4 GI	- Secondary 2nd cycle, lower general
4 GS	- Secondary 2nd cycle, higher general
4 PI	- Secondary 2nd cycle, lower vocational
4 PS	- Secondary 2nd cycle, higher vocational
4 PC	- Secondary 2nd cycle, supplementary vocational
4 TI	- Secondary 2nd cycle, lower technical
4 TS	- Secondary 2nd cycle, higher technical
5	- Special secondary

╋ : Type of school

☐ : Pupils' nationality

II. ENROLMENT OF FOREIGN CHILDREN IN FRENCH SCHOOLS

GENERAL FOREIGN POPULATION DATA

a) **Broad Trend**

Two factors are symptomatic of developments in recent years:

-- The levelling off (or very slight increase) in the total population, due to the continuation of family reunion policy and to the surge in the birthrate among the foreign population;

-- The fall in the number of foreign workers following the Government's decision in July 1974 to end admission for employable first-time immigrants (except EEC nationals).

Moreover, a breakdown by sex would show that for the population as a whole, numbers of women are rising more rapidly than men and that within the labour force, numbers of female workers are continuing to rise while numbers of male workers are declining.

b) **Foreign Birthrates**

The number of foreign-origin births (i.e., to parents at least one of whom is a foreigner) has been constantly rising over some 30 years, both in absolute numbers and proportionately, the latter increase being even more rapid because the indigenous French birth rate has been dropping.

Although in 1982, total legitimate births were almost back to their 1975 levels (683 825 in 1982, 681 636 in 1975) the foreign birthrate advanced over the same period by 14.8 per cent, thus partly concealing the decline in legitimate births where both parents are French (Table 2).

c) **Present Position**

Retracing some of the demographic and socio-economic findings deriving from an examination of one in 20 of the 1982 census returns brings out various quantitative and/or qualitative influences on the position of foreign children in the French school system and on the forms their enrolment can take.

Table 1

Foreign Population Trend in France

Year	Total Foreign Population ('000)	%	Foreign Labour Force ('000)	%
1975*	3 442.4	6.5	1 584.3	7.3
1977	3 518.9	6.9	1 550.1	7.0
1978	3 645.5	7.0	1 518.0	6.8
1979	3 567.8	6.9	1 498.0	6.6
1980	3 599.2	6.9	1 458.2	6.4
1981	3 636.7	7.0	1 427.1	6.3
1982*	3 680.1	6.8	1 556.3	6.6

Notes: The data from the two sources used are not strictly comparable, so much that it would be hazardous to calculate a trend between the results of a census and those of an employment survey (or vice-versa).

The employment survey, conducted among a sample of ordinary households, tends to underestimate the size of the foreign population, both total and working.

Sources: *For 1975 and 1982: INSEE: Recensement général de la population.

1977 to 1981: INSEE, Enquête Emploi (March annual employment survey).

i) Demographic structures

Whatever the indicators used, all emphasize the relatively greater proportion of the young in the foreign population and, therein, the unequal breakdown by constituent nationality.

The foreign proportion becomes greater the further down the age range, and this over-representation at the base of the age pyramid results in a rise in the numbers of foreign school-age children (Table 3).

The distribution differs appreciably by nationality, depending on whether the whole of the population (including all age groups) is considered or only the under 16 age group (Table 4).

Another consideration of direct relevance to the question to be addressed below is the average number of children age 0 to 16 per family (1) by nationality of the reference person (so-called instead of head of household): French-born families average 1.76, while foreign-born families average 2.36, the breakdown around that average being: Italian, 1.86; Spanish, 1.84; Portuguese, 1.99; Algerian, 3.15; Moroccan, 3.07; Tunisian, 2.62; but only 1.74 for EEC nationals, other than Italians.

Table 2

Foreign Origin Birthrate Trend in France

	Total Legitimate Births	Total Legitimate Births where at least One Parent is Foreign	
Year	nb.	nb.	%
1975	681 636	82 151	12.0
1976	658 926	81 529	12.4
1977	679 346	85 435	12.6
1978	667 841	85 784	12.8
1979	679 521	87 377	12.9
1980	709 261	90 316	12.7
1981	703 337	93 484	13.3
1982	683 825	94 322	13.8

Note: In this table, all births to French/foreign couples (of the order of 18 000 to 20 000 over the period examined) have been added to total births where both parents are foreign -- giving the data in column 2. Another method is to take only half the births registered where only one parent is foreign.

Source: INSEE, Statistique de l'Etat Civil.

Table 3

Total Population and Foreign Population by Age, March 1982

	Total Population	Foreign Population	
Age Group	nb.	nb.	%
0- 4 years	3 129 440	280 080	8.9
5- 9 years	3 820 840	341 080	8.9
10-14 years	4 282 700	326 920	7.6
15-19 years	4 361 980	277 740	6.4
20-24 years	4 231 540	266 420	6.3
All ages	54 273 200	3 680 100	6.8

Source: INSEE, Recensement général de la population.

Table 4

Foreign Population by Nationality and by Age Group, March 1982
(as percentages)

	Total	Algeria	Morocco	Tunisia	Spain	Portugal	Italy	Other EEC	Others
All ages	100.0	21.6	11.7	5.1	8.7	20.8	9.1	4.3	18.7
Under 16	100.0	25.7	13.5	5.9	8.6	22.7	8.6	2.4	12.6

Source: INSEE, Recensement général de la population.

Table 5

Manpower by Nationality and by Selected Socio-economic Category (1)
(Situation at 31st March 1982)

Nationality	Total Labour Force (2)	Managerial Professional	Non-manual	Domestic Service	Manual	Skilled	Unsk., Farming
French + Foreigners	100.0	8.2	23.1	3.8	33.5	17.7	15.8
French	100.0	8.5	24.0	3.6	31.0	17.1	13.9
Foreign	100.0	3.4	10.4	7.2	68.9	26.1	42.8
of which:							
EEC other than Italian	100.0	24.1	15.3	4.0	19.9	11.1	8.8
Spanish	100.0	1.6	10.0	13.3	62.7	28.4	34.3
Portuguese	100.0	0.3	8.1	11.7	76.0	29.1	46.9
Algerian	100.0	0.6	8.4	2.7	56.5	20.3	36.2
Moroccan	100.0	0.9	7.3	3.8	83.9	22.5	61.4

1. The figure for each nationality is a percentage of the total labour force (which combines headings 1 to 6 of the INSEE socio-economic categories).

2. Refers to the employed and unemployed working population, except for the jobless who have never worked.

Source: INSEE, Recensement général de la population, 1982.

ii) Distribution by socio-economic category

Several studies have shown that children from less skilled socio-economic categories are inclined to have difficulties at school. It is therefore interesting to consider the distribution of French and foreign children from that standpoint.

A majority of the foreigners (two out of three) are in the working class, as opposed to only one French person in three. Similarly, foreigners are proportionally twice as numerous as French nationals in domestic service.

By nationality, the manual worker percentage, especially unskilled, is especially high among Moroccans (83.9 per cent manual worker, 61.4 per cent unskilled) and Portuguese (76 and 46.9 per cent) (Table 5).

This probably goes some way towards explaining the large numbers of young Moroccans and Portuguese (though of others too) in certain very specific types of education: special education, and also short secondary and vocational cycles.

FOREIGN CHILDREN IN FRENCH SCHOOLS

The most recent complete statistics to hand, for the school year 1983-84, give the number of children identified as being of foreign nationality attending public and private schools in the primary and secondary levels as 1 062 263, representing 8.7 per cent of total enrolment. By level the breakdown is:

-- Preschool: 241 924 (22.8 per cent);

-- Elementary: 464 345 (43.7 per cent);

-- Secondary: 355 994 (33.5 per cent).

French schools now, for the first time, have over one million foreign children among their pupils. This is the outcome of a lengthy process of steady growth which has been monitored in primary education since 1974-75; for this secondary education some data were collected in 1976-77; and full figures are available from 1978-79 onwards. But the increase has not occurred uniformly in every type of education, special and short-cycle education, for instance, having higher proportions of foreign children.

a) Past Development by Level

Table 6 illustrates the steady increase in the proportion of foreign children in each level of education. The only exception over the review period was the school year 1980-81, when there was a slight (and temporary) drop in the proportion of immigrants' children in preschool classes (9.1 per cent as against 9.2 per cent in 1979-80).

The trend is the outcome of two contrasting movements:

-- An increase in the number of foreign children due to the higher birth-rate among the foreign population and because of the continuation of family review policy;

-- A fall in the number of French children in the primary level and virtual stability in the secondary level, due to the levelling out and subsequent decline in the French birth-rate.

A comparison covering the only period for which full data on enrolments are available (the five school years 1978-79 to 1983-84) shows the following trends:

-- Preschool

Total enrolment:	- 41 481 (-1.7 per cent)
of which French children:	- 71 675 (-3.1 per cent)
Foreign children:	+ 30 194 (+14.3 per cent)

-- Elementary

Total enrolment:	- 440 953 (-6.6 per cent)
of which French children:	- 529 069 (-8.1 per cent)
Foreign children:	+ 88 116 (+12.7 per cent)

-- Secondary

Total enrolment:	+ 262 791 (+4.9 per cent)
of which French children:	+ 186 589 (+3.7 per cent)
Foreign children:	+ 76 202 (+21.4 per cent)

-- Total Enrolment (primary + secondary)

Total enrolment:	- 221 640 (-1.8 per cent)
of which French children:	- 383 573 (-3.5 per cent)
Foreign children:	+ 161 933 (+15.2 per cent)

These figures, drawn from a relatively short period (2), point up the considerable changes that have occurred in the make-up of the school population, even if they were not always clearly perceived at the time. Averaged overall, from preschool to the end of secondary education, the proportion of foreign children per hundred enrolled rose from seven to nine over the six-year period.

This quantitative assessment is only one aspect of the research however, and it is also important to see how the French education system has catered for schoolchildren of a certain type (to the extent that foreign children can be taken as a single category). For this purpose a number of specific indicators will be used to compare the average school career of French and immigrants' children.

b) <u>A Markedly Different Education Pattern</u>

The difference in the way foreign children are educated can be seen in two ways:

Table 6

Enrolment of Foreign Children in Primary and Secondary Education (private and public)
(as percentage of total enrolment)

Level	1974/75	1975/76	1976/77	1977/78	1978/79	1979/80	1980/81	1981/82	1982/83	1983/84
Primary of which:	7.4	7.7	7.9	8.4	8.5	9.0	9.2	9.5	10.0	10.4
Pre-school	7.2	7.4	7.7	8.3	8.5	9.2	9.1	..	9.8	9.8
Elementary	7.5	7.8	8.0	8.5	8.5	9.0	9.3	..	10.1	10.7
Secondary (including special schools)	..	..	..	..	5.5	5.7	6.0	6.2	6.4	6.7
Secondary (including special schools) of which:	..	..	4.7	5.0	5.3	5.5	5.8	5.9	6.2	6.4
- First cycle	..	..	5.0	5.2	5.4	5.7	6.0	6.2	6.5	6.7
- Second cycle	..	..	4.2	4.5	5.1	5.2	5.4	5.5	5.7	5.9
Total primary and secondary	..	..	..	..	7.3	7.7	7.9	8.1	8.4	8.7

Source: French Ministry of Education.

62

-- First, the proportion of foreign children found in special education, which contains children with intellectual deficiencies or who are so behind in their schooling that they cannot follow an ordinary course of instruction;

-- Second, as a factor of the streaming process, the proportion of foreign children in each secondary cycle, whether the longer cycle providing general education leading on to further studies or the shorter cycle preparing children to join the labour market at an earlier stage and hence with a lower qualification.

The indicator that was used for Table 6 (the proportion of foreign children in total enrolment) can also be used to bring out the differences in the level of enrolment according to the type and purpose of particular courses.

i) Special education

Table 7 shows that:

-- The proportion of foreign children is consistently higher in special education than in overall education at the same level (in 1976-77, for instance, eight in every 100 children enrolled in primary education were foreign, but the figure for special education was 14 in every 100);

-- The ratio between the two enrolment rates has not changed at the elementary level and has declined only very slightly at the secondary level, meaning that the discrepancy indicative of the less favourable situation of children of foreign nationality is disappearing very slowly, if at all, even though their numbers are in fact increasing.

Table 7

Enrolment of Foreign Children in Special Education
(as percentage of total enrolment)

Level	1975/76	1976/77	1977/78	1978/79	1979/80	1980/81	1981/82	1982/83	1983/84
Primary:									
All primary (1)	7.8	8.0	8.5	8.5	9.0	9.3	..	10.1	10.7
Special education (2)	13.1	13.9	13.3	13.6	15.1	15.2	..	17.3	17.8
Ratio (2)/(1)	1.7	1.8	1.6	1.6	1.7	1.6	..	1.7	1.7
Secondary:									
All secondary (1)				5.5	5.7	6.0	6.2	6.4	6.7
Special education (2)				15.4	14.8	15.8	16.0	15.2	16.7
Ratio (2)/(1)				2.8	2.6	2.6	2.6	2.4	2.5

Note: Lines 1 and 4 in Table 2 are identical to lines 3 and 4 in Table 1.

ii) Academic and vocational streaming

The earlier findings, from the review of special education, are both matched in the case of the academic (and hence vocational) streaming of foreign children (see Table 8):

-- First, a higher proportion of foreign children in the short stream in each cycle, i.e. CPPN and CPA in the first cycle and the short second cycle as from the first year;

-- Second, the disparity between the proportion of foreign children in the short streams of each cycle and the proportion of foreign children enrolled in all secondary education has held steady, though there has been a slight improvement in the first cycle.

Table 8

Enrolment of Foreign Children by Stream in Each Cycle of Secondary Education
(as percentage of total enrolment)

Cycle and Level	1976/77	1977/78	1978/79	1979/80	1980/81	1981/82	1982/83	1983/84
First cycle (1) of which:	5.0	5.2	5.4	5.7	6.0	6.2	6.5	6.7
CPPN–CPA excluded (2)	4.7	4.9	5.0	5.4	5.7	5.9	6.2	6.4
CPPN–CPA (3)	9.5	10.4	10.8	11.2	10.7	11.3	11.4	11.8
Ratio (3)/(1)	1.9	2.0	2.0	2.0	1.8	1.8	1.8	1.8
Second cycle (4) of which:	4.2	4.5	5.1	5.2	5.4	5.5	5.7	5.9
Long cycle (5)	2.4	2.6	3.0	3.0	3.2	3.4	3.5	3.7
Short cycle (6)	6.6	7.3	7.9	8.2	8.4	8.5	8.8	9.1
Ratio (6)/(4)	1.6	1.6	1.6	1.6	1.6	1.6	1.6	1.5
All secondary (7)=(1)+(4) (Special education excluded) of which:	4.7	5.0	5.3	5.5	5.8	5.9	6.2	6.4
Short streams (8)=(3)+(6)	7.1	7.9	8.5	8.8	8.8	9.0	9.2	9.5
Ratio (8)/(7)	1.5	1.6	1.6	1.6	1.5	1.5	1.5	1.5

Notes: CPPN: Classes pré-professionnelles de niveau
CPA: Classes préparatoires à l'apprentissage, for example vocationally-oriented streams in the first cycle of secondary education.
Lines 1, 5 and 9 in table are identical to lines 6, 7 and 5 in Table 1.

c) Conclusions

What significant conclusions can be drawn from this preliminary overall approach, which considers all foreign children of whatever nationality?

The uneven impact of schooling, apparent as soon as statistics become available, can be seen throughout the observation period, the same pattern of distribution for foreign children between ordinary and special education, and between the short and long streams having persisted with virtually no change over time. This means that inequality at school (the consequences of social inequality but also -- perhaps above all -- a factor in reproducing it) is continuing.

The second part of this investigation involves a similar review, by nationality, to demonstrate how the nationalities involved in the most recent waves of migration and those whose cultural norms are farthest removed from the values of the host society are to be found, in larger proportions, in those areas of education which most seriously constrain pupils' occupational futures.

ANALYSIS BY NATIONALITY AND IMPACT OF PARENTS' SOCIO-ECONOMIC STATUS

The first stage in this research compared the school careers of two categories of children considered to form two homogeneous units, i.e. French children and children of foreign nationality. We may now take the analysis further by introducing a breakdown by nationality which will situate each national group in relation to the two major indicators already identified: a higher (average) rate of enrolment in special education than in education as a whole, and a higher (average) proportion in the shorter streams.

This detailed review will be based on statistics for the school year 1980-81, the most recent ones to provide information on all levels and types of education separately.

a) Special Education

The data for the school year 1980-81 given in Table 7 show that:

-- At elementary level, children of foreign nationality represented 9.3 per cent of total enrolment (ordinary + special education), but 15.15 per cent of enrolment in special education;

-- At secondary level, the proportion of foreign children enrolled in all classes (1st and 2nd cycles + special education) was 6 per cent, but rose to 15.8 per cent when special education alone was considered.

Put another way:

-- At elementary level, out of 100 foreign children enrolled, 4.1 are in special education (as against only 2.4 for every 100 French children);

-- At secondary level, out of 100 foreign children enrolled, 6.3 per cent are in special education (as against only 2.1 for every 100 French children).

That is the basis for Table 9, which shows how these figures vary when calculated per 100 children by nationality.

The uneven distribution across the various types of education is clear from these figures:

-- The enrolment of foreign and French children in special education is in a ratio of 1:2 at elementary level and 1:3 at secondary level;

-- Among the individual groups of foreign children, the extremes are represented on the one hand by children of EEC nationals other than Italians (about one child per 100 in special education), and on the other by Algerian children (five per 100 in special primary education and nearly nine per 100 in special secondary education).

Compared to the average for all foreign children combined, the following nationalities are unfavourably placed:

-- At elementary level, children of migrants from the three Maghreb countries: Algeria (5.1), Tunisia (4.7), Morocco (4.3);

-- At secondary level, children of migrants from the Maghreb countries and Turkey and Portugal: Algeria (8.55), Turkey (8.4), Morocco (8.1), Tunisia (7.4) and Portugal (7.1).

b) Academic and Vocational Streaming

Table 8 showed that foreign children are over-represented in the short streams of secondary education. For the school year 1980/81 the following averages were found:

-- 6 per cent of foreign children in the 1st cycle as a whole, but 10.7 per cent in the CPPN and CPA classes;

-- 5.4 per cent of migrants' children in the 2nd cycle as a whole, but 8.4 per cent in the short stream;

-- 5.8 per cent of foreign children in all secondary education (special education excluded), but 8.8 per cent in the two short streams.

A detailed nationality breakdown was arrived at by considering what proportion of children in the 1st cycle, the 2nd cycle and secondary education as a whole received education aimed at an early entry to working life. The results are set out in Table 10.

Table 9

Enrolment in Special Education at Each Level, by Nationality
(School Year 1980/81)

Nationality	Special Education Elementary Level	Special Education Secondary Level (SES-GCA-ENP)
Total Enrolment	2.5	2.3
of which:		
French	2.4	2.1
Foreigners	4.1	6.3
Total Foreign Enrolment	4.1	6.3
of which:		
Algeria	5.1	8.6
Morocco	4.3	8.1
Tunisia	4.7	7.4
Other Africa	2.8	1.6
Spain	3.8	3.6
Portugal	4.0	7.1
Italy	3.5	4.3
Other EEC	0.9	1.0
Yugoslavia	2.2	2.7
Turkey	3.9	8.4
Laos, Cambodia	1.3	..
Others	2.3	1.1

Notes: SES: Section d'éducation spéciale
GCA: Groupes de classes-ateliers
ENP: Ecole nationale de perfectionnement

$$\text{Column 1} = \frac{\text{children enrolled in special education}}{\text{children enrolled in elementary as a whole (ordinary + special)}}$$

$$\text{Column 2} = \frac{\text{children enrolled in special education (SES-GCA-ENP)}}{\text{children enrolled in secondary education as a whole (1st and 2nd cycles + special)}}$$

Table 10

**Enrolment in Classes with Low Level of Recruitment
of Secondary Education, by Nationality**
(School Year 1980/81)

Nationality	Children of 1st Cycle of Secondary Education Enrolled in CPPN-CPA	Short Stream 2nd Cycle	Columns 1 and 2
Total enrolment	6.0	41.2	19.1
Of which:			
French	5.7	39.9	18.5
Foreigners	10.7	64.5	29.4
Total foreign enrolment	10.7	64.5	29.4
Of which:			
Algeria	11.2	72.5	33.7
Italy	8.8	62.3	30.1
Morocco	14.3	67.8	32.0
Portugal	12.0	76.9	30.9
Spain	7.9	60.3	27.0
Tunisia	9.5	64.6	29.6
Turkey	30.0	78.3	37.6
Yugoslavia	5.9	59.0	23.4
Other Africa	4.3	34.3	19.1
Other CEE	2.8	19.2	8.7
Others	6.0	34.2	16.1

Notes:

$$\text{Column 1} = \frac{\text{Children enrolled in CPPN-CPA}}{\text{Children enrolled in all 1st cycle classes}}$$

$$\text{Column 2} = \frac{\text{Children enrolled in short stream, 2nd cycle}}{\text{Children enrolled in 2nd cycle}}$$

$$\text{Column 3} = \frac{\text{Children enrolled in CPPN-CPA and the short stream, 2nd cycle}}{\text{Children enrolled in secondary education (excluding special education)}}$$

Here again the distribution by nationality is clearly uneven:

-- First between French and foreign children, since fewer than 6 per cent of French children are enrolled in CPPN-CPA classes compared to over 100 per cent of foreign children, and the short 2nd cycle receives less than half of French children (39.9 per cent) but far more (64.5 per cent) foreign children; and

-- Secondly among other nationalities, since there is a big disparity between children from EEC countries other than Italian and Turkish children.

Between those two extremes, which in fact involve very small numbers of children (about 5 000 in each case), there is a wide range of cases above or below the average for all foreign children combined. There is a higher than average proportion of children in one or other short stream in the case of children from the following countries:

-- In the 1st cycle, Turkey (30 per cent), Morocco (14.3 per cent), Portugal (12 per cent) and Algeria (11.2 per cent);

-- In the 2nd cycle, Turkey (78.3 per cent), Portugal (76.9 per cent), Algeria (72.5 per cent), Morocco (67.8 per cent) and Tunisia (64.6 per cent).

The difference in streaming at this level is noteworthy. Some figures may be given for children reaching the final stage of secondary education without receiving the general instruction (provided in the long stream of the 2nd cycle) which leads on to university education: two French children out of every five, three foreign children (all nationalities combined) out of five, and four out of every five Turkish, Portuguese or Algerian children.

c) Conclusions

It is thus clear that the term "foreign children" covers a great variety of situations, with children from the most recent waves of migration (for instance, Moroccan and Turkish children) and/or farthest removed in cultural terms from the norms of the host society (children from the Maghreb countries) being most disadvantaged. The education of these children ends at a lower level and leads on to low-skilled occupations.

Important though this first set of factors is, it should not be allowed to mask other factors relating to the socio-economic and socio-cultural level of the childrens' parents. Although no accurate yardsticks are available, it is possible by analogy to verify that the education of foreign children tends to follow the same pattern as the education of children from working class families (a category which moreover contains a substantial proportion of immigrants).

A survey concerning the occupation and status of foreign manpower, covering employees in the private industrial and commercial sector only (firms with ten or more staff), brings out the disparities in skills to the disadvantage of foreign workers (data for October 1979).

The second step is to incorporate various items from sample surveys or studies indicating how the parents' membership of a given socio-economic category affects their children's school careers.

The examples given in Tables 12-14 clearly demonstrate that social factors (belong to a given socio-economic and socio-cultural environment, socio-economic status of parents, parents' level of education -- all closely interlinked) play a decisive part in the school career of children, whatever their nationality.

Immigrants' children have thus to contend with two types of handicap, being foreigners in an education system which marginalises children who have not absorbed the cultural and behavioural patterns of the country, and by and large belonging to a social environment which in itself is already in a position of inferiority and lacks equality of opportunity from the outset.

Table 11

Labour Force in Firms with Ten or More Staff by Nationality and by Socio-economic Status

	Operatives	All Manual Workers	Unskilled Workers	Skilled Workers	Non-manual Workers	Supervisor Staff, Technicians	Executives
Foreigners	13.4	85.8	34.5	37.9	9.2	2.6	2.1
All employees (Foreigners included)	5.5	52.6	19.7	27.4	25.6	11.4	9.8

Table 12

Educational Retardation in the Elementary Sector

	Total (1)	Foreigners (1)	Unskilled (2)	Skilled (2)	Executive (2)
Percentage of children one year of more behind	27.0	49.0	49.2	42.1	20.5

1. 1977/78 survey on immigrants' children and French schools (INED).
2. 1964/65 survey on the intellectual level of school-age children.

Table 13

**Probability of Reaching a Given Level or Class
According to Socio-economic Status (1)**

Status of Parents	Entering Short Vocational Stream (CPPN-CPA-1st Year CAP)	Entering Short 2nd Cycle	Entering Long 2nd Cycle
Manual workers	50.0	19.3	26.7
Domestic services	48.6	19.8	26.6
Non-manual workers	32.9	19.3	42.7
Junior executives	12.9	14.2	65.8
Senior executives, professions	3.2	5.0	84.4

1. Combination of three samples of children entering the lowest class of secondary school (6e) in 1972, 1973 and 1974, base = 100 for each category.

Source: SEIS, October 1980.

Table 14

**Socio-economic Origin of 100 Pupils Entering
Special Secondary Education, by Status of Parents**

Manual workers	57.8
Non-manual workers	6.2
Senior executives, Professions	0.6
Junior executives	1.5

Source: Service des études informatiques et statistiques, October 1980.

NOTES

1. For families with at least one child aged 0 to 16.

2. Observation over a longer period (possible in the case of primary education because statistics have been available since 1974-75) illustrates the scale of the change still more clearly. Over ten years primary education (preschool and elementary combined) "lost" some 640 000 children, as a result of two trends: -790 000 French children, +150 000 foreign children.

FRANCE

RESULTAT D'UNE ANALYSE FACTORIELLE DES CORRESPONDANCES ENTRE LE DEGRE D'ENSEIGNEMENT ET LA NATIONALITE POUR L'ANNEE SCOLAIRE 1980/81

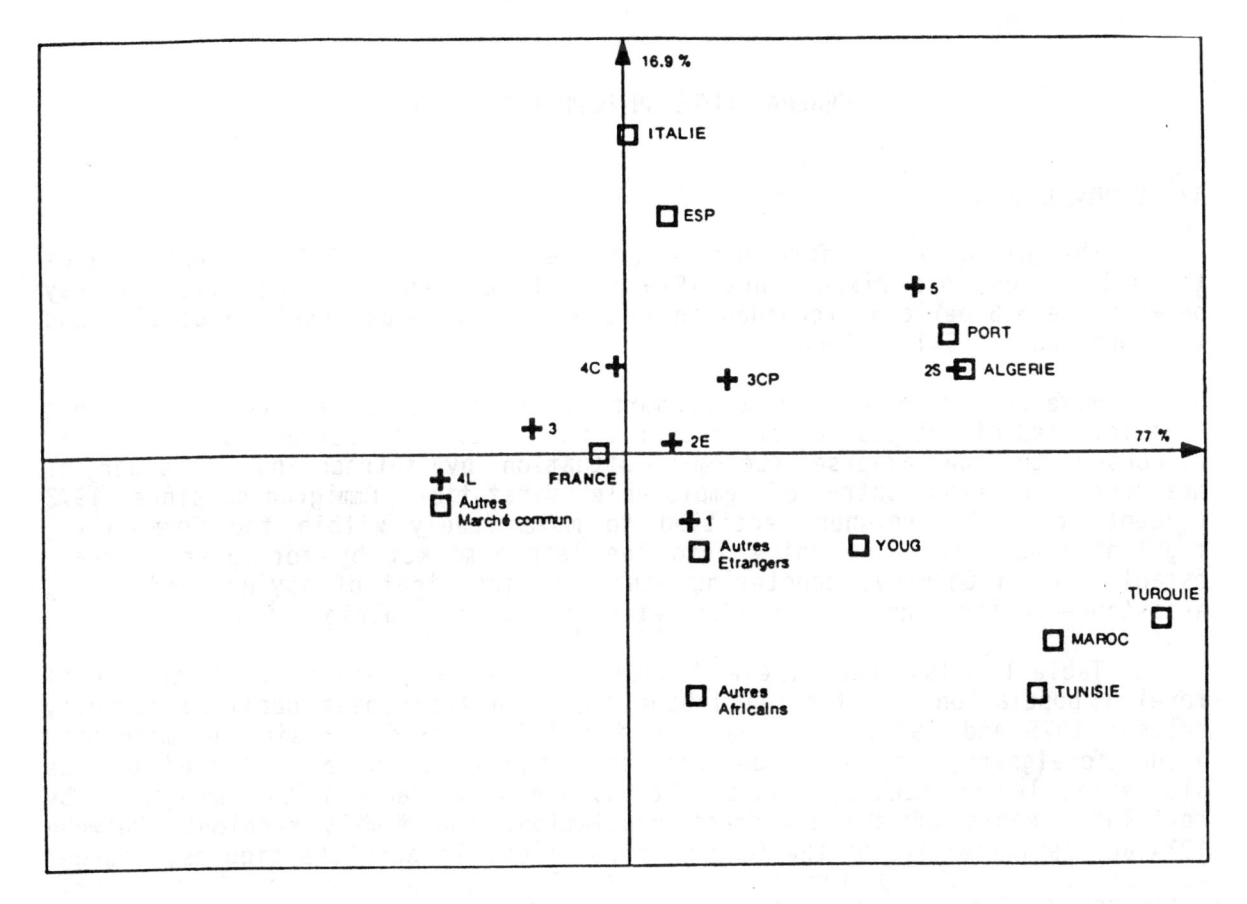

1.   Préscolaire
2E.   Primaire
2S.   Primaire spécial
3.   Secondaire 1er cycle sans CPPN
3CP.   Secondaire 1er cycle avec CCPN et CPA
4C.   Secondaire 2e cycle court
4L.   Secondaire 2e cycle long
5.   Secondaire spécial

➕ : Type d'école

☐ : Nationalité des élèves

III. ENROLMENT OF FOREIGN CHILDREN IN GERMAN SCHOOLS

GENERAL FOREIGN POPULATION DATA

a) <u>Recent Trends</u>

The proportion of foreigners in Germany, at about 6.5 per cent towards the late 1970s, has risen since 1979 to 7.6 per cent in 1982, i.e. mid-way between the 6.8 per cent recorded in France and the 9 per cent in Belgium and 14.5 per cent in Switzerland.

However, foreigners as a proportion of the labour force in employment have levelled off at just under or over 9 per cent. The German government has responded to the adverse economic situation by introducing a number of measures: halting entry of employable first-time immigrants since 1973 (except for EEC foreigners entitled to move freely within the Community), tightening up control on entry into the labour market by foreigners already established in Germany, countering abuses of the right of asylum, and giving assistance to foreigners wishing to return to their countries of origin.

Table 1 illustrates these tendencies. As a proportion of the total foreign population the foreign labour force in employment declined steadily between 1975 and 1982. Explanations for this included rising umemployment among foreigners, who were quicker than nationals to be affected by the slackening labour market, the conditions governing access to employment by certain segments of the immigrant population, and family reunion. Between 1974 and 1981 the size of the foreign population, in absolute figures, changed as follows: - 39 369 for men over 16 (i.e. a decline of 1.9 per cent), + 149 781 for women over 16 (an increase of 11.7 per cent) and + 397 501 for children under 16 (an increase of 51.8 per cent).

b) <u>The Foreign Birthrate</u>

Table 2 shows that between 1970 and 1974, the number of German births declined by 30.7 per cent and that of foreign births increased by 71.8 per cent, whereas between 1975 and 1983, the number of German births rose by 5.6 per cent and the number of foreign births dropped by 35.9 per cent. The reason was that new legislation has since 1975 given German nationality at birth to any child with at least one German parent. These children have accordingly helped "boost" the number of German births and check the decline in indigenous births (Germany having one of the lowest fertility rates in western Europe).

Table 1

Trend of Total and Employed Foreign Population in Germany

Year	Total Foreign Population (1) ('000)	% (3)	Foreign Population in Employment (2) ('000)	% (3)	Ratio (2)/(1)
1975	4 089.6	6.6	2 070.7	10.3	1.56
1976	3 948.3	6.4	1 937.1	9.7	1.52
1977	3 948.3	6.4	1 888.6	9.5	1.48
1978	3 981.1	6.5	1 869.3	9.3	1.43
1979	4 143.8	6.7	1 933.7	9.4	1.40
1980	4 453.3	7.2	2 071.7	9.9	1.37
1981	4 629.7	7.5	1 929.7	9.2	1.23
1982	4 666.9	7.6	1 809.0	8.8	1.16

1. At 30th September of each year.

2. At 30th June of each year. Figures refer to members of the labour force making compulsory social security payments. Data on the total working population (those in and seeking work and frontier workers) are available only for 1980 to 1982. At 30th June 1982, the foreign labour force amounted to 2 037 000 and represented 9.2 per cent of the total labour force.

3. Percentages are calculated in relation to the entire population (nationals and foreigners) in each category.

Source: Statistisches Bundesamt.

c) **Present Position**

i) **Total population**

At 30th September 1982, of the 4 666 917 foreigners resident in Germany, 1 580 671 were Turkish (33.9 per cent of the foreign population), 631 692 were Yugoslav (13.5 per cent), 601 621 Italian (12.9 per cent), 300 824 Greek (6.4 per cent), 311 579 were EEC nationals other than Italian and Greek (6.7 per cent), 174 988 Austrian (3.75 per cent), and 173 526 Spanish (3.7 per cent).

The age breakdown reveals a higher proportion of foreigners in the younger age groups, with 10.1 per cent for the under-15s as opposed to 7.5 per cent for the total population, all ages combined (Table 3).

Table 2

Live Births

Year	All Births nb.	Of Which Foreign nb.	%
1970	810 808	63 007	7.8
1971	778 526	80 714	10.4
1972	701 214	91 441	13.0
1973	635 633	99 086	15.6
1974	626 373	108 270	17.3
1975	600 512	95 873	16.0
1976	602 851	86 953	14.4
1977	582 344	78 271	13.4
1978	576 468	74 993	13.0
1979	587 984	75 560	13.0
1980	620 657	80 695	13.0
1981	624 557	80 009	12.8
1982	621 173	72 981	11.8
1983	594 177	61 470	10.3

Source: Bundesminister für Arbeit und Sozialordnung.

The same figures broken down by nationality show the very high proportion of Turkish children among the younger foreign age-groups: one the 409 500 immigrants under 6 years of age, 199 400 (48.7 per cent) were of Turkish nationality, whereas taking all age groups, Turkish immigrants make up only 33.9 per cent of the foreign population.

By contrast, there are remarkably few young Dutch nationals (0.4 per cent of the foreign population under six) indicating that they stay in their own country even when their parents emigrate; thus Dutch nationals in the 21-35 age group constitute 30.5 per cent of the total immigrant Dutch population, whereas children under six represent only 1.9 per cent of this same population. Spanish immigrants are relatively older: 23.5 per cent of them are aged between 21 and 35, 21 per cent between 35 and 45 and 19 per cent between 45 and 55, whereas only 6.4 per cent are under six.

The immigrant population from Yugoslavia, Italy, Portugal and, to a lesser extent, Greece, tend to be rather younger.

ii) Labour force

At 30th June 1982, the 1 808 981 foreigners in employment included 564 567 Turks (31.2 per cent of the employed foreign workers), 320 335 Yugoslavs (17.7 per cent), 261 020 Italians (14.4 per cent), 116 421 Greeks (6.4 per cent) and 76 754 Spanish (4.2 per cent).

Table 3

Total and Foreign Population in Germany by Age Group, 1981

Age Group	Total Population	Foreign Population ('000)	%
0- 5 years	3 560.8	409.5	11.5
6- 9 years	2 604.2	326.4	12.5
10-14 years	4 637.9	360.3	7.8
15-17 years	4 268.5	218.1	5.1
All ages	61 628.0	4629.7	7.5

Source: Statistisches Bundesamt 1982.

Table 4

Workers Employed in Selected Branches of the German Economy
(Situation at 31st March 1982)

	Total Employed nb.	Foreign Employed nb.	%
Overall German economy	20 385 600	1 808 981	8.9
Of which			
Manufacturing	8 207 959	1 016 403	12.4
Construction	1 512 946	167 578	11.1
Banking, insurance	777 970	12 726	1.6
Retail	2 860 320	116 704	4.1
Services	3 632 651	291 724	8.0

Source: SOPEMI/OCDE, 1983

Table 4 shows how the total labour force and the foreign labour force are employed in selected sectors.

Foreigners are relatively more numerous in secondary sector activities. Conversely, except for services, fewer are employed in the tertiary sector; it is possible that this is the result of stricter legislation in regard to the foreign population.

FOREIGN STUDENTS IN GERMAN SCHOOLS

The figures given in Table 5 show that over the period 1974-84 there was a steady upward trend in the percentage of foreign enrolment in the pre-school, primary and secondary levels. But, in absolute numbers, there has been a decrease in 1983/84 of 14 200 foreign pupils compared with the preceding year.

As regards technical and vocational education, however, no clear trend can be discerned.

a) <u>Nursery Schools</u>

There is no data concerning the presence of foreign pupils in pre-elementary schools as such but only data referring to pre-elementary classes attached to primary school education. These classes are institutions for children under compulsory school law who, because of development of these institutions, cannot attend regular education.

Enrolment in these institutions is not compulsory, but in some cases, school authorities may insist on it.

There has been a dramatic increase in foreign enrolment in these classes; currently out of every hundred children enrolled in these schools, just over 17 are of foreign nationality, compared with a figure of only 6 in 1974. This is the result of the combined effects of two contrasting trends: firstly, the increase in the foreign population aged under 16 and, secondly, the fall in the German birthrate over the past few years (Germany has one of the lowest fertility rates in western Europe). These two trends are illustrated by the following figures: in 1974, total enrolment in <u>Schulkindergärten</u> was 85 973, which included 5 284 foreign children; however, by 1981 total enrolment was 65 456 and the number of foreign children 22 439 -- in other words, a drop of 33 per cent in the number of German children and an increase of 116 per cent in the number of foreign children.

b) <u>Primary Schools</u>

The situation is much the same as regards foreign enrolment in primary school education: here, statistics also include foreign pupils enrolled in the <u>Grundschulen</u> and <u>Hauptschulen</u> and do not differentiate between the foreign pupils in primary schools and those in some other types of secondary school

Table 5

Trend of Foreign Enrolment in German Schools as a Percentage of Total Enrolment

		1974/75	1975/76	1976/77	1977/78	1978/79	1979/80	1980/81	1981/82	1982/83	1983/84
Pre-school education (1)	Schulkindergarten	6.2	6.8	8.2	9.6	12.4	15.5	16.3	17.5	18.1	19.5
Primary education	Grundschulen + Hauptschulen (2)	4.7	5.1	5.4	6.0	7.1	8.6	10.4	11.9	12.9	13.1
1st cycle secondary	Realschulen + Gesamtschulen	1.3	1.4	1.5	1.6	1.8	2.1	2.5	3.1	3.7	4.4
1st and 2nd cycles secondary	Gymnasien	1.3	1.4	1.5	1.6	1.6	1.7	1.9	2.1	2.4	2.7
Special education	Sonderschulen	2.7	3.2	3.8	4.6	5.4	6.5	7.8	9.5	11.3	13.0
Part-time vocational education	Berufsschulen	3.1	2.9	2.8	2.8	2.9	3.2	4.3	5.1	5.1	5.2
Full-time vocational education	Berufsfachschulen	1.9	2.2	1.9	2.1	2.2	2.6	3.3	4.2	4.7	4.6
Vocational extension education	Berufsaufbau-schulen	1.6	1.4	1.3	1.6	1.9	1.7	1.8	1.8	1.8	1.9
Technical education	Fachoberschulen	1.4	1.4	1.6	1.8	1.9	1.9	2.0	2.3	2.5	2.7
Technical education	Fachschulen	3.2	3.0	2.8	2.5	2.2	2.2	2.1	2.4	2.4	2.2

1. Data including only pre-elementary classes attached to primary school education.

2. The Hauptschulen belong to secondary school education and pupils who attend should not be included with those enrolled in Grundschulen which are attached to primary school enrolment. Nevertheless, in the German official statistics on foreign pupils' enrolment, the two categories of pupils are always together with no distinction between pupils in primary school education and those in the Hauptschulen which is a particular type of secondary school education. This confusion is understandable in the mean that pupils attending the Hauptschulen are those who are unable to attend a more difficult general secondary school education course and who, thus, are immediately guided towards vocational training.

Sources: Statistisches Bundesamt (Fachserie II, Bildung und Kultur, Reihe 1.1, 1981)).
Grund und Struktur Daten 1984/85 der Bundesminister für Bildung und Wissenschaft.

education (for example, the Hauptschulen). Foreign enrolment was in 1984 close to 13 per cent, whereas in 1974, it was only about 4.7 per cent.

c) General Secondary Schools

Foreign enrolment is slightly higher in Realschulen and Gesamtschulen (4.4 per cent in 1983-84) than in Gymnasien (2.65 per cent in 1983-84). The explanation for this is probably that foreigners tend to abandon the so-called "academic" stream in favour of vocational education. The traditional type of education dispensed in Gymnasien is the most prestigious and academic path to university, whereas the type of education dispensed in the Realschulen can lead on either to second-cycle general secondary education in a lycée (usually only for the brightest students), or to a technical or vocational school, or directly to employment combined with part-time vocational training. The Gesamtschulen, which is a combination of the different types of education provided by the Realschulen, the Hauptschulen and the Gymnasien, works on a large scale in five Länder in which they live with the Hauptschulen, the Realschulen and the Gymnasien and also exist on an experimental basis in the other Länder.

Graph 1.

**TRENDS IN THE FOREIGN POPULATION
(CALCULATED AND COMPARED WITH TOTAL PUPILS ENROLLED)
IN EACH TYPE OF GENERAL SECONDARY SCHOOL
EDUCATION IN GERMANY**

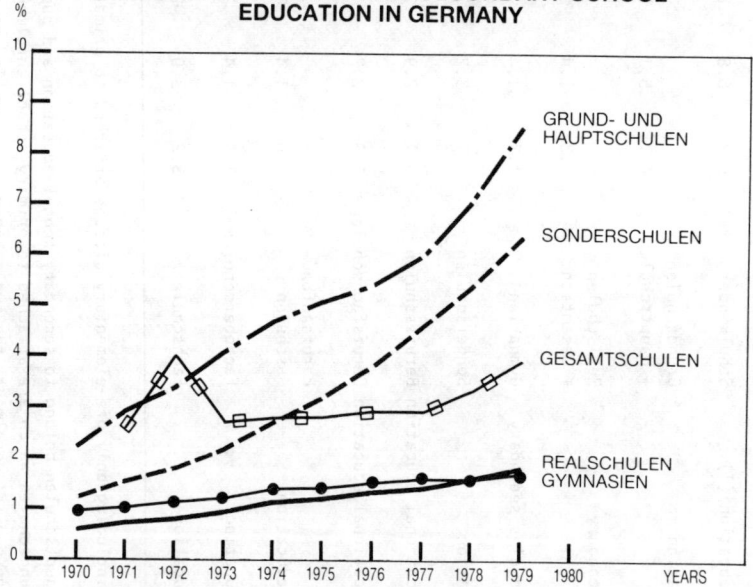

Note: For *Grund- und Hauptschulen*, refer to note 2 of Table 5

Source: *Ausländer in der Bundesrepublik Deutschland*, by Luitgard Trommer and Helmut Köhler (1981), DJI Deutsches Jugendinstitut.

d) Vocational Secondary Schools

Once they have completed the first cycle of secondary education, foreign children tend more towards vocational education (where their level of enrolment in 1983-84 was approximately 4.5 per cent) than towards second-cycle general education (2.65 per cent in 1983-84).

Several forms of vocational education are available both to Germans and foreigners, and these are described briefly below. There are three main types of vocational education:

-- <u>Berufsschulen</u>: establishments enabling students to complete their general education and acquire the necessary theoretical knowledge for the exercise of a particular trade. According to the German system for vocational training, enrolment in these schools is on a part-time basis and the most important part (apprenticeship) is working with firms. General training only is provided in schools whose courses last at least three years.

-- <u>Berufsfachschulen</u>: full-time vocational training with school apprenticeship.

-- <u>Berufsaufbauschulen</u>: complementary vocational training giving access to upper vocational training.

-- <u>Berufssonderschulen</u>: vocational training for the handicapped.

-- <u>Fachoberschulen</u>: technical secondary education.

-- <u>Fachgymnasien</u>: specialised technical secondary education.

These last two types of school provide long-course vocational training.

Foreigners hardly show a slight preference for short-course vocational education (4.9 per cent in 1983-84) rather than long-course (4.6 per cent) or extension education.

e) Special Education

The figures in Table 5 relating to special education need to be viewed with caution in the context of this analysis of foreign enrolment in German schools.

Data relating to special education in Germany only include institutions for the physically and mentally handicapped people (<u>Schulkindergärten für Behinderte, Sonderschulen</u>). Institutions for foreigners are not included in these data. Then, the comparison between these data and those for other European countries which include the two types of institutions, requires a lot of precautions.

<u>Schulkindergärten für Behinderte</u> and <u>Sonderschulen</u> are intended solely for physically and mentally handicapped children of school age (six and over), whereas in other Western European countries special education covers not only handicappd children but also those who have reading or writing difficulties or who are educationally backward in some way or other, and includes therefore children of immigrants with language problems.

Similarly, these special schools in Germany (<u>Sonderschulen</u>), like ordinary schools, provide not only primary education but also general secondary, technical and vocational education for handicapped children, whereas in other countries special education is provided at each level, i.e. there are special classes for the primary level, others for the first-cycle secondary level and so on.

The figures for special education in Table 5 cover only this particular type of school and are therefore incomplete since they do not include children in special classes for foreigners.

The German authorities have taken steps to ensure better integration of foreigners; in particular, preparatory classes have been created for foreigners with no knowledge of the German language and to help these children adjust to German schools. About 17 per cent of foreign schoolchildren attend these preparatory classes, although this percentage varies from Land to Land. Unfortunately, the system is tending to break down due to differences among the students (age, social class, language, etc.), a shortage of teaching staff, etc. The number of these classes is decreasing because an increasing number of migrants' children, born in Germany, attends pre-primary schools and starts enrolment with good knowledge of the German language, which thus makes a preparatory class unecessary.

In the German school system, bilingual classes for the immigrants' children include not only their mother tongue but also German as a foreign language for the first four years. Their main aim is either to fit these pupils into the German school system or to allow them to return to their own country. Enrolment in bilingual classes varies from Land to Land: in 1978/79, 25 per cent of the full-time foreign pupils in North Rhine-Westphalia and 46 per cent in Bavaria were enrolled in these classes.

In Bavaria, at the end of enrolment, pupils attending these classes, receive the German certificate of "End of <u>Hauptschule</u>".

Generally, in order to facilitate the foreign pupils' insertion into German classes, the number of these pupils must not exceed a fifth of the total number of pupils in these classes. In areas in which there is a great concentration of foreigners, special classes for immigrants have been created. There are only a few of these classes (in 1978/79 there were 107 special classes in the whole of Germany). German authorities assert that the number of these classes will probably decrease in the years to come because an increasing number of foreign children have enough knowledge of the German language at their admission to school and consequently do not need to go through these special classes to adapt to the German school system.

Not all of the figures for these different types of education for foreign children are included under the heading Sonderschulen in Table 5, which makes it even harder to calculate the actual proportions of foreign students in the German education system as a whole.

f) Breakdown by Nationality

Breaking down the statistics by type of education and by nationality provides some useful information and throws light on the behaviour patterns and problems facing each ethnic group. It would seem at first sight from factor analysis of correspondence that there are two more or less homogeneous groups: firstly, immigrants from the Mediterranean countries (Turkey, Yugoslavia, Italy, Greece, Spain, Portugal and North Africa) who are enrolled predominantly in nursery and primary schools and, secondly, foreigners from the so-called "rich" countries (America and Western Europe -- Austria, Holland, United Kingdom, France, Belgium, Switzerland, Denmark, Luxembourg, Norway, etc.) of whom there are proportionately more enrolled in secondary education (See Diagram).

It follows from this that there is a correlation between the level of education and the date when immigrants arrived: between 1974 and 1981 the number of Turkish children under 16 rose by 145 per cent and currently they account for slightly more than half of all foreigners in this age group so that it is not surprising to find that 64 per cent of foreign children enrolled in Schulkindergarten are of Turkish nationality. The same applies to Moroccan children (the number of those under 16 rose by 482 per cent between 1974 and 1981), Tunisian children (+373 per cent), Yugoslav children (+75 per cent) and Portuguese children (+49 per cent). On the other hand the Europeans and Americans, who have been resident in Germany for a number of years, have a proportionately higher enrolment in Realschulen, Gesamtschulen and Gymnasien (with their lower birthrate, the number of children of these nationalities is even diminishing: between 1974 and 1981 the number of children of Austrian and EEC nationalities, with the exception of the Italians, declined by about 17 per cent).

Austrian children -- although they represent scarcely 2 per cent of the foreign population enrolled in German schools -- account for about 10 per cent of foreign enrolment in Gymnasien. It must be remembered that German is the language spoken in Austria, so that Austrian children have far less difficulty integrating into the German school system. American and French children also have a disproportionately high level of enrolment in the second cycle of secondary education: whereas American children make up 1.25 per cent of all foreigners enrolled in German schools, they account for almost 8 per cent of those attending Gymnasien, with French children accounting for 3 per cent of foreign enrolment in these schools although they represent only 0.5 per cent of total foreign enrolment. By contrast, barely 18 per cent of Turkish children are enrolled in Gymnasien, whereas they represent almost half of total foreign enrolment in secondary education.

Table 6 highlights the differences between Turks, Italians, Austrians and Dutch at secondary education level:

-- Austrian children are noticeably more numerous in general secondary education and are therefore more likely to be contemplating a

Table 6

Foreign Enrolment in the Different Types of Secondary Education (1), 1981/82

	Turks	Italians	Austrians	Dutch	Ratios (2) Turks	Italians	Austrians	Dutch
Enrolment in the system of education as a whole	52.6	11.3	1.7	0.9				
Enrolment in secondary education as a whole (3)	44.6	10.3	4.2	2.0				
Enrolment in Realschulen and Gesamtschulen (comprehensive schools)	35.0	11.6	3.5	2.0	0.78	1.13	0.82	0.98
Enrolment in Gymnasien (1st and 2nd cycles secondary)	17.8	7.3	10.6	3.2	0.40	0.71	2.51	1.56
Enrolment in Berufsschulen für Vollzeitschüler (year of intensive vocational education)	75.8	5.9	0.5	1.0	1.70	0.57	0.12	0.48
Enrolment in Berufsschulen für Teilzeitschüler (variant of the preceding type of school)	58.7	12.0	2.2	1.5	1.32	1.16	0.53	0.73
Enrolment in Berufsfachschulen (full-time vocational education)	42.5	11.5	2.6	2.8	0.95	1.11	0.62	1.38
Enrolment in Berufsfachbauschulen (vocational extension school)	28.7	10.1	7.7	3.4	0.65	0.99	1.82	1.67
Enrolment in Fachoberschulen (technical education)	48.3	3.7	6.2	2.9	1.08	0.36	1.45	1.44
Enrolment in Fachgymnasien (specialised technical education)	22.6	11.2	5.6	1.7	0.51	1.09	1.33	0.83

1. Percentages are calculated in relation to the foreign population.

2. The above ratios are obtained by dividing the enrolment levels for the different types of secondary education by the foreign enrolment level in secondary education as a whole.

3. Foreign pupils enrolled in the Hauptschulen are not included in secondary education: refer to note Table 5.

Source: Statistisches Bundesamt 1982 (Bildung und Kultur, Fachserie II, Reihe 1 et 2).

university career rather than vocational education (it should be noted though that when they do opt for vocational education, they prefer to do so at a more intensive level and enrol in long-cycle vocational education). By contrast, Turkish children tend primarily to enter short-cycle vocational education and are less numerous in the academic streams.

-- As for Italian children, despite their long-standing immigration going back more than 30 years, they are enrolled mainly in the lower-grade streams of secondary education.

Thus the German school system can be seen to be rigid where immigrants are concerned. Only a foreigner from a country where the educational background is more or less similar to Germany's seems to be able to integrate into the German system in the same sort of way as a German national.

As regards special education, and subject to the above point about the comprehensiveness of the statistics available, there are fewer foreigners than Germans (1981/82, foreigners accounted for no more than 9.5 per cent of enrolment in special education). However, this foreign enrolment includes large numbers of Turks (50.5 per cent of foreign students in special education), then Italians (19.7 per cent) and Yugoslavs (8.6 per cent), but very few Austrians (0.8 per cent) and Dutch (0.7 per cent).

Calculating the ratios (the ratio of the enrolment rate in specialised education to the enrolment rate in the overall system of education) bears out that there are proportionately more Turks and Italians than Austrians or Dutch (the ratio for Turks being 0.96, for Italians 1.75, for Austrians 0.47 and for the Dutch 0.71).

Factor analysis of correspondence aims, among other things, to group together individuals with more or less the same profiles, and it shows (though the results must be interpreted cautiously) that Mediterranean nationals are disadvantaged compared with American and Europeans as regards education, and are more often than not enrolled in short-cycle technical or vocational education. In most cases, accordingly, they can only enter the labour market on less favourable terms (type of job, remuneration etc.) and find it harder to make their way into working and social life.

FEDERAL REPUBLIC OF GERMANY

**FACTOR ANALYSIS DIAGRAM OF CORRESPONDENCE BETWEEN
EDUCATIONAL LEVELS AND NATIONALITIES FOR THE SCHOOL YEAR
1981/82**

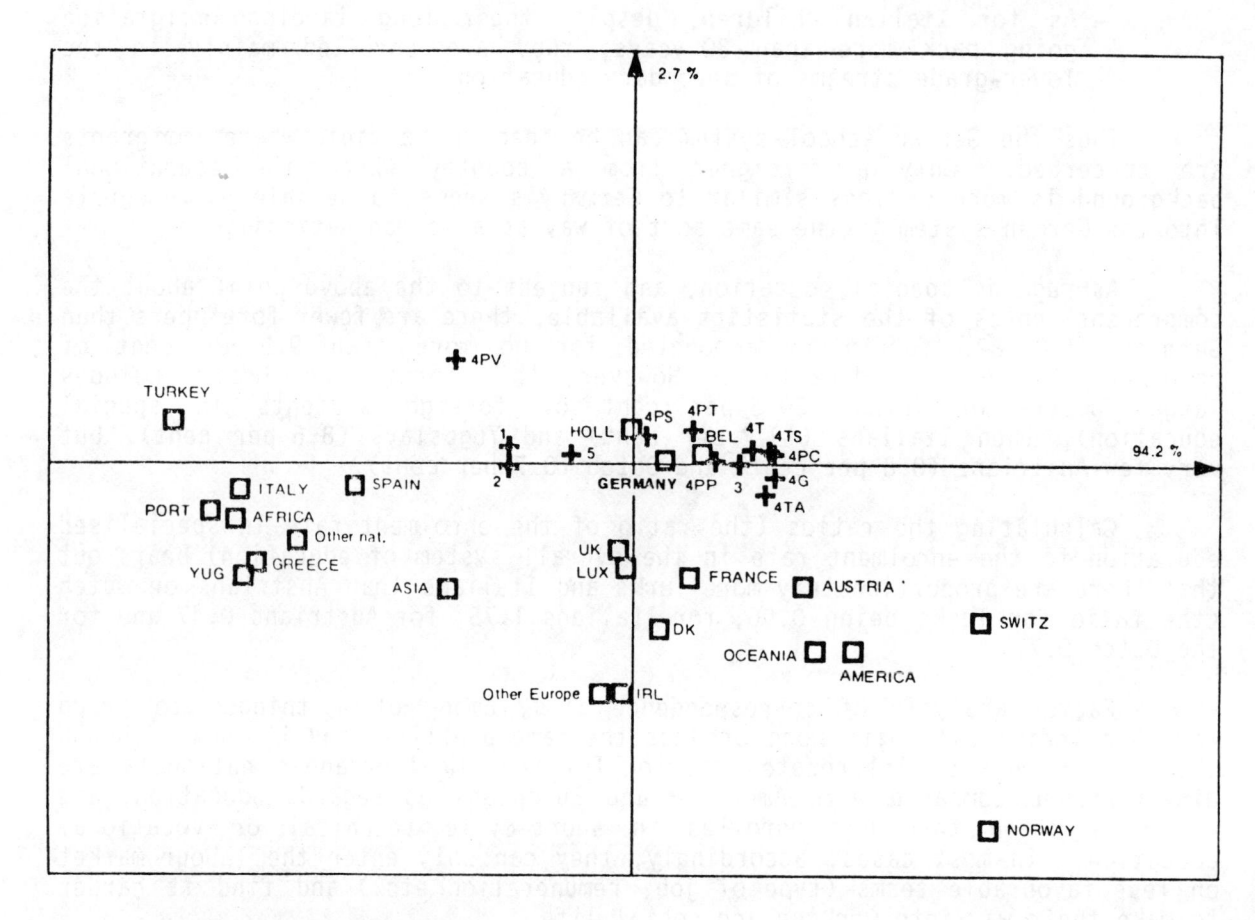

1.	Schulkindergarten : pre-school
2.	Grund und Hauptschulen : Primary
3.	Realschulen und Gesamtschulen : Secondary 1st cycle
4G.	Gymnasien : Secondary 1st and 2nd cycles
4PV.	Berufsschulen für Vollzeitschüler : Vocational schools : short cycle (one year of "intensive" courses)
4PT.	Berufsschulen für Teilzeitschüler : Vocational schools : short cycle (alternative)
4PP.	Berufsfachschulen : Vocational schools : long cycle
4PC.	Berufsaufbauschulen : Vocational extension schools
4PS.	Berufssonderschulen : Special vocational schools
4T.	Fachoberschulen : Technical secondary schools
4TS.	Fachgymnasien : Specialised technical schools
4TA.	Fachschulen : Specialised technical secondary schools for adults
5.	Sonderschulen : Special schools.

+ : Type of school

☐ : Pupils' nationality

IV. ENROLMENT OF FOREIGN CHILDREN IN LUXEMBOURG SCHOOLS

GENERAL DATA ON THE FOREIGN POPULATION

To give a better idea of the scale of foreign enrolment in the Luxembourg school system, it may be useful to outline certain of the current demographic and socio-economic characteristics of the foreign population and the changes that have taken place since 1975.

a) <u>Recent Trends</u>

Luxembourg has the highest proportion of foreign residents of all Western European countries. According to the census carried out in 1981 by the STATEC (the central service for statistics and economic studies), 96 000 out of about 365 000 people resident in the country -- 26.3 per cent -- are non-Luxemburgeois. In other words, rather more than one inhabitant in four is of foreign nationality.

This is not altogether a recent phenomenon, since for almost a hundred years foreign residents have accounted for at least 10 per cent of the total population -- in 1900, for instance, for 12.3 per cent. Moreover, without massive recourse to immigrant labour, Luxembourg firms would not be able to operate, since one-third of the total labour force is foreign.

For Luxembourg, therefore, immigration is a structural rather than a cyclical phenomenon.

Between 1975 and 1981 the total foreign population grew at a rather more rapid rate than the foreign labour force, due to family reunification and a high number of foreign births (Table 1).

b) <u>The Foreign Birth Rate</u>

Although the foreign birth rate has levelled out in recent years, foreign births continue to account for a substantial part of the total number of births recorded -- over one-third (between 38 and 40 per cent).

In 1981, 776 out of 1 700 foreign births were Portuguese (45.6 per cent), 293 Italian (17.2 per cent) and 173 French (10.4 per cent). This is an appreciable contribution to demographic growth in Luxembourg and helps counteract the decline in the national birth rate, which is one of the world's lowest (Table 2).

Table 1

Trend of Total Foreign Population and Foreign Labour Force (1)

Year	Total Foreign Population nb.	% (2)	Employed Foreign Labour Force (3) nb.	% (2)
1975	88 300	24.5	48 600	31.0
1976	84 500	23.4	48 700	31.3
1977	84 000	23.2	49 100	31.5
1978	91 000	25.1	49 800	32.0
1979	92 100	25.3	50 400	32.2
1980	94 000	25.7	51 900	32.8
1981	95 789	26.3	52 200	33.0
1982	95 900	26.2	52 300	33.0

1. All figures are estimates, except for the 1981 total foreign population figures, which are taken from the 31st March 1981 census.

2. Percentages are calculated in relation to the total population (nationals + foreigners) in each category.

3. The employed foreign labour force includes self-employed and frontier workers, but not Luxembourgeois frontier workers, international civil servants and the unemployed.

Source: STATEC.

c) The Current Situation

i) The total population

Distribution by age group shows that the younger the age group the higher the ratio of foreign to total population (Table 3).

It is interesting to see that in the case of Portuguese nationals -- who constitute almost 28 per cent of the foreign population -- 33 out of 100 are under 15, while in the case of Italians (23 per cent of the foreign population), 25 out of 100 have not yet reached their 15th birthday; or, to bring this point home still more vividly, of 1 000 people aged 15 or over resident in Luxembourg, 627 are Luxemburgeois, 143 Portuguese and 84 Italian. Hence the large numbers of Portuguese and Italian children enrolled in pre-primary and primary schools.

Table 2

Number of Births

Year	Total Number of Births	Number of Foreign Births	%
1975	3 982	1 653	41.5
1976	3 915	1 680	42.9
1977	4 053	1 651	40.7
1978	4 072	1 576	38.7
1979	4 078	1 561	38.3
1980	4 169	1 558	37.4
1981	4 414	1 700	38.5
1982	4 300	1 668	38.8

Source: STATEC.

Table 3

Breakdown by Age Group of Total and Foreign Populations
(Situation at 31st March 1981)

Age Group	Total Population	Foreign Population	%
0- 4	20 850	8 413	40.3
5- 9	21 262	8 630	40.6
10-14	25 386	8 120	32.0
15-19	27 948	7 427	26.6
20-24	29 118	7 652	26.3
All ages together	364 602	95 789	26.3

Source: STATEC 1983/84.

ii) The labour force

The data set out in Table 4 -- derived from the 1981 census and thus corresponding to a definition of the labour force which is not the same as the one used in the retrospective analysis (see Note to Table 4) -- show the distribution of the total and foreign labour force in certain economic sectors.

As in the majority of host countries, most foreigners belong to the working class (42 per cent of immigrants in the labour force are skilled or unskilled workers). But the number of foreign "white-collar" workers must also be taken into consideration, since this small country houses the headquarters of several international bodies such as the European Parliament and Court of Justice, as well as a number of multinationals.

Thus, in continuing the study on the enrolment of foreign children in Luxembourg schools, it will be particularly important to take into account not only their nationality but also their parents' socio-economic status.

ENROLMENT OF FOREIGN CHILDREN IN LUXEMBOURG SCHOOLS

Tables 5, 6 and 7 show how the proportion of foreign children in the Luxembourg school system changed over the period 1974-1983.

In all types and at all levels of education the proportion of foreign children increases year by year. There are two reasons for this -- the increase in the number of foreign residents, and the determination of the Luxembourg authorities to integrate immigrants into the host society.

Between 1974 and 1983, while the school population as a whole fell by 5 534, the number of foreign children attending school rose by 3 326. In other words, the number of Luxembourg nationals attending school fell by 8 770. Even more striking is the fall in the numbers of Luxembourg nationals attending pre-primary and primary school between 1974 and 1983 -- down 21 per cent and 36.6 per cent respectively. Patently Luxembourg has not avoided the general fall in the birth rate that is affecting the whole of Western Europe.

It should, however, be noted that with the proportion of immigrant children reaching 39.3 per cent of pre-primary school enrolment in 1981/82 -- so that in the coming years these same children will account for a correspondingly high proportion of primary and secondary school enrolment -- a peak has been reached, since in the following year, 1982/83, the relative weight of foreign enrolment declined to 37 per cent. This decline is probably due to a very slight upturn in the birth rate of Luxembourg nationals, a downturn in that of the foreign population (which shows a tendency to adopt the fertility patterns of the host country), and the fact that in view of the current economic difficulties some immigrants have returned, with their families, to their country of origin.

a) Analysis by Level of Education

The figures in Table 5 show that the proportion of immigrant children in special classes is higher than that of Luxembourg nationals and that

Table 4

Employed Labour Force — Breakdown by Socio-economic
Status and Nationality, 1981

Socio-economic Status	Total Population	Foreign Population	%
All economic activities	150 720	46 159	30.6
Of which:			
Farmers	3 514	122	3.5
Employers	6 265	1 083	17.3
Directors, members of legislative bodies, senior civil servants	1 594	710	44.5
Liberal professions	16 276	3 716	22.8
Administrative personnel, distributive trades, salesmen and women and specialised service workers	50 009	15 222	30.4
Charge hands and supervisors	2 998	564	18.8
Skilled and semi-skilled workers	40 086	16 266	40.6
Unskilled workers	6 598	3 181	48.2

Note: The national employment concept used in the census to measure the labour force differs from the interior employment concept used for STATEC surveys (from which the data shown in Table 1, for example, have been drawn). Without entering into detail, the essential difference is that the former concept covers employment of people resident in Luxembourg, while the latter includes all those employed in Luxembourg, whether they are resident there or not.

Source: 31st March 1981 census.

foreign enrolment in vocational training is higher than in general secondary education; in supplementary classes, more than one child in three is of foreign nationality.

i) Special education

Three categories of class come under this heading -- classes for children with learning difficulties, induction classes for foreign children and classes for the physically or mentally handicapped.

Generally speaking, the linguistic situation in Luxembourg is fraught with difficulty. Teaching is in three languages: the mother tongue is

Table 5

Proportion of Foreign Children in the Luxembourg
School System Between 1974 and 1983

	1974/75	1975/76	1976/77	1977/78	1978/79	1979/80	1980/81	1981/82	1982/83
Pre-primary school	28.7	30.3	33.0	35.9	37.8	37.7	39.1	39.3	37.0
Ordinary primary school	24.8	25.7	27.1	28.5	30.0	31.4	33.2	34.6	36.0
Special classes	48.7	56.0	56.2	55.8	58.2	58.8	57.6	57.7	61.2
Supplementary education	27.1	27.8	30.3	32.7	35.3	36.2	38.2	40.3	44.2
Post-primary education	13.6	14.2	14.2	15.0	15.4	16.3	17.0	17.9	19.3
Of which:									
Technical secondary	17.2	17.8	17.8	18.5	19.1	20.1	21.0	22.0	..
General secondary	7.7	7.8	7.9	8.5	8.6	9.3	9.8	10.3	..
Total	22.4	23.4	24.3	25.2	26.2	27.1	28.1	28.9	30.0

Source: Courrier de l'Education Nationale -- Grand Duché du Luxembourg.

Luxembourgeois, children learn to read and write in German, and written and oral French is taught from the second year of primary school on. The foreign child, with his fourth language -- that of his parents' country of origin -- is at a considerable disadvantage as compared with nationals, especially as regards German, which is not an "everyday" spoken language.

This has led the Luxembourg authorities to set up induction classes for immigrant children where the number of pupils is limited to 15, with teaching personalised as far as possible and adapted to the children's needs; the intention is that children should not remain in such classes for more than one year.

Tables 6 and 7 show the proportion of foreign children in these three quite separate types of special education.

When classes for children with learning difficulties, classes for the physically and mentally handicapped and induction classes are differentiated in this way, the proportion of foreign children in special education is seen to be lower, but it is still too high in comparison with that of Luxembourg nationals. The latest statistics even indicate that the number of foreigners in special education in the strict sense of the term is increasing. This leads one to wonder whether transfers are not made automatically from induction classes to other special classes.

ii) Supplementary education

This type of education marks the end of compulsory schooling for certain 12-15 year-olds. If, on completing the 6th year of primary education, children are unable to pass an entrance examination giving access to either general or technical secondary education, the result of this "elimination" process is that they enter supplementary education.

As Table 5 shows, the situation for immigrant children is by no means improving since they continue to account for an ever-increasing proportion of enrolment here -- in relative terms, at least, since the numbers of both nationals and foreigners in this type of education are declining. In 1982/83, foreign children accounted for over 44 per cent of total enrolment in supplementary education.

iii) Post-primary education

Here the proportion of foreign children, while still lower than in other types of education, has risen steadily, from 13.6 per cent in 1974/75 to 19.3 per cent in 1982/83. This increase is due not only to the larger numbers of foreign residents in the country, but also to the measures taken by the government of the Grand Duchy -- institution of transition classes to ease the transition from primary to post-primary education and classes with a special linguistic regime in the lower cycle of secondary education.

But the biggest difference between immigrant children and Luxembourg nationals is that so many of the former opt for the technical stream of post-primary education, while the latter are more attracted towards secondary education, which gives them access to university. In 1981/82, for instance, the proportion of foreign children in general education was about 10 per cent, against 22 per cent in technical or vocational education.

Table 6

Distribution of Foreign Children in the Various Types of Special Class

	1974/75	1975/76	1976/77	1977/78	1978/79	1979/80	1980/81	1981/82	1982/83
Of 1 000 foreign children in special education, the following numbers are enrolled in									
Classes for children with learning difficulties	457	374	464	458	400	445	441	435	423
Classes for handicapped children	17	21	27	22	43	26	27	72	89
Induction classes	526	605	509	520	557	529	542	493	488

Source: Dossiers Statistiques du SIRP (Service d'Innovation et de Recherche Pédagogique).

Table 7

Proportion of Foreign Children in Special Education

	1974/75	1975/76	1976/77	1977/78	1978/79	1979/80	1980/81	1981/82	1982/83
Special classes Of which:	48.6	55.9	56.2	55.8	58.2	58.8	57.6	57.6	61.2
Classes for children with learning difficulties	34.8	37.6	43.0	42.5	44.9	44.7	48.8	48.0	52.7
Classes for handicapped children	7.8	11.6	13.9	11.4	16.8	15.1	17.4	21.4	22.6
Induction classes	100.0	99.2	99.8	100.0	97.8	99.8	99.2	99.8	98.3

Source: Dossiers Statistiques du SIRP (Service d'Innovation et de Recherche Pédagogique).

The relative weight of foreign enrolment may thus double according to the type of education concerned. It is highest in the training courses which prepare young people for an early entry into working life takes first place, and this again points up the fact that foreign students are at a disadvantage compared with Luxembourg nationals.

b) <u>Breakdown by Nationality</u>

Since the terms "immigrant" and "foreigner" are too broad, a breakdown by nationality is called for.

i) <u>The Portuguese</u>

Table 8 shows the predominance of Portuguese children in pre-primary and primary education, where they account for about half the foreign enrolment. In the nine years 1974/75 to 1982/83 their numbers in pre-primary schools have increased from 569 to 1 511 and in primary schools from 2 224 to 4 912 .

Similarly, Table 9 shows that in the case of the Portuguese the ratio of pupils in post-primary education to those in the education system as a whole is less than 0.5 -- whereas for children of other nationalities it is greater than 1. This is due to the fact that young Portuguese are more recent immigrants, while other nationalities (e.g., German and Italian) have been established longer.

Another way of neutralising the "age" variable effects is to calculate the number of foreign primary schoolchildren in special or supplementary education, taking 100 as the base. The calculations covering total foreign enrolment are then repeated for 100 Portuguese, 100 Italians, etc. The same procedure can be followed as regards post-primary education (see Table 10).

As already indicated, the Portuguese come up against special difficulties in the Luxembourg school system; in primary education, 10/100 are enrolled in special classes, against 7/100 for foreign children as a whole. Similarly, when they do reach the post-primary level, they usually choose -- to a greater extent than other young immigrants -- technical, vocational or agricultural courses, i.e. the short cycle, which leads on to rapid entry into the job market. The proportion here is 76/100, against 61/100 for all foreign nationals taken together.

ii) <u>EEC nationals</u>

Numbers of schoolchildren of other nationalities (Italian, French, German, Belgian, Dutch, etc.) all dropped to a greater or lesser extent over the same period (i.e. between 1976/77 and 1982/83). No EEC country has escaped the general fall in the birth rate throughout the developed countries, and numbers of nationals have either levelled off (France) or fallen -- sometimes sharply (Germany, Italy).

In post-primary education, it is for German and Dutch nationals that the ratios are highest -- 1.75 and 1.64 respectively (see Table 9). Table 10 confirms this favourable position.

Table 8

Breakdown by Nationality at Pre-primary and Primary Level for School Year 1982/83
(as percentages)

	Foreigners	Portuguese	Italians	French	Germans	Belgians	Dutch	Spaniards	Other
Pre-primary education	100.0	53.9	16.0	9.7	4.1	4.6	1.9	2.5	7.3
Primary education	100.0	48.4	23.0	7.7	4.5	4.2	1.9	3.0	7.2
School system overall	100.0	41.5	25.1	9.1	6.1	4.8	2.5	3.0	7.8

Source: Courrier de l'Education Nationale.

Table 9

Breakdown by Nationality at Post-primary Level for School Year 1982/83
(as percentages)

	Foreigners	Portuguese	Italians	French	Germans	Belgians	Dutch	Spaniards	Other
Pre-primary education (1)	100.0	20.0	34.8	11.6	10.7	6.3	4.1	3.3	9.3
School system overall (2)	100.0	41.5	25.1	9.1	6.1	4.8	2.5	3.0	7.8
Ratio (1)/(2)	1.0	0.5	1.4	1.3	1.8	1.3	1.6	1.1	1.2

Source: Courrier de l'Education nationale.

The complex bilingual situation characteristic of the Luxembourg school system, which requires fluency in both German and French, leads certain parents of Latin origin to send their children to school in neighbouring countries. Some foreign children go to French-speaking schools in Belgium (Province of Luxembourg) or France (Lorraine), where the linguistic system suits them better, since teaching is in French, whereas in Luxembourg the command of both French and German that is required greatly reduces their chances of getting on at school or acquiring vocational skills. At present no detailed statistics on this trend or on its extent is available.

Among the foreign pupils usually classified in Luxembourg as "French-speaking" (e.g. those of Italian, Spanish and Portuguese origin), Italian youngsters are beginning to be represented at the higher levels of general and technical secondary education as well as in higher and/or university studies. This favourable development is largely due to the fact that Italian immigration is longer-established than Portuguese and therefore more firmly rooted in Luxembourg society.

CONCLUSIONS

Factor analysis of correspondence derived from two sets of variables (level of education and nationality) makes it easier to depict young immigrants' schooling patterns. The results arrived at in the Analysis Diagram are approximately the same as those obtained through calculations.

Later it should be possible to refine this analysis by taking into account other sets of variables such as foreigners' mother tongue (whether closely related to Luxemburgeois or German, or not), the chronology of migratory flows (Italians, Spaniards, Portuguese, etc.), parents' socio-economic status and demographic features.

This essay in retrospective analysis of the foreign enrolment situation has enabled us to identify its main features. Between 1974 and 1983 there was a substantial increase in foreign enrolment at all levels of education. The trend has not, however, been undifferentiated. Because Portuguese immigration is relatively recent, there are disproportionately large numbers of Portuguese children in pre-primary and primary schools and in special and supplementary education, while the number of German, Dutch, Belgian and French children in secondary education continues to rise. Italian enrolment falls midway between these two categories.

Thus the Luxembourg authorities, while endeavouring to facilitate the integration of the ever-increasing numbers of foreigners in their education system -- which is bound to involve long-term problems -- will at the same time have to take steps to enable the most disadvantaged immigrant groups to fit more easily into that system.

Table 10

Average Foreign Enrolment in Education by Nationality
(as percentages)

	All Foreign Nationalities Together	Portuguese	Italians	Germans	Dutch
School Year 1982/83					
Of 100 pupils in primary and supplementary education the following numbers are enrolled in:					
Special classes	7.2	9.9	4.8	1.7	2.6
Supplementary education	11.7	11.3	15.5	13.8	5.2
School year 1981/82					
Of 100 pupils in secondary education the following are enrolled in:					
General secondary education	20.7	8.0	17.1	27.6	24.5
Technical secondary education	79.3	92.0	82.9	72.4	75.5

Note: The average foreign enrolment in a given type of education is calculated as follows:

Foreign enrolment in the type of education concerned
―――
Foreign enrolment in the level category (primary or secondary) which includes the type of education concerned

Source: Courrier de l'Education nationale.

LUXEMBOURG

FACTOR ANALYSIS DIAGRAM OF CORRESPONDENCE BETWEEN EDUCATIONAL LEVELS AND NATIONALITIES FOR THE SCHOOL YEAR 1981/1982

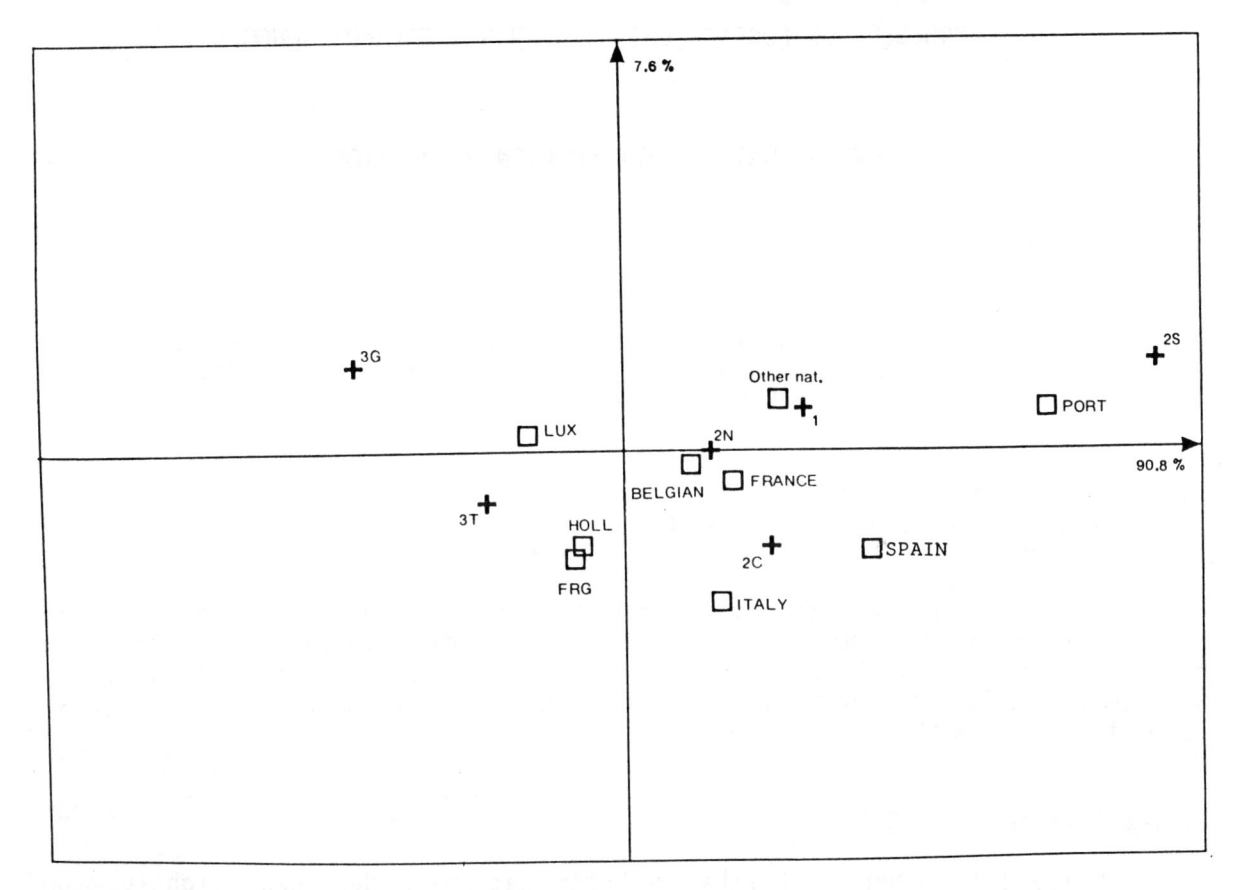

1 - Pre-primary
2N - Ordinary primary
2S - Special primary
2C - Supplementary education
3G - General secondary education
3T - Technical secondary education

+ : Type of school

☐ : Pupils' nationality

V. ENROLMENT OF FOREIGN CHILDREN IN NETHERLANDS SCHOOLS

GENERAL DATA ON THE FOREIGN POPULATION

a) Recent Trends

In recent years the changes in the total foreign population and in the employed foreign labour force have been strikingly different. In seven years the former has increased by 70 per cent (from 316 000 to 538 000), while the latter has increased by only 5 per cent and is barely at the 1977 level.

As shown by the ratios in the right-hand column of Table 1, the proportion of the total foreign population in employment continues to decline, indicating the combined effects of two factors -- the scale of family reunification and the increase in foreign natality.

A third factor -- one which works in the opposite sense -- also has to be taken into account. This is the rapidly increasing number of naturalisations (3 392 in 1970, 6 022 in 1975 and 15 312 in 1981). It is among Surinamese immigrants that the rate of naturalisation is by far the highest (almost 60 per cent).

b) The Foreign Birth Rate

While the number of births to Dutch nationals declined slightly from 169 730 to 164 100 (-3.3 per cent) between 1975 and 1981, in the foreign population it rose steadily during the same period, from 8 150 to 14 470 (+77.5 per cent) -- pratically doubling in the Turkish population and even tripling for Moroccans. Age specific fertility rates for all foreigners decreased modestly in 1983 after rather sharp fall in 1982. The same holds for Moroccans and Turks. Thus the proportion of foreign births in total live births was correctly 7.7 per cent in 1982, against 4.6 per cent in 1975 (Table 2).

This situation is due to the fertility differential between Dutch and foreign women (Table 3).

c) The Current Situation

i) Demographic structure

Of the 14 million people at present resident in the Netherlands, nearly 550 000 are foreigners and about 200 000, although they have Dutch nationality, are of Moluccan, Surinamese or Dutch East Indian origin. In addition, on 1st January 1982 the total population of the Netherlands also

Table 1

Trend of Foreign Population ('000)

Year	Foreign Population (1) nb.	% (3)	Foreign Labour Force (2) nb.	% (3)	Ratio (2)/(1)
1975	316.3	2.3	176.0	..	..
1976	350.5	2.6	180.5	..	..
1977	376.3	2.7	187.0	..	..
1978	399.8	2.9	196.4	..	..
1979	431.8	3.1	182.3	4.3	1.39
1980	473.4	3.4	188.1	4.3	1.26
1981	520.9	3.7	192.7	4.4	1.19
1982	537.6	3.8	185.0	4.3	1.13

1. Data at 1st January of each year.

2. Data at 31st March of each year. Figures show the numbers of the employed labour force, including frontier workers but not self-employed workers and their families.

3. Percentages are calculated in relation to the total population (nationals + foreigners) in each category.

Sources: CBS Standstatistiek tabel 5 Maandstatistiek Bevolking 83/2
CBS for ₋stimates of employed foreign workers; Ministry of Social Affairs and Employment for registered unemployed foreigners.

included a minority of 6 000 Moluccans and 17 700 Surinamese who had not acquired Dutch nationality.

Numbers of Turks and Moroccans rose substantially during the period 1979-83; the Turkish population increased from 105 227 in 1979 to 154 201 in 1983 (a 46.5 per cent increase), and the Moroccan population from 62 929 in 1979 to 101 511 in 1983 (up 61.3 per cent).

These are the two nationalities primarily concerned by a high rate of family immigration and a growing number of births. This explains two major features that differentiate them from the other nationalities:

-- A lower-than-average employment rate as compared with the total population (Table 4);

Table 2

Number of Live Births in the Netherlands, 1975-82

Year	Total Number of Live Births	Number of Foreign Births	%	Number of Dutch Births	Number of Turkish Births	Number of Moroccan Births
1975	177 800	8 150	4.6	169 730	2 370	1 280
1976	177 090	8 790	5.0	168 300	2 550	1 610
1977	173 300	10 180	5.9	163 120	3 300	2 030
1978	175 550	11 070	6.3	164 480	3 680	2 370
1979	174 980	12 110	6.9	162 870	4 080	2 810
1980	181 290	13 580	7.5	167 720	4 700	3 130
1981	178 570	14 470	8.1	164 100	5 150	3 480
1982	172 070	13 320	7.7	158 750	4 460	3 710

Source: CBS Maandstatistiek van de Bevolking.

Table 3

Total Fertility Rates (1) for 1 000 Women According to Their Nationality

	All Nationalities	Dutch	Foreigners	Turkish	Moroccan	Surinamese
1976	1 642	1 596	2 969	4 545	7 951	2 343
1981	1 559	1 489	3 464	4 592	6 658	1 906

1. That is, the mean number of children that would be born to a woman if she were subject to the age-specific fertility rates observed for the year concerned (the values of this synthetic measure of fertility being indicated for 1 000 women).

Source: CBS Maandstatistiek van de Bevolking.

-- A disproportionate number of Turkish and Moroccan children in the 0-9 age group (see Table 5).

Thus Turks and Moroccans predominate in a foreign population whose average age is already lower than that of the population as a whole. Foreign children account for 31.7 per cent of the 0-9 age group (38 000 out of 120 000), and Turks and Moroccans for 20.6 per cent, though for all age groups together foreign nationals represent only 26.6 per cent and Turks and Moroccans 16 per cent.

ii) <u>The labour force</u>

The figures in Table 4 show the high proportion of Turks and Moroccans in the foreign labour force (22.4 per cent and 15.6 per cent respectively). The relative weight of the two nationalities is higher than that of the total

Table 4

Foreign Resident Population in the Netherlands and Employed Foreign Labour Force (by Nationality), 1st January 1982

Nationality	Foreign Population nb.	Foreign Labour in Employment (1) nb.	% (2)
All Foreign Nationalities	537 571	185 000	34.4
Of which:			
Non-EEC (3)	397 349	118 900	29.9
Including:			
Turkish	147 970	41 400	28.0
Moroccan	93 077	28 800	30.9
Spanish	22 706	9 500	41.8
Yugoslav	14 148	6 200	43.8
EEC	140 222	66 100	47.1
Including:			
Italian	21 038	8 200	38.5

1. See Table 1 for definition of foreign labour force.

2. The percentages are calculated for each nationality in relation to the corresponding foreign population.

3. EEC: Belgium, Denmark, F.R.G, France, Italy, Ireland, Luxembourg, the United Kingdom and Greece.

Source: Centraal Bureau voor de Statistiek.

Table 5

Resident Population of the Netherlands in 1981
According to Age and Nationality ('000)

Age Group	Total Population nb.	Foreign Population nb.	%	Turkish	Moroccan
0- 9 years	1 910.5	120.3	6.7	38.1	24.8
10-14 years	2 485.4	92.2	3.7	32.1	14.0
All ages	14 208.6	520.2	3.7	138.5	83.3

Source: Migration, Minorities and Policy in the Netherlands. 1983, Rinus Penninx, OECD/SOPEMI Report.

Table 6

Total and Foreign Labour Force Breakdown
According to Economic Activity ('000)
(Situation as of 31st March 1981)

	Total Labour Force (1)	Foreign Labour Force	%
Agriculture	65.5	2.6	4.0
Industry, Mining	1 089.9	100.5	9.2
Construction	365.1	10.5	2.9
Distributive Trades	689.9	25.7	3.7
Transport	293.2	8.8	3.0
Banking and Insurance	415.7	9.2	2.2
Other Services	1 242.4	35.4	2.8
Total	4 162.2	192.7	4.6

1. This table gives numbers of workers employed at least 15 hours a week. For this reason, percentages differ slightly from those in Table 1.

Source: Centraal Bureau voor de Statistiek.

labour force of EEC nationals (35.7 per cent). All nationalities taken together (1), the foreign penetration rate in the secondary sector is higher than in the other sectors. On 31st March 1981, of 100 foreigners working in the Netherlands, 52 were employed in industry or mining, about 19 in the service sector, five in banking or insurance and less than two in agriculture (2).

Table 6 confirms the disproportionate number of foreigners in industry as compared with other economic activities as a whole.

These figures give a clearer idea of the scale of foreign enrolment in pre-primary and primary classes and in establishments providing certain specific types of education.

FOREIGN CHILDREN IN DUTCH SCHOOLS

a) How the Education System is Organised

An account of the Dutch education system will make it easier to understand the statistics on school enrolment broken down according to nationality and level of education.

In the Netherlands, after attending pre-primary school (Kleuteronderwijs) and primary school (Gewoon lager onderwijs), children can opt for general secondary education (Algemeen voortgezet onderwijs) or lower-level vocational and technical education (LBO -- Lager beroeps onderwijs).

Those who opt for the first alternative then have to make a further choice -- whether to enter a junior secondary school (MAVO -- Middelbaar algemeen voortgezet onderwijs, length of studies three or four years); or a senior secondary school (HAVO -- Hoger Algemeen Voortgezet Onderwijs, length of studies five years); or pre-university education (VWO -- Voorbereidend Wetenschappelijk onderwijs, length of studies six years). There are three types of pre-university school: the gymnasium (classical secondary school); the atheneum (modern secondary school); and the lyceum (where education may be either classical or modern).

Some of the pupils who have opted for vocational training may, after completing lower-level training (LBO) go on to the middle level, and some again may continue to the higher level (HBO -- Hoger beroeps onderwijs).

Similarly, pupils leaving MAVO may opt for either MBO (Middelbaar beroeps onderwijs) or HAVO.

Alongside this standard education, special education is provided for children between 3 and 18 who suffer from physical, mental, sensory or locomotor handicaps.

The Dutch education system has remained, on the whole, a selective one, with two distinct streams from the outset in secondary education, one for the elite and the other for the also-rans, and high repeat rates. In recent years, there has been a broad and intensive debate on the desirability and possibilities of a more integrated system for the first years of secondary education.

b) <u>Overview</u>

Table 7 shows the development of foreign enrolment rates in the Netherlands education system from 1974/75 to 1982/83. It can be seen at once that at all levels enrolment of foreign children has increased much faster than that of Dutch nationals. As regards pre-primary and primary education this is not surprising, since the number of live births has grown faster among the foreign population than among nationals, and in the case of certain nationalities family reunification has continued at a rapid rate.

As regards secondary education, it is clear from the 1981/82 column of Table 7 that:

-- The majority of foreigners opt for vocational training -- even at lower level, provided it gives them a skill -- rather than for so-called general education (only 1.7 per cent of students enrolled at MAVO, HAVO and VWO are foreign, against 2.6 per cent at LBO, MBO and HBO);

-- As regards this vocational and technical training, it is quite clear that there are far more foreigners (both as a percentage and in absolute figures) at the lower level than at the middle and higher levels, since they account for 4.1 per cent of total enrolment at LBO but only 0.7 per cent at MBO and barely 1 per cent at HBO. However, the "age" effect may be an important factor here, since because of recent immigration many children are still in the lower age groups (3).

The distribution of foreigners (of all nationalities) as compared with that of Dutch nationals is shown in Table 8 (foreign enrolment by nationality in the various types of secondary education), which highlights the differences in educational expectations. There is a differential of some ten points between the two groups. Fifty-two per cent of Dutch nationals enter general secondary education and 48 per cent vocational and technical training, while for foreigners the percentages are reversed -- 42 and 58 per cent respectively.

c) <u>Breakdown by Nationality</u>

Differences in school careers can be studied from a number of standpoints according to the nationality or group of nationalities to which pupils belong.

First, factor analysis of correspondence between level of education and nationality for the year 1982/83 gives a clearer picture of the educational pattern specific to each nationality (4).

On the one hand are the Turks, Moroccans and Yugoslavs, the nationalities whose numbers are highest in pre-primary and primary education, because of their recent arrival in the Netherlands and the high proportion of

Table 7

Foreign Enrolment Rates in the Netherlands Education System

		1974/75	1975/76	1976/77	1977/78	1978/79	1979/80	1980/81	1981/82	1982/83
Pre-primary school	Kleuteronderwijs	..	..	2.2	2.8	3.6	4.4	5.1	5.4	5.9
Primary school	Gewoon Lager Onderwijs	1.4	1.6	1.9	2.2	2.7	3.3	3.9	4.4	4.8
General secondary education	Algemeen Voortgezet Onderwijs (MAVO, HAVO, VWO)	..	0.5	0.6	0.8	0.9	1.1	1.4	1.7	1.9
Vocational training lower level	LBO (Lager Beroeps Onderwijs)	..	..	..	..	1.9	2.5	3.3	4.1	4.4
Vocational training intermediate level	MBO (Middelbaar Beroeps Onderwijs)	..	..	..	..	0.3	0.4	0.5	0.7	0.8
Vocational training higher level	HBO (Hoger Beroeps Onderwijs)	..	..	..	..	0.8	0.9	1.0	1.0	1.1
Special education	Buitengewoon Onderwijs	..	..	..	..	..	..	2.3	2.8	3.3

Note: Percentages correspond to number of foreign pupils divided by total number of pupils at each level.

Source: Centraal Bureau voor de Statistiek.

young children among them. On the other hand, Italians and Spaniards, and also nationals of "other EEC" countries (i.e., France, Belgium, the Federal Republic of Germany, the United Kingdom, Denmark, Luxembourg, Ireland and -- since 1981 -- Greece) are more numerous in general secondary education and in intermediate- or higher-level vocational training.

Secondly, a detailed breakdown of enrolment in secondary education (by type of education and nationality) shows the widely divergent paths followed by young foreigners according to their geographical origin.

The sharpest contrast in school careers is between young Turks and Moroccans on the one hand and EEC nationals on the other. Of the former, between 70 and 75 per cent of those in secondary education are receiving vocational and technical training, against under 40 per cent of the latter. In general secondary education, the proportions are reversed -- under 30 per cent of Turks and Moroccans, but over 60 per cent of EEC nationals.

Table 8

Foreign Enrolment by Nationality in the Different Types of Secondary Education (School Year 1982/83)

	Total Enrolment in Secondary Education	Enrolment in General Secondary Education		Enrolment in Vocational and Technical Secondary Education	
	nb.	nb.	% (1)	nb.	% (1)
Total Enrolment Of which:	1 604 391	836 220	52.1	768 171	47.9
Dutch	1 567 763	820 763	52.4	747 000	47.6
Foreigners Of which:	36 628	15 457	42.2	21 171	57.8
Non-EEC Including	20 555	6 257	30.4	14 298	69.6
Turkish	12 253	3 572	29.2	8 681	70.8
Moroccan	5 923	1 407	23.8	4 516	76.2
Spanish	1 938	1 037	53.5	901	46.5
Yugoslav	441	241	54.6	200	45.4
EEC Including	8 540	5 263	61.6	3 277	38.4
Italian	2 127	1 355	63.7	772	36.3
Other EEC	6 413	3 908	60.9	2 505	39.1

1. Percentages are calculated as a proportion of the corresponding population enrolled in secondary education.

Source: Centraal Bureau voor de Statistiek.

Pupils of other nationalities are in an intermediate position; the distribution of Spanish pupils is about the same as that of the Dutch, while that of Yugoslavs is nearer that of the foreign pupils (all nationalities taken together).

d) Special Education

At both primary and secondary levels this type of education is sub-divided into sections according to the nature of handicap -- aural or visual, physical or locomotor, mental retardation, learning difficulties (in reading and writing), multiple handicaps.

According to the nature of the handicap there is little difference between foreigners and Dutch nationals, except that almost one in two foreigners in special education is mentally retarded, against a corresponding ratio of barely one in three among Dutch nationals.

Given the high proportion of Turks, Moroccans and Surinamese in the Netherlands education system as a whole, it is not surprising to find that these nationalities are among those most often found in special education.

Table 9

Foreign Enrolment in Special Education
(Situation at 16th April 1984)

	Total Enrolment	Foreigners (1)	%
Special education at primary level	72 792	3 870	5.3
Special education at secondary level	26 009	1 529	5.7

1. Including children of Surinamese and Moluccan origin.

Source: Ministerie van Onderwijs en Wetenschappen.

e) Ethnic Minorities in Dutch Schools

It must not be forgotten that the population of the Netherlands comprises many people from the Dutch West Indies, Surinam (5) and the Moluccan Islands, who constitute clearly defined ethnic minorities. Since most of them have Dutch nationality, estimates of their numbers are unreliable.

Similarly, statistical data on school enrolment are based on place of birth, and so, since most children of Surinamese or Dutch West Indian origin were born in the Netherlands, do not give any clear picture of the differences between the Dutch-born children and the ethnic minorities.

Because of the wide cultural differences between Moluccans, Surinamese, Dutch West Indians and Dutch -- and within each group -- it would be helpful to have a better understanding of the educational problems that arise for each ethnic minority. Unfortunately, in the absence of detailed statistical data the analysis cannot be refined.

Table 10

School Enrolment (Absolute Figures, Breakdown According to Nationality)
School Year 1982/83

Nationality	Kleuter onderwijs	Gewoon lager onderwijs	Algemeen voortgezet- onderwijs	LBO	MBO	HBO	Buiten- gewoon onderwijs
Dutch	375 303	1 144 411	820 763	405 000 (c)	205 000 (c)	137 000 (c)	92 537
Turks	8 808	22 225	3 572	8 152	340	189	1 228
Moroccons	6 790	14 929	1 407	4 369	110	37	864
Italians	500	1 903	1 355	565	150	57	150
Spaniards	748	2 344	1 037	728	129	44	146
Yugoslavs	661	1 249	241	176	16	8	49
Other EEC (b)	1 800	5 466	3 908	1 580	384	541	274
Non-EEC (c)	4 194	8 985	3 937	2 394	491	711	460

a) Figures are estimates.
b) Other EEC: French, Germans, Luxembourgeois, Irish, Greek (from 1981), Danish, Belgians, British.
c) Non-EEC: Americans, Asiatics, Africans and Oceanians.

Source: Centraal Bureau voor de Statistiek, 1982/83

NOTES

1. No data broken down by both nationality and economic activity are available.

2. These calculations are based on the Central Bureau for Statistics estimates of the foreign labour force and numbers of foreigners in employment.

3. It was not possible to carry out the same analysis as regards general education, since no statistics combining streams (MAVO, HAVO, VWO) with nationality were available.

4. See Annex 2 for a table giving absolute figures broken down according to nationality.

5. A special reference should be made to the Surinamese; following the proclamation of Surinam's independence in 1975, the number of Surinamese applying for Dutch nationality tripled in three years, from 2 869 in 1979 to 9 087 in 1981 (Statistical Yearbook of the Netherlands, 1982).

NETHERLANDS

FACTOR ANALYSIS DIAGRAM OF CORRESPONDENCE BETWEEN EDUCATIONAL LEVELS AND NATIONALITIES FOR THE SCHOOL YEAR 1982/1983

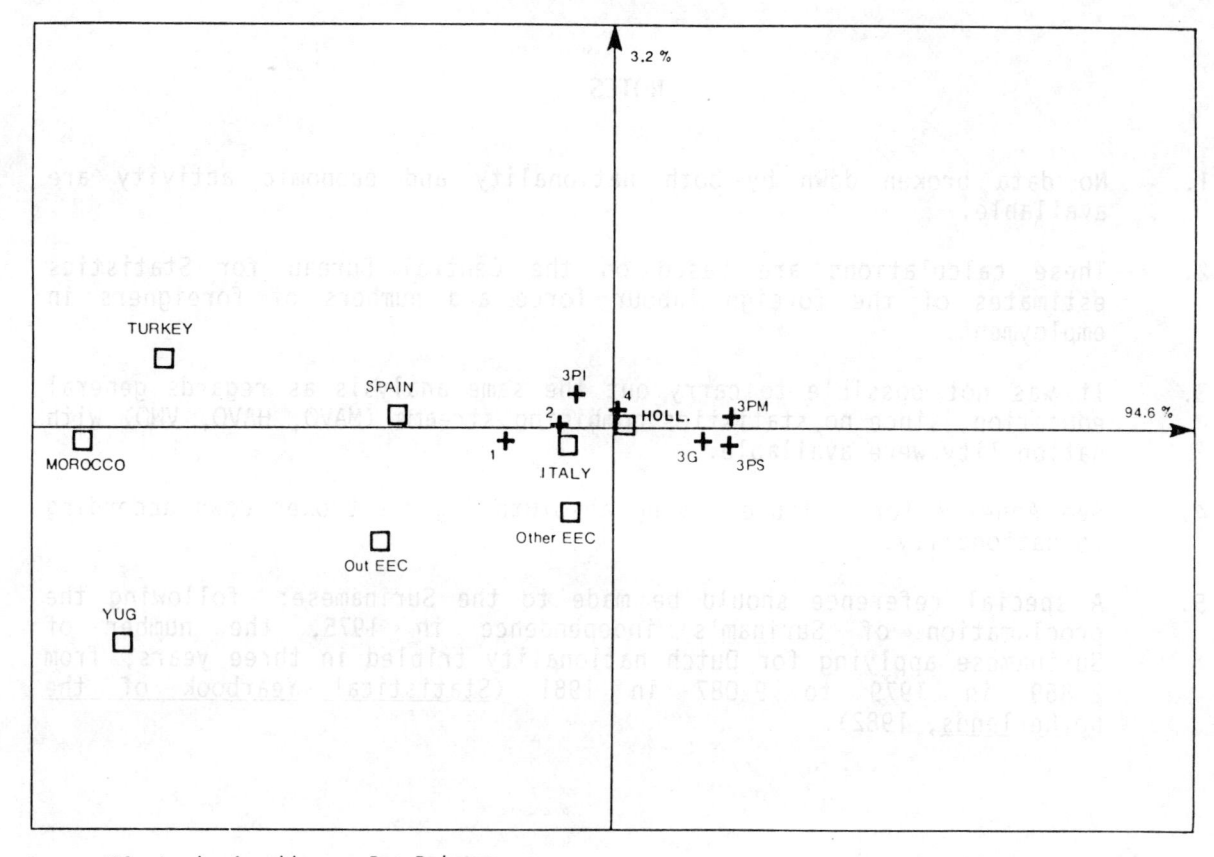

1	Kleuterionderwijs :	Pre-Primary
2	Gewoon lager onderwijs :	Primary
3G	Algemeen voortgezet onderwijs :	General secondary
3PI	Lager beroeps onderwijs :	Vocational training (lower level)
3PM	Middelbaar beroeps onderwijs :	Vocational training (intermediate level)
3PS	Hoger beroeps onderwijs :	Vocational training (higher level)
4	Buitengewoon onderwijs :	Special education

+ : Type of school

□ : Pupils' nationality

VI. ENROLMENT OF FOREIGN CHILDREN IN SWEDISH SCHOOLS

BASIC FACTS AND FIGURES ON THE FOREIGN POPULATION

a) The Trend in Recent Years

In the 1970s an increasing number of foreigners entered Swedish society, which has itself changed a great deal in the past few years, from a homogeneous ethnic structure to a much more heterogeneous one.

This change has taken place in several clearly marked stages:

-- Between 1943 and 1945, most foreigners came from countries devastated by the war: thirty thousand Estonians, 60 000 Norwegians and Danes, 70 000 Finns. Later on, many refugees (from Hungary, Czechoslovakia, Poland, Turkey and Latin America) tried to settle in Sweden, some of them only for a short period;

-- In the 1950s Italians recruited in their country of origin arrived, followed by small numbers of West Germans, Dutch and Austrians;

-- In 1954, renewed in 1982, an agreement was signed between Norway, Denmark, Finland and Sweden establishing a Nordic labour market with free movement of persons. Thus, the differences in the economic developments of the countries led to massive migratory flows (particularly from Finland) and explains why there are so many Nordic nationals in Sweden;

-- In the 1960s the labour market expanded and manpower sources diversified to include Greeks, Yugoslavs and Turks;

-- During the 1970s immigration to Sweden changed character. All foreigners wishing to take up employment (except those from Nordic countries) have been required since 1967 to obtain a labour permit before entering Sweden, and since the early 1970s immigration of workers from non-Nordic countries has virtually ceased. On the other hand, the number of refugees coming to Sweden has increased substantially. In recent years, the average annual immigration has totalled 27 000 and of these more than two-thirds have come from non-Nordic countries. As many as a fourth of all immigrants coming to Sweden are children, including a large number of adopted children.

-- In recent years the flow of migration tends to go from Sweden to the countries of origin. This is very clear in the case of e.g. Finland.

Table 1 shows the trend of the total and foreign population during the years 1975-1983.

Data on the foreign population in the strict sense show that since 1975 its numbers have remained more or less stable, around 5 per cent. This is largely due to the high proportion of naturalisations each year (about 18-20 000), which drains the "foreigners" category and swells that of nationals. In 1975 there were some 230 000 naturalised citizens (2.8 per cent of the total population); in 1979 there were 357 000 (4.3 per cent); and in 1980 378 000 (4.5 per cent).

Table 1

Resident Population in Sweden, 1975-83

Year	Total Population nb.	Alien Population nb.	% (1)
1975	8 208 442	409 894	5.0
1978	8 284 437	424 188	5.1
1979	8 303 010	424 113	5.1
1980	8 317 937	421 667	5.1
1981	8 323 033	414 001	5.0
1982	8 327 484	405 475	4.9
1983	8 330 573	397 140	4.8

1. The percentages are calculated in relation to the total population (nationals + foreigners).

Source: Statistisk Arsbok 1984.

b) **Foreign Natality**

Taking the national/foreigner distinction in the strictly legal sense (although this does not correspond to the sociological reality of Swedish society), the fall in the number of births registered between 1975 and 1982 was more marked for foreigners than for nationals. This situation is not surprising, but may be due to the following reasons:

-- First, the increasing number of naturalisations, which alters the nationality of children born later;

-- Secondly, i.e. from July 1979, statistics record as Swedish children born to foreign fathers (but Swedish mothers) and also children of mothers of foreign origin but who have adopted Swedish nationality (about 10 per cent). This partly explains the decline in births between 1975 and 1983. Another explanation is that the immigrant population grows older.

Table 2

Number of Births in Sweden between 1975 and 1983

Year	Total Births nb.	Foreign Births nb.	%
1975	103 632	8 852	8.5
1976	98 345	8 929	9.1
1977	96 057	8 696	9.1
1978	93 248	8 680	9.3
1979	96 255	8 052	8.4
1980	97 064	7 246	7.5
1981	94 065	6 823	7.3
1982	92 748	6 354	6.9
1983	91 780	5 880	6.4

Source: Swedish Commission on Immigration Research (EIFO), 1983.

Table 3

Breakdown of the Number of Births by Nationality in 1975 and 1983

Nationality	1975	1983	Change between 1975 and 1983
Total	103 632	91 780	-11.4
Of which:			
Swedish	94 780	85 900	-9.4
Foreign	8 852	5 880	-33.6
Of which:			
Finnish	3 628	2 337	-35.6
Yugoslav	935	430	-54.0
Turkish	277	621	124.2
Others	3 523	2 492	29.3

Source: EIFO -- Commission on Immigration Research, 1983.

-- Furthermore, one of the features of the Swedish statistical system is that "there are practically no (demographic) data at all concerning aliens who are living in Sweden, and perhaps also gainfully employed there, without being registered "residents" (SOPEMI Report 1984). But recently, via the Swedish Statistical Bureau, it is possible to obtain more precise information on the situation of residents born outside Sweden and also on that of naturalised citizens.

On that strictly defined basis, the ratio of foreign to total births fell from 8.5 per cent in 1975 to 6.9 per cent in 1982 (Table 2); on average, foreign natality declined by 28 per cent between these two dates, as compared with a 10.5 per cent fall in the number of Swedish births (Table 3).

A more precise estimate of the contribution made by foreigners (or immigrants) to Swedish population growth can be obtained by comparing the values of the current fertility indicator (calculated here for 1 000 women) according to the mothers' country of origin (Table 4).

Table 4

Current Fertility Indicator (Calculated for 1 000 Women)
According to the Mothers' Country of Origin

Year	Sweden	Finland	Greece	Yugoslavia	Turkey
1978	1 564.0	1 764.5	2 591.0	1 994.0	4 953.0
1980	1 640.0	1 908.0	2 558.0	1 942.5	4 898.0
1982	1 582.0	1 704.0	2 058.5	1 683.0	3 932.5

Source: EIFO -- Commission on Immigration Research, 1983.

c) The Current Situation

i) Distribution by nationality

Tables 5 and 6 show the distribution of the eight million residents in Sweden at the beginning of the 1980s by nationality and place of birth.

A high proportion of foreigners resident in Sweden are from the Nordic countries, although their relative weight in the flow of entries has fallen since the 1960s, while that of nationals of the Mediterranean countries has increased. In 1982, Finns accounted for 39.5 per cent of the foreign population, Danes for 6.7 per cent and Norwegians for 6.1 per cent; in other words over half the residents formally possessing a foreign nationality are natives of the countries which together with Sweden constitute the Nordic labour market.

Table 5

Foreign Population Broken Down by Citizenship
(Situation at 31st December 1983)

	nb.	%
Foreign Population	397 140	100.0
Of which:		
Finns	150 641	37.9
Yugoslavs	38 272	9.6
Danes	26 195	6.6
Norwegians	25 131	6.3
Turks	20 900	5.3
Poles	14 852	3.7
Germans	12 459	3.1
Greeks	11 810	3.1
From Mediterranean Countries (1)	11 604	2.9
British	8 978	2.3
French	2 297	0.6
Dutch	2 290	0.6
Others	71 711	18.1

1. Mediterranean countries: Algeria (540), Italy (4 151), Morocco (1 309), Portugal (1 555), Spain (3 156), and Tunisia 893).

Source: The National Swedish Immigration and Naturalization Board.

Table 6

National and Alien Population Resident in Sweden
(Situation at 31st December 1983)

Nationality	Born in Sweden	Born Abroad	Total
Swedish	7 606 126	323 307	7 933 433
Aliens	86 987	310 153	397 140
Total	7 693 113	637 460	8 330 573

Source: Folkmangd 31 december 1983, del 3, SOS.

ii) Distribution by age group

The number of foreigners is highest in the youngest age-groups. In Sweden, as in many other European countries with a high rate of immigration, nearly half the foreigners are under 25.

Table 7

Distribution by Age Group of the Total and Alien Population
(Situation at 31st December 1983)

Age Group	Total Population	Alien Population	%
0- 4 years	473 365	30 354	6.4
5- 9 years	505 855	31 761	6.3
10-14 years	554 708	32 671	5.9
15-19 years	607 423	28 132	4.6
All ages	8 330 573	397 140	4.8

Source: Statistisk Arsbok, 1984.

Table 8

Swedish Labour Force (Aged 16-74) in 1983

	Total Population	Foreign Population	Finns	Other Nordics	Yugoslavs
Labour force	4 375 000	221 600	91 200	31 300	20 200
Of which:					
Employed	4 223 800	207 700	85 800	29 900	18 900
Unemployed	151 200	13 900	5 300	1 400	1 200
Unemployment rate (%)	3.5	6.3	5.8	4.5	6.0

Source: SOPEMI/OECD, 1984.

iii) The labour force

In 1983 the average number of foreigners in employment was 221 600; foreigners thus accounted for 5.1 per cent of the total labour force estimated at 4 375 000 persons; the number of foreign unemployed, however, was 13 900, i.e. 6.3 per cent of the total foreign labour force (whereas only 3.5 per cent of the Swedish labour force were unemployed). This represents an increase in the foreign unemployment rate, compared with 4.8 per cent in 1981 and 5.8 per cent in 1982. A detailed breakdown by nationality (see Table 8) shows that nationals of the Nordic countries are in a less unfavourable position than other foreigners; the unemployment rate among Finns was 5.8 per cent, and among nationals of other Nordic countries 4.5 per cent.

As regards distribution by sector of activity, Table 9 shows that -- as in other European countries -- the rate of penetration of foreign labour in the industrial sector is considerably higher than the average rate for all sectors as a whole (9.4 per cent, against 5.6 per cent). However, the distributive trades (5.6 per cent) and other services (5.0 per cent) come second and third respectively, a long way ahead of the building and civil engineering sector (2.7 per cent).

d) Conclusion

In the end, it seems that the idea of "the foreigner" is gradually giving way to that of the citizen of foreign origin. This change is partly due to the large number of naturalisations every year and the presence of a second generation consisting of children and adolescents born in Sweden but having another language than Swedish as their first or home language.

Table 9

Distribution of the Total and Alien Labour Force
by Sector of Activity in 1980

	Total Population	Alien Population	
	nb.	nb.	%
Agriculture	225 498	2 900	1.3
Industry	1 012 548	94 900	9.4
Building and Civil Engineering	277 984	7 500	2.7
Distributive Trades	553 337	31 100	5.6
Transport	284 906	11 600	4.1
Banks and Insurance	280 961	8 800	3.1
Other Services	1 364 891	67 800	5.0
Total	4 000 125	224 700	5.6

Source: Folk och Bostadsrakningen, 1980.

Swedish educational statistics -- unlike those of most other European countries -- are broken down not by nationality but by home language. It is therefore according to this criterion (which reflects the child's true linguistic situation) that distribution by educational level will be studied here.

FOREIGN CHILDREN AND CHILDREN OF FOREIGN ORIGIN IN SWEDISH PRE-SCHOOLS AND SCHOOLS

a) <u>Pre-school System</u>

There are pre-schools (daycare and nursery school) where the child may attend from the age of seven months until school age at seven.

For pre-school children of foreign origin, a number of municipalities offer home-language support for 5-6 year olds, sometimes even younger children participate.

b) <u>The School System</u>

The school system is organised at two levels after pre-school :

-- Compulsory school, which lasts nine years and is divided into three levels:

  . Junior level: grades 1 to 3; average age: 7 to 10;

  . Middle level: grades 4 to 6; average age: 10 to 13;

  . Senior level: grades 7 to 9; average age: 13 to 16;

-- Secondary (or "upper secondary") school, the voluntary prolongation of compulsory school, where the child opts for one of several streams:

  . "Three- and four-year lines", giving access to the universities and colleges;

  . "Two-year theoretical lines", giving basic education and to some extent access to university courses;

  . "Vocational training (two-year lines)", providing training for direct entry onto the labour market;

  . "Specialised upper secondary school courses (varying length)", the least advanced secondary education stream.

c) <u>Schooling for Children with a Home Language other than Swedish</u>

For a number of years now Sweden has been interested in the problems of integrating young immigrants in pre-schools and schools and has taken various measures to promote this. In 1977, the "Child Care Act" stipulated that the very young children should get backing in their mother tongue. State allowance has been available from 1977 to give home language support for 6-year olds in pre-school. In 1979, even the 5-year olds were allowed four hours a week home-language support in their mother tongue. The children with a home language other than Swedish are in pre-school organised either in home language groups, integrated groups or in the ordinary Swedish groups depending e.g. on the numbers of children of foreign accent and their parents' wishes. In 1979, the Riksdag voted in favour of the extension of home-language courses and the provision of financial resources for municipalities.

As a result, four types of class were introduced in the compulsory schools:

-- "Ordinary classes", where the child (attending the class together with Swedish and other children) may temporarily leave his class in order to take courses in his home language or receive coaching in Swedish;

-- "Compiled classes", which comprise a group of Swedes and a group of foreigners with one common home language other than Swedish alongside one another and where teaching is mainly in the respective home languages;

-- "Home language classes" which include only children speaking one common language other than Swedish; teaching is in the home language and Swedish is taught as a foreign language. This is gradually changed through the first six years so that the language of instruction can be Swedish all through senior level;

-- "Preparatory classes" (temporary arrangement) where there are several groups speaking different languages and teaching concerns building up a basic command of Swedish, but the children can also have coaching in their home language and attend courses on other subjects given in that language.

d) School Enrolment in Sweden of Children Speaking a Home Language other than Swedish (at the various educational levels)

Table 10 shows the enrolment rate trend at the various levels of education between 1979 and 1983, not of foreigners of children speaking a language other than Swedish (1).

i) Pre-primary schools (2)

In 1983-84, there were 243 314 children in pre-primary schools (according to Statistical Reports, Series S 1984: 16, p. 26), including 20 355 (8.4 per cent) speaking a language other than Swedish. Of these 20 355 children, 5 867 (28.8 per cent) speak Finnish; 2 453 (12.1 per cent) Spanish; 1 876 (9.2 per cent) one of the languages spoken in Yugoslavia; 1 418 (7.0 per cent) Polish; 1 111 (5.5 per cent) Syrian; 973 (4.8 per cent) Greek; 1 186 (5.8 per cent) Turkish; 859 (4.2 per cent) Arabic; and 5 585 (27.4 per cent) speak other languages.

Table 10

School Enrolment Rates of Children Speaking a Language Other than Swedish, by Education Level

	1979/80		1980/81		1981/82		1982/83		1983/84	
	nb.	%	nb.	%	nb.	%	nb.	%	nb.	%
Pre-school	16 356	7.3	17 266	7.6	17 304	7.4	18 910	7.9	20 355	8.4
Compulsory education										
Primary level	30 296	9.0	30 131	8.9	29 644	8.9	29 045	8.9	29 131	9.3
Middle level	29 315	8.6	29 655	9.0	29 793	9.0	30 055	9.0	30 261	9.1
Senior level	25 838	7.1	26 810	7.3	27 565	7.7	27 618	8.1	28 266	8.6
Sub-total	85 449	8.2	86 596	8.4	87 002	8.5	86 718	8.7	87 658	9.0
Secondary education										
3- and 4-year lines	4 475	4.6	4 951	4.7	5 701	5.0	6 267	5.1	6 734	5.2
2-year lines theoretical	1 568	4.8	1 618	4.8	1 643	4.9	1 639	5.2	1 519	5.1
Vocational training	3 967	4.9	4 442	5.0	4 763	4.8	5 177	4.9	5 507	4.8
Specialised upper secondary school courses	1 547	4.7	1 764	5.3	1 901	5.5	1 986	5.1	2 049	3.5
Sub-total	11 557	4.7	12 775	4.9	14 008	5.0	15 069	5.0	15 809	4.8
Total	113 362	7.5	116 637	7.7	118 314	7.7	120 697	7.9	123 822	8.0

Source: Statistiska Centralbyran, 1984. Series Statistical reports, sub-series S (Social Welfare) and U (Education, Research and Culture).

ii) Compulsory schooling

During the school year 1981-82, 1 018 631 children were enrolled in compulsory education; 87 002 (8.5 per cent) of them speak a language other than Swedish. The Finns make up by far the largest group (44.4 per cent of the population speaking a language other than Swedish). They are followed by the Yugoslavs (9.3 per cent), the Germans (6.3 per cent), the Spanish (5.3 per cent), the Poles (4.4 per cent), the Danes (4.3 per cent), the English (3.9 per cent), the Greeks (3.2 per cent), the Syrians (3 per cent) and the Turks (2.2 per cent).

iii) Secondary education (upper secondary schools)

This optional education is the prolongation of compulsory education for those over sixteen. Access depends on procedures which emphasise the difference in school career according to the language spoken.

In the 1981-82 school year, out of the 282 013 pupils in secondary education, 14 008 spoke a language other than Swedish; 43.2 per cent spoke Finnish, 8.1 per cent a Slav language and 7.2 per cent a Germanic language, while 5.5 per cent speak Spanish, 4.6 per cent Polish, 3.7 per cent Danish, 3.4 per cent English, 3.2 per cent Greek, 2.6 per cent Italian and 2.3 per cent Norwegian.

At first sight, young people speaking Swedish and those speaking a foreign language are in a similar position with regard to admission to the various streams of secondary education (Table 11).

However, some differences should be noted. Pupils whose home tongue is Danish, Finnish and, above all, Spanish have a below-average rate of enrolment in the higher stream ("three and four-year lines"); children of Finnish and Danish origin have an above-average enrolment rate in vocational training; and Spanish, Greek and Polish-speaking children in specialised education. Lastly, it may seem surprising that in the higher streams there are fewer children from the Nordic countries (except for Norway) than children of Italian or Slavonic origin. But as will be shown below, few Nordic nationals have lessons in their home language or coaching in Swedish, and they are more likely to enter working life as soon as their compulsory education has ended (3).

e) Enrolment in Home Language Courses and Swedish Courses by School Level

These courses have an important place in Swedish schools, since many children speaking a language other than Swedish can take advantage of lessons in their own home language, or Swedish lessons, or both.

During the past decade these types of education have been considerably developed. In 1980-81, 50 523 children enrolled in compulsory education received teaching in their home language, against only 3 854 in 1970-71. Enrolments rose frm 10 262 in 1970-71 to 40 598 in 1980-81.

Table 12 shows that over half the children speaking a language other than Swedish receive lessons in their home language.

A 1978-79 school year survey of children in compulsory education (Grade 9) confirms the connection between level of competence in Swedish and date of arrival in Sweden. Seventy-seven per cent of those who had entered the country before 1970 or were born there were proficient in Swedish, whereas 79 per cent of those who had arrived between 1976 and 1978 had little or no poor knowledge of the language.

Most of children speaking Esthonian, Italian or German (belonged to the first group), whereas the second group -- which represented only 17 per cent of the school population surveyed -- consisted among others of the majority of those speaking Arabic, Spanish, Turkish or the Tzigane language.

Table 11

Enrolment in Secondary Education Broken down by Streams and by Home Language
1982/83

(in percentages)

Education Level	All Languages Other Than Swedish	Swedish	Finnish	Danish	Norwegian	Yugoslav	Greek	Spanish	German	Italian	Polish
3- and 4-year lines	41.6	41.2	34.9	34.3	51.0	47.1	45.1	25.0	64.8	59.6	52.2
2-year lines theoretical	10.9	10.5	12.4	10.1	12.2	10.3	8.6	10.2	10.5	11.9	9.7
Vocational training	34.3	35.2	43.1	45.1	30.0	34.6	31.7	25.3	21.0	24.9	24.0
Specialised upper secondary school courses	13.2	13.1	9.6	10.3	6.8	7.9	14.6	39.5	3.6	3.6	14.0
Total	100.0	100.0	100.0	100.0	100.0	100.0	100.0	100.0	100.0	100.0	100.0

Source: Official Statistics of Sweden, 1984.

Table 12

Percentage of Children Speaking a Language Other than Swedish Receiving Lessons in Their Home Language
1981/82

Home Language	Pre-school	Compulsory Education	Secondary Education	Total School System
All languages other than Swedish	59.2	64.0	34.8	59.9
Of which:				
Arabic	45.8	78.5	55.4	67.2
Finnish	74.1	65.8	27.7	62.2
Greek	53.7	77.8	54.3	70.5
Polish	41.2	66.2	40.6	56.6
Spanish	61.3	80.5	22.4	69.4
Turkish	51.3	83.0	58.1	71.7
Yugoslav	58.4	65.1	41.5	61.6
Other	46.7	54.9	39.7	51.9

Source: "Immigrants and Immigrant Teaching in Sweden", 1983.

i) Pre-school education

Pre-school children of foreign origin can have support in their home language from the age of four and thus find it easier to integrate themselves in Swedish society when the time comes for compulsory education.

In 1983-84, of the 20 355 children 0-6 years old with a home language other than Swedish, 11 760 (57.8 per cent) had support in their home language, 11 060 of them more than four hours a week and 700 less (4). The majority of children receiving this support were Finns, probably because Finnish immigration is long-established.

ii) Compulsory education

In 1981-82, 63.4 per cent of the so-called "foreign" children had lessons in their home language and 50.1 per cent extra tuition in Swedish.

But the proportion of children attending varied according to language. Few Danish or Norwegian-speaking children took advantage of these lessons, whereas a large proportion of those speaking Chinese, Syrian or Spanish did.

iii) Secondary education

As the educational level rises, the number of pupils speaking a language other than Swedish receiving lessons in their home languages and special coaching in Swedish falls. Of the 14 009 "foreign" pupils in secondary schools, only 4 882 (i.e. 34.8 per cent) receive lessons in the home language, and 2 071 (14.8 per cent) special coaching in Swedish.

f) Some Features Typical of the School Careers of Children Speaking a Language other than Swedish

It should be pointed out, to begin with, that the way Swedish educational statistics are collected and processed does not allow the same analyses to be made as in other countries. However, if a few modifications are made it is possible to identify certain differences in the course and conclusion of children's school careers according to home language, date of arrival in Sweden, etc. This study is based on statistics for the year 1978-79 (5) showing what happened to the 111 685 children (7 096 speaking a language other than Swedish) who completed the ninth grade of compulsory education that year.

Most of them wished to continue their studies and enter one of the streams leading to upper secondary education (90.6 per cent in all, sub-divided into 96.8 per cent of the Swedish-speaking children and 83.5 per cent of those speaking another language).

The overall average percentage of applicants admitted to upper secondary education was 83.2 per cent, but this percentage varied sharply according to home language (Table 13).

Of the total number of young immigrants who completed Grade 9, it was among the larger language groups mainly Italian and pupils of Yugoslavian descent speakers who wanted to enter secondary education and whose applications were successful. Spanish, Turkish and Danish nationals on the other hand, obtained the poorest results.

So in spite of the different way in which Swedish data are presented, divergency in school careers emerges quite clearly. Over 80 per cent of the young Swedes who completed compulsory education and were then filtered through the application and admission procedures went on to upper secondary schools. The corresponding percentages for the other nationalities were respectively: 81 Italians, 77 Germans, 77 Yugoslavians -- but only 60 Danes, 52 Turks and 43 of those from Spanish speaking countries.

Other information may be gleaned from these same statistics, regarding first choice of educational orientation and the influence on subsequent studies of the ability to speak good Swedish (Table 14).

As already shown, over half the Finns and Danes opted for vocational training, whereas nearly two-thirds of the French wanted to go on to the

Table 13

Children Applying to and Enrolled in Upper Secondary Schools
1978/79

Home Language	Applicants (a) nb.	%	Enrolled (b) nb.	%
Swedish	101 296	96.8	84 271	83.2
All languages other than Swedish	5 928	83.5	4 910	82.8
Of which: Danish	363	79.2	274	75.5
Finnish	3 147	85.6	2 579	81.9
Italian	124	90.5	111	89.5
Yugoslav	417	85.1	378	90.6
Spanish	139	66.2	90	64.7
Turkish	99	77.3	67	67.7
German	473	86.6	419	88.6

a) Percentage of applicants:

$$\frac{\text{Number of applicants}}{\text{Number who completed Grade 9 of compulsory education}}$$

b) Percentage of children enrolled:

$$\frac{\text{Number enrolled}}{\text{Number of applicants}}$$

Source: "Immigrants and Immigrant Teaching in Sweden", report issued in 1983 by Statistics Sweden.

Table 14

First Choice of Educational Orientation of Young People Wishing to Continue Their Education According to Their Home Language
1978/79

	3- and 4-year Lines	2-year Theoretical Lines	2-year Vocational Lines	Specialised Courses
All pupils as a whole	33.2	13.9	45.6	7.3
Pupils speaking a language other than Swedish	31.4	12.5	48.7	8.4
Of which:				
Turkish	20.6	9.3	44.3	25.8
Finnish	23.6	12.5	56.4	..
Danish	19.8	13.2	53.4	13.5
French	60.7	3.6	28.6	7.1

Source: "Immigrants and Immigrant Teaching in Sweden", report issued in 1983 by Statistics Sweden.

Table 15

Proportion of Young People Choosing One or Another of Secondary Education Streams According to Their Degree of Mastery of Swedish
1978/79

Degree of Mastery of Swedish	3- and 4-year Lines	2-year Theoretical Lines	Vocational Lines	Sub-total	2-year Specialised Courses	Total
Very good	30.9	11.9	28.3	71.1	4.5	75.6
Good	15.3	11.6	38.0	64.9	4.6	69.5
Fair, weak or nil	9.0	6.6	25.0	40.6	5.0	45.6

Source: Immigrants and Immigrant Teaching in Sweden, report issued in 1983 by Statistics Sweden.

university; the Turks are among the largest group of "foreigners" to need special coaching.

As for the influence exerted by the ability to speak good Swedish, the figures from table 15 show that of those admitted to secondary schools, the better their Swedish, the more they seek to enter the more highly valued streams of secondary education:

In fact, 75.6 per cent of those with very good Swedish are admitted to one of the secondary school streams (30.9 per cent of them to the "3 and 4-year lines"); whereas of those whose Swedish is poor, only 45.6 per cent are admitted, and only 9 per cent of them in the upper stream.

g) <u>The Factor Analysis of Correspondence</u>

Lastly, factor analysis of correspondence -- while neither comprehensive nor able to elimate the "age"factor -- confirms the relations existing between level of education achieved and language spoken.

Young Swedish-speakers are near the centre of gravity, since they are represented at all educational levels, whereas "foreigners" as a whole are placed from left to right along a descending hyperbolic curve -- first nationals of countries which are members of the European Communities, then those of the Nordice countries, and lastly those of the Mediterranean countries, are least well represented in the upper streams of secondary education because their immigration is recent (thus implying a higher percentage of young and even very young children, as well as problems of insertion in a society whose standards and values are very unlike those of the country of origin).

NOTES

1. It is important, in this report, not to confuse the two terms "nationality" and "speaking a language other than Swedish". Take, for example, the case of a child whose father is Greek and whose mother is Swedish. Although he has Swedish nationality, his home language may be Greek (but most probably also Swedish!)

2. The figures quoted are taken from the report "Immigrants and Immigrant Teaching in Sweden" published in 1983 by the Statistical Office, and the report "Compulsory School Leavers in 1979 with Home Languages other than Swedish", published by the Swedish National Board of Education in 1981.

3. According to report 3 in "Compulsory School Leavers in 1979 with Home Languages other than Swedish" issued by the Swedish National Board of Education in 1981, some children speaking a foreign language -- particularly those from Denmark and Finland -- more than other

pupils in the compulsory school prefer to enter working life directly, while others -- mainly the Turks -- would like to go on studying, but the families could not afford it (although upper secondary education is free of charge).

4. At preschool level there is no extra Swedish coaching for children speaking a language other than Swedish.

5. More recent data suitable for this kind of analysis are not available.

SWEDEN

FACTOR ANALYSIS DIAGRAM OF CORRESPONDENCE BETWEEN EDUCATIONAL LEVELS AND HOME LANGUAGE FOR THE SCHOOL YEAR 1982/1983

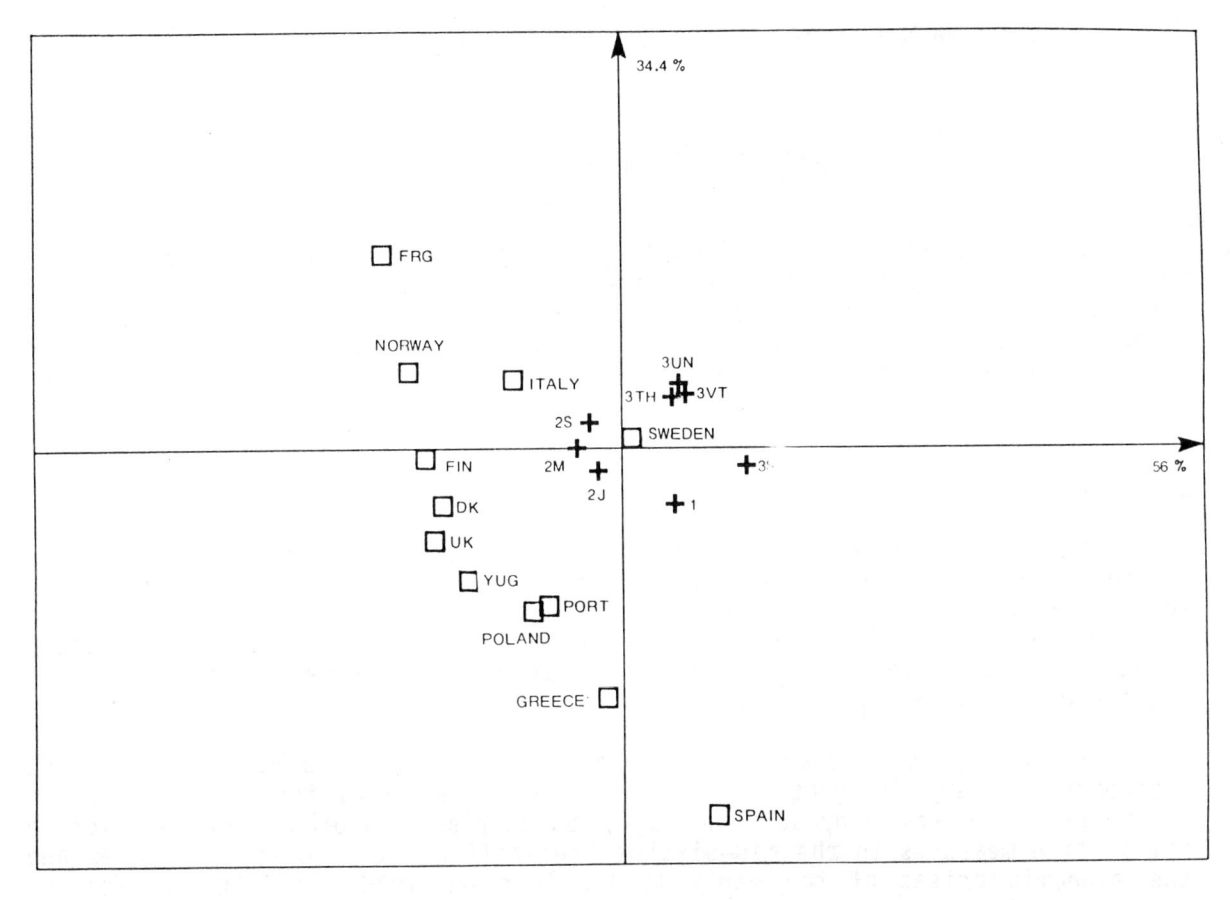

1.	Pre-primary
2J.	Compulsory education : junior level
3M.	Compulsory education : middle level
2S.	Compulsory education : senior level
3UN.	Secondary education : "3 and 4 year lines"
3TH.	Secondary education : "2 year lines theoretical"
3VT.	Secondary education : "vocational training"
3S.	Secondary education : "special courses"

+ : Type of school

☐ : Pupils' nationality

VII. ENROLMENT OF FOREIGN CHILDREN IN SCHOOLS IN SWITZERLAND

GENERAL FOREIGN POPULATION DATA

An overview of the following demographic aspects: the foreign population trend over recent years, the trend in the number of births and the present size of the total foreign population and of the foreign labour force reveals various quantitative data which should help to clarify the findings and commentary on the numbers of foreign children in Swiss schools and the forms their enrolment can take.

a) <u>Recent Trends</u>

For several years Switzerland has played host to considerable numbers of foreigners, in terms both of the total foreign population and of the foreign labour force. Foreigners account for something like 15 per cent of the overall population, as against under 10 per cent in most western countries. As Table 1 shows, however, that percentage has been tending to decline over the last few years.

Following the years of prosperity after World War II, and the accompanying heavy immigration associated with the rapid turnover of workers in response to its manpower shortage, Switzerland adopted very restrictive immigration measures in the mid-sixties, reflecting "xenophobic" pressures and the economic crises of the early 1970s. Between 1970 and 1980 the foreign population therefore decreased.

The foreign labour force/foreign population ratio, a yardstick for measuring the scale of family reunion and birth rate trends, changed hardly at all between 1975 and 1983, reflecting two self-cancelling pressures. The economic recession began to be felt as from 1974, and this, coupled with the pressure exerted by "xenophobic" movements, prompted the government to restrict annual and seasonal residence permits (although issue of the latter has no immediate effect on the size of the foreign population, it can have in the long run because after several years' residence in Switzerland seasonal permits can be converted to annual residence permits).

On the other hand, a new hereditary right of citizenship introduced on 1st January 1978 gave a child born of a Swiss mother by birth and a foreign father full communal and cantonal rights from its mother and, thereby, Swiss nationality, provided the parents were resident in Switzerland when the child was born. This change has among other things had the effect of artificially reducing the size of the foreign population.

Table 1

Foreigners in Switzerland as of 31st December of Each Year (1)

Year	Total Foreign Population (a) ('000)	% (2)	Foreign Labour Force (b) ('000)	% (2)	Ratio (a)/(b)
1975	1 013	15.9	552.6	18.3	1.15
1976	959	15.2	516.0	17.7	1.16
1977	933	14.8	492.8	16.9	1.14
1978	898	14.3	489.4	16.6	1.16
1979	884	14.0	490.7	16.6	1.19
1980	893	14.1	501.1	16.6	1.18
1981	910	14.3	515.1	16.9	1.18
1982	926	14.5	526.2	17.3	1.19
1983	..	..	529.7	..	..

1. Refers to the resident foreign population (and the working population in employment), i.e. foreigners with establishment or residence permits, not seasonal or frontier workers or international organisation staff.

2. Calculated for the whole population (nationals + foreigners) in each category.

Source: Office Fédéral de la Statistique, Berne 1983.

b) The Foreign Birthrate

As Table 2 shows, the foreign birthrate has moved in the same direction as the Swiss birthrate, though with a slight lag. Swiss births rose steadily up until 1966, and then fell fairly steeply -- depending on the year -- before recovering slightly in 1981.

The number of foreign births declined not only in absolute but also in relative terms, their share in all births decreasing steadily from 31.4 per cent in 1974 to 16.6 per cent in 1982 and, in fact only levelling off in the 1980s. This marked drop in the foreign fertility rate in Switzerland reflects not only the highly restrictive immigration policy of the 1970s, but also the ageing of the foreign population, in which the over-40s have become much more numerous, rising to 34.5 per cent in 1981 from 23.2 per cent in 1973.

Table 2

Trend in the Number of Births In Switzerland

Year	Total Births	Total Foreign Births	%
1974	84 507	26 554	31.4
1975	78 464	23 167	29.5
1976	74 199	19 571	26.4
1977	72 829	17 991	24.7
1978	71 375	13 607	19.1
1979	71 986	11 927	16.6
1980	73 661	11 993	16.3
1981	73 747	12 136	16.5
1982	74 916	12 459	16.6

Source: Office Fédéral de la Statistique: Mouvement de la Population, Berne 1982.

c) The Present Position

i) Total population

At 31st December 1982, of the 925 826 foreigners resident in Switzerland, 411 993 were Italian (44.5 per cent of the foreign population), 102 559 Spanish (11.1 per cent), 84 814 German (9.2 per cent), 54 824 Yugoslav (5.9 per cent), 46 806 Turkish (5 per cent), 46 688 French (5 per cent), 30 637 Austrian (3.3 per cent) and 16 658 Portuguese (1.8 per cent).

The age distribution shows that there were relatively more foreigners among the younger age groups -- 16.2 per cent of the under 15s, as against 14.5 per cent of the total population (Table 3).

The age structure has an appreciable influence on education since there are still substantial though diminishing numbers of foreign children in Swiss schools (see below).

Table 4 shows that nearly one in two migrant children under sixteen are of Italian origin, and that among those of school age more than one in two are likewise of Italian origin.

This preponderance of Italian children clearly raises the problem of recognising Italian cultural identity, not just within the education system but in all other areas of social life. True, there is a Swiss population whose culture is Italian, but that is concentrated in particular areas of the country, whereas there are Italian children in all parts of Switzerland.

Table 3

Distribution of Foreign Population by Age Group
(Situation at 31st December 1982)

Age Group	Total Population	Foreign Population	%
Under 5	359 952	57 161	15.9
5- 9 years	384 965	67 171	17.4
10-14 years	465 174	72 077	15.5
15-19 years	517 490	74 837	14.5
20-24 years	482 642	68 589	14.2
All ages	6 384 349	925 826	14.5

Source: Office Fédéral de la Statistique, Bern 1983.

Table 4

**Nationality Breakdown of the Numbers of Children
under 16 and School-age Children**
(Situation at 31st December 1982)

Nationality	Total Population nb.	Children under 16 nb.	%	School-age Children (7 to 15) nb.	%
Total foreign children	925 826	211 139	22.8	128 088	13.8
Of which:					
German	84 814	12 189	14.4	9 084	10.7
French	46 688	7 908	16.9	5 441	11.6
Austrian	30 637	4 635	15.1	3 526	11.5
Italian	411 993	102 747	24.9	65 490	16.0
Spanish	102 559	24 375	23.8	13 253	12.9
Portuguese	16 658	3 381	20.3	1 667	10.0
Yugoslav	54 824	12 174	22.2	5 291	9.6
Turkish	46 806	16 015	34.2	7 894	16.9
Others	130 847	27 715	21.2	15 992	12.2

Source: SOPEMI Report, August 1983.

ii) <u>Labour force</u>

Of the 526 203 foreign workers, 233 118 are Italian (44.3 per cent), 64 880 Spanish (12.3 per cent), 46 332 German (8.8 per cent), 37 959 Yugoslav (7.2 per cent), 26 019 French (4.9 per cent), 24 060 Turkish (4.6 per cent) and 19 634 Austrian (3.7 per cent).

The data in Table 5 show the breakdown of the total labour force and foreign labour force in selected sectors of the economy.

As a general rule, foreigners are more numerous the less attractive the type of work and employment conditions.

Differences of the same order appear when the foreign labour force is broken down by nationality (Table 6).

Some industries are highly dependent on foreign manpower, especially Italians who, for example, alone account for 60 per cent of the manpower employed in building and civil engineering. Italians are in a unique position because of their numbers, and because of the growing variety of types of employment they take (being increasingly numerous in the tertiary sector, such as banking for example). The fact that they have been in Switzerland for a long time helps them to integrate, and current changes in educational orientation and vocational training may account for their occupational and social mobility.

Table 5

Manpower in Selected Branches of the Swiss Economy
(Situation at 31st December 1982)

Sector	Total Employed Labour Force ('000)	Foreign Employed Labour Force (1) ('000)	%
Total	3 033	526.2	17.3
Of which:			
Textiles	41	18.0	43.7
Building, civil engineering	195	60.2	30.9
Iron, steel, etc.	169	40.6	24.1
Clocks, watches	55	9.1	16.4
Banking	96	8.9	9.3
Public health	169	41.6	24.6
Hotels, catering	177	38.6	21.8

1. Refers to resident foreign labour force (excluding frontier and seasonal workers and international organisation staff).

<u>Source</u>: La Vie Economique, Office Fédéral de la Statistique, Berne 1983.

Table 6

Foreign Labour Force by Nationality
(Situation at 31st December 1982)

Sector	Foreign Labour Force (1) nb.	%	Italian nb.	%	Spanish nb.	%	Turkish nb.	%	German nb.	%	French nb.	%
Total	526 203	100.0	233 118	44.3	64 888	12.3	24 060	4.6	46 332	8.8	26 019	4.9
Of which:												
Textiles	18 023	100.0	8 563	47.5	2 004	11.1	3 585	19.9	645	3.6	63	0.3
Building, civil engineering	60 190	100.0	37 550	62.4	8 246	13.7	417	0.7	2 366	3.9	1 068	1.8
Iron, steel, etc.	40 574	100.0	21 343	52.6	4 725	11.6	3 126	7.7	2 687	6.6	1 124	2.8
Clocks, watches	9 152	100.0	5 310	58.0	1 580	17.3	205	2.2	205	2.2	1 028	11.1
Banking	8 864	100.0	3 015	34.0	654	17.4	79	0.8	1 429	16.1	819	9.2
Public health	41 601	100.0	10 260	24.7	6 091	14.6	1 037	2.5	4 999	12.0	2 870	6.9
Hotels, catering	38 642	100.0	10 783	27.9	7 708	19.9	1 332	3.4	2 582	6.7	2 134	5.5

1. Refers to the resident foreign labour force (excluding frontier and seasonal workers and international organisation staff).

Source: La Vie Economique, Office Fédéral de la Statistique, Berne 1983.

Table 7

Swiss and Foreign Labour Force by Socio-economic Category
(Situation at 2nd December 1980)

Nationality	Labour Force nb.	%	Senior Administrative Managerial nb.	%	Domestic, Services etc. nb.	%	Foremen, Supervisors nb.	%	Skilled, Semi-skilled, Unskilled nb.	%	Labourers nb.	%
Swiss and foreign	3 091 694	100.0	32 915	1.1	291 986	9.4	148 354	4.8	766 906	24.8	73 924	1.4
Swiss	2 522 542	100.0	28 396	1.1	211 748	8.4	129 721	5.1	541 370	21.5	28 457	1.1
Foreign	569 152	100.0	4 519	0.8	80 238	14.1	18 633	3.3	225 536	39.6	45 467	8.0

1. Partial breakdown only, covering some 40 per cent of the Swiss labour force and 65 per cent of the foreign force.

Source: Office Fédéral de la Statistique, Berne: Recensement fédéral de la Population du 2 décembre 1980.

Table 7, which is derived from the 1980 census data, gives the socio-economic distribution of Swiss and foreign workers. The latter's over-representation in the manual categories is clearly apparent, accounting as they do for nearly half (47.6 per cent) of the foreign labour force but under a quarter (22.6 per cent) of Switzerland's working population.

The various demographic and economic factors above inevitably influence both the type of education and the school careers of migrant children.

ENROLMENT OF FOREIGN CHILDREN IN SCHOOLS IN SWITZERLAND

Despite the fact that foreign enrolment in the school system as a whole remained stable at about 15 per cent over the years 1976-84, a number of trends were apparent during this period:

— First, there was a drop in enrolment of both Swiss and foreign nationals in pre-school and primary education;

— Secondly, enrolment in first- and second-cycle secondary education increased, this being more marked in the case of foreigners than in the case of Swiss nationals.

These figures reflect a number of factors: firstly, the decline in population which has affected most western countries since the early 1970s has put a stop to the rise in the number of children in infant schools. Secondly, the measures adopted to curb immigration have tended to slow the growth in the number of children in pre-school and primary education:

— In 1976 the number of foreigners in pre-school education was 25 795, whereas by 1984 there were only 22 186, i.e. a drop of about 14 per cent;

— The fall in enrolment in primary education is even more striking, i.e. 19 per cent.

Lastly, the younger generations who arrived in substantial numbers in the 1960s at a time when Switzerland's economy was expanding are now in secondary education where enrolment has been increasing steadily (a rise of 6.9 per cent between 1976 and 1984 in the first cycle and of 70.3 per cent in the second cycle.)

Table 8 shows the trend in foreign enrolment at each level of education for the years 1976-77 to 1983-84.

Two points need noting in connection with this overall analysis:

— The relatively higher enrolment of foreigners in special education;

— The enrolment of foreigners in secondary education where — strangely enough — there are relatively more enrolled in general education than the Swiss and relatively less in vocational education.

Table 8

Trend in the Level of Foreign Enrolment throughout the School System as a Whole (1976/77 to 1983/84)

	1976/77	1977/78	1978/79	1979/80	1980/81	1981/82	1982/83	1983/84
Pre-school	19.8	21.5	21.4	20.7	20.1	20.1	19.7	18.6
Normal primary	17.9	17.4	17.3	16.8	16.9	17.3	17.7	17.2
Special primary	22.9	22.6	23.0	23.5	24.9	26.4	27.7	27.9
Total primary	18.2	18.1	17.8	17.3	17.5	18.0	18.4	18.5
1st Cycle secondary	13.0	13.3	13.7	13.7	14.0	14.2	14.5	14.8
2nd Cycle secondary	8.8	9.6	9.8	10.4	10.6	11.2	11.5	12.1
Vocational secondary	8.2	9.0	9.2	9.8	10.0	10.6	11.0	11.7
General secondary	10.6	11.3	11.8	12.2	12.5	12.8	13.0	13.3
Total school system	15.0	15.4	15.3	15.0	15.1	15.5	15.7	15.9

Source: *Statistique des élèves*. Office Fédéral de la Statistique, Berne.

Table 9

Foreign Enrolment in Special Education

	1976/77	1977/78	1978/79	1979/80	1980/81	1981/82	1982/83	1983/84
Number of foreign children in 6-11 age group	115 205	110 392	97 756	90 289	87 913	86 142	..	..
Number of foreign enrolment in special education	9 176	8 772	8 926	8 824	9 069	9 331	9 567	9 171
Level of foreign enrolment in special education (1) [%]	22.9	22.6	23.0	23.5	24.9	26.4	27.7	27.9
Level of foreign enrolment in primary education (2) [%]	18.2	18.1	17.8	17.3	17.5	18.0	18.4	18.5
Ratio (1)/(2)	1.26	1.25	1.29	1.36	1.42	1.47	1.50	1.51

Source: *Statistique des élèves*. Office Fédéral de la Statistique, Berne.

a) Special Education

This type of education is included under primary education and thus involves children aged between six and eleven.

Although the total number of foreign children in this age group is declining, as is reflected in the reduced enrolment of foreign children throughout primary education, the number of foreign children in special education is rising. This is because through selective treatment of foreigners children repeating a year are more numerous in German-speaking and French-speaking Switzerland. Compared to corresponding classes of society, the difference is not so big.

This shows that foreigners still tend -- and to an increasing extent -- to be relatively more numerous in special education; currently, out of every 100 children enrolled in special education almost 28 (i.e. more than one in four) are foreigners, whereas out of every 100 children enrolled in primary education only 18 are foreigners (Table 9).

b) Secondary Education

A number of aspects revealed by the figures may, at first sight, seem surprising:

-- Firstly, the level of enrolment in compulsory secondary education in the case of foreigners is higher than in the case of the total school-age population (education is compulsory for children aged between 6 and 15 and comprises the primary and first-cycle secondary levels);

-- A more marked increase in foreign enrolment in second-cycle secondary than in first-cycle secondary;

-- At the upper secondary level, a higher level of foreign enrolment in the "general" stream than in the "vocational" stream.

By contrast, an analysis of the trend for the first cycle does not reveal any significant changes in pattern. What should however be noted are the differences in enrolment rates depending on the requirements for a particular type of education: in other words, in the case where there is no selection process, 26.6 per cent of students are of foreign nationality, whereas this figure drops to 18.3 per cent in the stream with "basic" entrance requirements and to only 11.5 per cent in the stream with "stricter" requirements.

There are several possible explanations for these findings which are illustrated by the figures in Table 10:

-- The fact that the level of enrolment of foreigners in compulsory education is higher than that for Swiss children is not after all so surprising; it simply means that many of them are content merely to complete their compulsory education, and only continue their secondary education when this is possible.

Table 10

Foreign Enrolment in Secondary Education

	1976/77	1977/78	1978/79	1979/80	1980/81	1981/82	1982/83	1983/84
Percentage of total population enrolled in compulsory secondary education compared with secondary education as a whole	58.4	57.5	57.1	56.1	58.5	53.4	52.5	51.4
Percentage of foreign population enrolled in compulsory secondary education compared with secondary education as a whole	67.4	65.3	64.9	62.7	61.5	59.4	58.3	56.5
1st cycle secondary								
Total	13.0	13.3	13.7	13.7	14.0	14.2	14.5	14.8
Basic entrance requirements	15.0	16.1	16.4	16.6	16.9	17.5	18.0	18.4
Stricter entrance requirements	11.3	11.0	11.3	11.1	11.4	11.3	11.3	11.5
No selection process	24.9	25.3	26.2	26.3	26.3	26.0	26.2	26.6
2nd cycle secondary								
Total	8.9	9.6	9.8	10.4	10.6	11.2	11.5	12.1
General education	13.6	13.5	13.5	13.8	13.9	14.3	14.6	15.0
Vocational training	8.2	9.0	9.2	9.8	10.0	10.6	11.0	11.7
Teacher training	3.4	2.9	2.7	3.0	2.8	2.6	2.3	2.4

Source: Statistique des élèves. Office Fédéral de la Statistique, Bern.

-- The sharper increase in foreign enrolment in the second cycle than in the first is probably due not only to the influx of migrants during the period of economic expansion of the 1960s, but also to an extraneous input of foreign children who are not immigrants (these children whose parents are German, French, Belgian, etc. have had normal school careers in their home countries and go directly into the second-cycle of secondary education).

Similarly, Hutmacher in his "Approach to the Social-cultural and Linguistic Problems of Migrant Children in Switzerland" (Etre Migrant, Editions Lang, Berne, 1981) -- a survey confined to the canton of Geneva [where the percentage of foreign population among the inhabitants of this canton is one of the highest (33 per cent) for all Switzerland] -- makes the very pertinent observation that many foreign children, whose parents are in the higher income brackets, enrol in general education (a point that is discussed further below).

There are a number of questions which stem from this quantitative analysis. What nationalities are numerically the most important amongst these foreign school children? To what socio-economic categories do their parents belong? What explains the fact that there are more foreign children in the "general" stream of second-cycle secondary education than in the "vocational" stream?

First of all, we need to define "general education" and "vocational education". By "general education" is meant education which leads to either of the two Federal polytechnic schools or to any university faculty.

There are several types of general education available to students, whether they be Swiss or not: schools preparing pupils for maturité examinations, general arts-oriented schools (which do not, however, lead on to university), other general education schools and schools providing access to the teaching professions (where foreigners are proportionately far less numerous than Swiss nationals).

On the other hand, vocational training is often coupled with apprenticeship, covering the following areas: industry, business and commerce, trades and crafts, agriculture and fine arts training, etc. Considering all the various systems of education, the most striking disparities between Swiss and foreign children occur at the apprenticeship level:

-- Foreign children are often uncertain as to the choice of a trade and fail to take the opportunities for training which are available to them.

-- There are a very limited number of apprenticeship contracts available to students on completion of compulsory education, which is precisely the time when foreign children are in doubt about their future because they lack the satisfactory exploitation of existing information.

-- The chances of getting an apprenticeship contract are affected to a marked degree by the candidate's level of education. Those who have successfully completed their secondary education in an establishment with "stricter entrance requirements" have an advantage over those with only primary education or secondary education in a school with "basic entrance requirements".

-- Lastly, the parents of foreign children -- uncertain as to how long they will be staying in Switzerland -- are faced with a difficult decision: should the choice of education be based on the assumption of continued residence in Switzerland or a return to the home country?

A clearer idea of the vocational choices made by these foreigners and thus of their possible future careers can be gained from a more detailed analysis by nationalities and by types of education at secondary level.

c) <u>Breakdown by Nationality</u>

Sixteen per cent of the children attending Swiss schools are children of immigrants, but within this global figure there are considerable disparities as between nationalities and types of education.

The two analyses which follow should give a clearer picture of the situation with regard to foreign children in Switzerland:

-- The first is a "structural" analysis illustrating the differences between schoolchildren of different nationalities enrolled in Swiss schools in a given year, and

-- the second is a "cyclical" analysis showing the trend for two or three nationalities over the period from 1976 to 1982.

i) <u>Structural analysis</u>

Table 11 gives a breakdown by nationality of foreign children enrolled in Swiss schools for the school year 1981-82. It will be seen that these nationalities fall into three categories:

-- Italian children, who alone account for more than half of total foreign enrolment in Swiss schools;

-- children from other Mediterranean countries (i.e. Spain, Yugoslavia, Greece and Turkey), who make up 18.35 per cent of foreign enrolment; and

-- German and French children who together make up 13.24 per cent of foreign enrolment.

Even more striking is the breakdown by nationality for second-cycle secondary education (Table 12). The ratios given in this table bear out the remarks made earlier concerning the patterns for the different nationalities.

For example, a much higher proportion of German and French children manage to continue their schooling beyond the compulsory level and to pursue studies of an academic nature leading on to higher education at university or elsewhere.

Table 11

Enrolment of Foreign Children by Nationality
1981/82

School Level	Foreign	German	French	Italian	Austrian	Liechtenstein	Spanish	Yugoslav	Greek	Turkish	Others
Pre-school	23 876	964	600	11 956	385	21	2 869	1 302	298	1 503	3 678
Primary	84 595	5 687	3 487	43 395	2 369	105	8 485	3 308	977	4 838	11 938
1st cycle Secondary	50 442	5 350	2 753	25 981	1 765	109	4 794	1 058	477	1 561	6 594
2nd cycle Secondary	34 425	4 192	2 254	16 733	1 283	758	2 870	443	230	445	5 217
Of which: Schools preparing for the Maturité Certificates	7 743	1 452	655	2 215	312	24	482	117	61	88	2 337
Vocational education	24 591	2 407	1 416	13 930	917	670	2 210	315	153	327	2 246
Total	193 338	16 193	9 394	98 065	5 802	993	19 018	6 111	1 982	8 347	27 427
Percentages	100.0	8.4	4.9	50.7	3.0	0.5	9.8	3.2	1.0	4.3	14.2

Source: Statistique des élèves. Office Fédéral de la Statistique, Bern.

Table 12

Breakdown by Nationality in Secondary Education
1981/82

	Foreign	German	French	Italian	Austrian	Liechtenstein	Spanish	Yugoslav	Greek	Turkish	Others
School system as a whole (1)	100.0	8.4	4.9	50.7	3.0	0.5	9.8	3.2	1.0	4.3	14.2
2nd cycle secondary (2)	100.0	12.2	6.6	48.6	3.7	2.2	8.3	1.3	0.7	1.3	15.2
Schools preparing for Maturité Certificates (3)	100.0	18.8	8.5	28.6	4.0	0.3	6.2	1.5	0.8	1.1	30.2
Vocational education (4)	100.0	9.8	5.8	56.6	3.7	2.7	9.0	1.3	0.6	1.3	9.1
Ratio (2)/(1)	1.0	1.45	1.35	0.96	1.24	4.31	0.85	0.41	0.65	0.30	1.07
Ratio (3)/(2)	1.0	1.54	1.29	0.59	1.08	0.14	0.75	1.17	1.18	0.88	1.99
Ratio (4)/(2)	1.0	0.80	0.88	1.16	1.00	1.24	1.08	0.99	0.92	1.03	0.60

Source: <u>Statistique des élèves</u>. Office Fédéral de la Statistique, Bern.

By contrast, Spanish, Yugoslav, Greek and Turkish children tend more towards vocational education although their chances are somewhat unequal; the Yugoslavs and Greeks are more disadvantaged in this respect than the Spanish and the Turks, who have a higher level of enrolment in the school system as a whole.

Lastly, whilst there are relatively large numbers of Italians in secondary education, they seem very little inclined or able to continue in general education, and a proportionately far greater number of them choose the vocational stream.

From this initial analysis it is clear that the general education stream continues to be the prerogative of nationalities which are not "immigrant" in the accepted sense of the term, and that vocational education, which gives more rapid access to the working world, is favoured by children from communities lower down the social scale.

ii) Cyclical analysis

To begin, look at the enrolment of Italian children. Table 13 shows the annual percentage change in the enrolment of Italian children in Swiss schools. Despite a slight drop in the total number of Italian children in the school system as a whole between 1977 and 1982, there has been a very sharp rise in enrolment in the second-cycle secondary level -- and this applies to both "general" and "vocational" education. At the same time, there has been a decline in the number of Italian children in special education, although this needs to be set against a much steeper decline in the overall number of Italian children enrolled in primary education.

As we have seen, because of the large numbers of Italians and increased recognition of their cultural identity, the integration of Italian children into Swiss schools is constantly improving.

In the case of children of German nationality, the total number enrolled in Swiss schools fell from 24 354 in 1976 to 16 193 in 1982, i.e. a drop of about 33.5 per cent. This was the result of an even bigger decline in the number of German children enrolled at pre-school level (-57.5 per cent), primary level (-54 per cent) and in the first-cycle secondary level (-14.3 per cent), offset to some extent by a substantial increase at the second-cycle secondary level (+36 per cent) where there was an even sharper rise in schools preparing students for their _maturité_ certificates (+53.5 per cent) than for schools providing vocational education (+31 per cent).

These figures are a clear indication both of the sharp population drop in progress in Germany and of the high store set on academic values in this country.

The reverse is true however in the case of children of nationals from Mediterranean countries -- that is to say, there has been an increase in their rates of enrolment at every level of education, as is shown in the figures for the period 1977-82 in Table 14.

In Switzerland, contrary to what is happening elsewhere in Europe, the birthrate in these countries is still rising while the pace of family reunion is speeding up. However, the difficulties are also multiplying, with special

Table 13

Trend in the Enrolment of Italian Children
(Annual percentage change)

	1977/78	1978/79	1979/80	1980/81	1981/82
Pre-school	2.0	-3.0	-6.7	-7.6	-4.6
Primary	-1.1	-4.6	-5.5	-4.3	-3.4
Of which:					
Special education	-4.6	-2.9	-3.3	-3.0	-2.8
1st cycle secondary	3.5	4.2	1.1	-0.1	-0.1
2nd cycle secondary	23.4	8.6	14.0	8.3	11.0
Of which:					
Schools preparing for					
Maturité Certificates	18.1	16.8	22.5	14.2	15.5
Vocational					
education	25.4	7.9	14.4	7.5	11.5
Total	2.7	-0.1	-1.7	-2.1	-0.1

Source: *Statistique des élèves*. Office Fédéral de la Statistique, Bern.

classes being increasingly filled with the children of these immigrants (70 per cent increase between 1976 and 1982).

As was mentioned earlier, these foreigners are at a disadvantage when the time comes to make a decision as regards their future and, being in most cases uncertain and unable to seize the opportunities available to them, find themselves "dropped" into "general" education -- which explains why there are more Spanish, Yugoslav, Greek and Turkish children in this type of education (an increase of 124 per cent between 1976 and 1982) than in vocational education (+61 per cent).

These comparisons between different nationalities raise the question of the limitations of the definition of a "foreigner"; the Germans in Switzerland are not foreigners in the same way as the others, since not only have they been living there for some time (for the most part in German Switzerland where the cultural differences are slight), but they also belong to the higher socio-economic categories (teachers, research-workers, engineers, bankers, etc.).

Table 14

Trend in the Enrolment of Nationals of Mediterranean Countries
(Yearly variations in percentages)

	1977/78	1978/79	1979/80	1980/81	1981/82
Pre-school	13.5	9.7	10.2	7.2	6.3
Primary	3.0	3.5	4.0	9.5	27.0
Of which: Special education	-1.0	11.9	9.8	10.8	27.6
1st cycle secondary	-1.0	10.2	10.2	7.4	18.5
2nd cycle secondary	4.1	5.2	16.5	11.6	15.7
Of whch: Schools preparing for Maturité Certificates	15.0	17.3	13.9	17.3	29.9
Vocational education	1.6	3.3	18.3	10.8	17.7
Total	3.9	6.2	7.8	8.8	19.9

Source: Statistique des élèves. Office Fédéral de la Statistique, Bern.

VOCATIONAL EDUCATION IN SWITZERLAND

As was mentioned earlier, the number of foreign children in vocational education in Switzerland is small, representing barely 11 per cent of total enrolment for the school year 1981-82. Of these foreign students, 15.5 per cent are of French or German nationality and 65.5 per cent of Italian or Spanish nationality.

The figures in Table 15 highlight the differences between French and German children on the one hand and Italian and Spanish children on the other. It is noticeable that, in comparison with the average for all types of vocational training, the enrolment levels for "advantaged" foreign children (German and French) are always the reverse of the levels for Spanish and Italian children, and these differences are particularly marked in the case of the following types of vocational training: "The hotel trade and domestic science", "health care" and "public health and hygiene, personal and beauty care."

It is therefore important when studying the enrolment of foreign children to take into account their nationality and their parents' socio-economic status, both of which have a direct influence on their educational opportunities and their subsequent working lives and careers.

Table 15

Foreign Enrolment in Vocational Education in Switzerland
1981/82

	Total	Foreigners nb.	%	As Percentage of Total Foreign Enrolment French + Germans	Italians + Spaniards
Agriculture	12 600	241	1.9	39.4	32.8
Crafts and trades	89 591	10 535	11.8	11.7	72.5
Technical occupations	15 495	1 906	12.3	17.2	60.1
Business and administration	72 006	7 942	11.0	15.6	64.5
Transport	5 517	236	4.3	23.0	47.7
Hotel trade and domestic science	9 386	505	5.4	23.1	47.7
Public health and hygiene, personal and beauty care	6 492	1 767	22.6	11.8	79.1
Health care	14 860	1 001	6.7	26.7	41.0
Art and decorative trades	4 127	717	17.4	42.7	24.7
Pastoral care and social work	498	10	2.0	20.0	60.0
Other	101	31	30.7	32.3	58.1
Total	230 673	24 591	10.7	15.5	65.6

Source: Statistique des élèves, année scolaire 1981/82. Formation professionnelle (Degré secondaire II). Office Fédéral de la Statistique, Bern.

SWITZERLAND

FACTOR ANALYSIS DIAGRAM OF CORRESPONDENCE BETWEEN EDUCATIONAL LEVELS AND NATIONALITIES FOR THE SCHOOL YEAR 1981/82

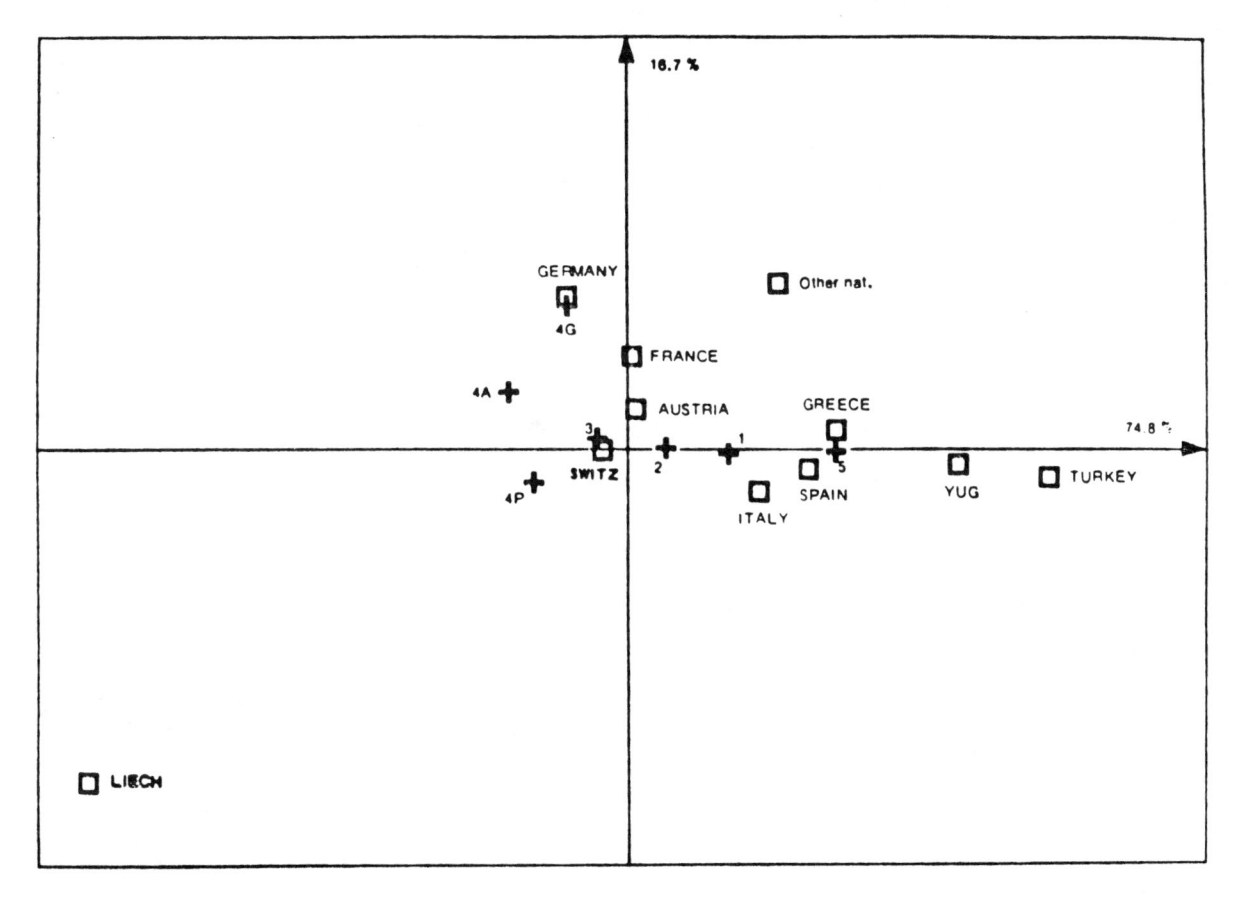

1. Pre-school
2. Primary
3. Secondary 1st cycle
4G. Secondary 2nd cycle, general
4P. Secondary 2nd cycle, vocational
4A. Secondary 2nd cycle, others
5. Special Education

✚ : Type of school

☐ : Pupils'nationality

Part Three

OTHER CONTINENTS, OTHER PROBLEMS

I. OVERSEAS-BORN CHILDREN AND CHILDREN OF IMMIGRANT DESCENT IN AUSTRALIAN SCHOOLS

Bearing in mind the context of the wider general report on the CERI project, the need to keep this one short has led to some obvious simplifications. One factor nevertheless requires emphasis: the difference between Australia and Europe: immigrants to Australia come essentially with the intention of settlement. In Europe (at least, initially) they moved to another country just for work. This gives partially a different framework for both the immigrants themselves and for the receiving government and society.

GENERAL DATA ON THE OVERSEAS-BORN POPULATION AND POPULATION OF IMMIGRANT DESCENT

a) Trend in Recent Decades

Australia's population of immigrant origin has more than quadrupled in 35 years since the end of World War II, as the number of residents born abroad rose from 744 187 in 1947 to 3 182 465 in 1981 (or respectively 9.8 and 21.8 per cent of all residents in Australia). This is a massive increase in immigration and raises issues concerning the relationship and acceptance of the various ethnic and linguistic groups on the Australian continent.

Data given in Table 1 show that the ethnic composition of Australia's resident population is changing from one which was regarded as almost homogeneous to a much more heterogeneous type. While the proportion of those born in the United Kingdom and Ireland among residents in Australia has remained fairly steady -- that of those born in non-English speaking countries is rising.

b) Present Situation

i) Population by age

Table 2 shows that the proportion of Australian residents in the younger age groups (0-24 years) is much greater among those residents born in Australia than it is among those born outside Australia.

Although almost 30 per cent of those born in Australia are under 15, only 18.1 per cent and 15.3 per cent, respectively, of Australian residents born in New Zealand and Asia are under 15.

Table 1

Changing Composition of the Australian Population Between the 1947 and 1981 Census

Place of Birth	1947 nb.	%	1954 nb.	%	1961 nb.	%	1966 nb.	%	1971 nb.	%	1976 nb.	%	1981 nb.	%
Australia	6 835 171	90.2	7 700 064	85.7	8 729 406	83.1	9 419 542	81.6	10 176 320	79.8	10 829 616	79.9	11 393 861	78.2
Outside Australia	744 187	9.8	1 286 466	14.3	1 778 780	16.9	2 130 920	18.4	2 579 318	20.2	2 718 832	20.1	3 182 469	21.8
in:														
United Kingdom and Ireland		7.1		7.4		7.2		7.8		8.5		8.2		7.8
Other Europe		1.5		5.5		8.1		8.5		8.7		8.1		7.5
Asia		0.3		0.6		0.8		0.9		1.3		1.8		2.2
America		0.2		0.2		0.2		0.3		0.4		0.6		0.7
Other		0.8		0.7		0.8		0.9		1.3		1.4		3.6
Total	7 579 358	100.0	8 986 530	100.0	10 508 186	100.0	11 550 462	100.0	12 755 638	100.0	13 548 448	100.0	14 576 330	100.0

Source: Australian Bureau of Statistics. 1981 Census of Population and Housing.

Among those residents born outside Australia, the proportion in the younger age groups who were born in Europe is significantly less than the corresponding proportion for all overseas born: only 6.1 per cent of the UK-born, 2.6 per cent of Greek-born and 1.7 per cent of Italian-born are in the 0-14 age bracket.

The split between those born in Australia and those born abroad does not enable a distinction to be made between descendants of immigrants and those who have been in Australia for generations. A high percentage of young people born in Australia are of non-English speaking origins, but these young people are of Australian nationality by law even if both their parents are of foreign nationality, for according to Australian legislation, anyone born on national territory may obtain Australian nationality. But these children, especially those who do not usually speak English at home, may have the same educational problems as children born abroad.

Similarly, in some immigrant families, the older children may have been born abroad while the younger ones have been born in Australia.

ii) <u>Demographic structure by parents' place of birth</u>

The breakdown of Australia's resident population by parents' place of birth may provide some useful information on "second-generation immigrants".

As the years pass, the number of individuals of immigrant descent is increasing: of Australia's 14 576 330 inhabitants in 1981, 8 445 526 (57.9 per cent) were of parents born in Australia and 6 130 804 (42.1 per cent) of parents of whom at least one was born abroad, as compared with 1976

Table 2

Australia's Resident Population, by Age

Age Group	Total	Born in Australia nb.	%	Born Abroad nb.	%
0-14 years	3 656 904	3 388 475	29.7	268 429	8.5
15-19 years	1 259 028	1 067 592	9.4	191 436	6.0
20-24 years	1 247 784	1 008 999	8.9	238 845	7.5
All ages	14 576 330	11 393 861	100.0	3 182 469	100.0

<u>Source</u>: Australian Bureau of Statistics. 1981 Census of Population and Housing.

figures of 13 548 448, 8 094 780 (59.8 per cent) and 5 453 668 (40.2 per cent). This means that the large wave of immigration is coming to an end, that the population of immigrant descent is seeking to establish its place in Australia and that integration issues ("integration" is used in the meaning the term has in Europe, which is slightly different from the one the same term has in Australia) associated with the development of an Australian multicultural society will need new solutions for the problems associated with the multicultural nature of Australian society.

An interesting report by the Italian Ministry of Foreign Affairs confirms the large number of second-generation Italians among residents in Australia: in 1981, of the 560 866 persons of Italian descent, 275 883 (49.2 per cent) were born in Italy and 284 983 (58.8 per cent) in Australia. This same report shows that second-generation immigrants are very young: almost 64 per cent are not yet 15 and about 16 per cent are between 15 and 19. In this particular case, the question may thus arise of the identity of these young Australians of Italian descent and their reactions to social, cultural and occupational integration in Australian society. Here too the educational implication is obvious.

iii) Birthrates of overseas-born

Data on parents' place of birth used in birth counts in Australia provides more information on the origins of "young Australian citizens" (1): in 1981, parents born in Australia accounted for 129 344 out of 202 579 legitimate births (or about 64 per cent), while 73 235 children (or almost 36 per cent) were registered to parents born outside Australia. Thus, due to the fact that one birth out of three occurs in families of foreign descent, the proportion of "young Australian citizens with foreign roots" among young Australians is rising, whereas on the basis of the statistics broken down by place of birth, the ethnic origin factor loses much of its significance since most young people are born in Australia.

In the case of births with at least one parent of overseas origin, the mothers of 15 181 were born in the United Kingdom, those of 11 409 in Asia (including 2 868 in the Lebanon), those of 3 543 in Italy, those of 2 701 in Yugoslavia and those of 2 289 in Greece (2).

iv) Labour force

In 1981 Australia had a labour force of 6 292 631 (or 43.2 per cent of the total population) of whom 4 591 213 (73 per cent) were born in Australia, 599 928 (9.5 per cent) in the United Kingdom and 162 635 (2.6 per cent) in Italy: thus more than one person out of four in the labour force was born outside Australia (3). It is interesting to study -- in relation to occupational categories -- the breakdown of the labour force by place of birth (4).

Table 3 shows that those from southern Europe and the Lebanon belong mainly to the working class. Of those persons in the labour force who were born in Italy, Greece, Poland or Lebanon, almost one in two were of the working class while the corresponding proportion for those born in Yugoslavia was almost two in three. By contrast, professional, executive and administrative staff are recruited more among those born in Australia, the United Kingdom, Germany, New Zealand and the Netherlands.

Table 3

Labour Force by Selected Occupational Categories and Place of Birth

Place of Birth	Total Labour Force nb.	Professional, Executive, Administrative and Related %	Tradesmen, Production, Process Workers and Labourers %	Service Sport and Recreational %
All places of birth combined	6 292 631	18.9	28.1	8.4
Australia	4 591 213	19.6	25.2	8.1
New Zealand	90 102	21.1	29.4	9.9
United Kingdom	599 928	21.3	30.4	9.6
Germany	66 974	20.2	36.6	8.9
Greece	88 998	7.5	49.7	11.3
Italy	162 635	7.8	51.3	9.7
Lebanon	21 088	6.9	49.1	7.2
Netherlands	56 328	20.6	34.0	9.1
Poland	29 442	17.1	46.3	10.9
Yugoslavia	89 603	5.2	64.2	10.2
Other (a)	496 325	18.4	30.4	8.6

a) Including those whose birthplace is not known.

Source: Australian Bureau of Statistics. 1981 Census of Population and Housing.

v) Conclusions

These few demographic statistics show that the population of foreign descent is very large in Australia (which in itself is not surprising since this country is mainly an immigration country) and that almost one resident out of two (42.1 per cent of Australian residents) -- whether with Australian nationality or not and whether born in Australia or overseas -- has ties with people living overseas. Despite strong political resolve in support of integration in Australian society (as seen in the concept for population statistics, the regulations for obtaining an Australian nationality, etc.), a threefold problem remains: integration of the working population born overseas; integration of the second-generation immigrants through schools; social mobility and career access for inhabitants who are not from English-speaking backgrounds.

c) Knowledge of English in Australia

As the national language is English, it is obvious that those who speak it very little or not at all will find it more difficult than others to become integrated in Australian society: this is especially the case of immigrants from non-English speaking countries, although quite a large number of them speak English properly. Of the 1 491 287 persons from non-English speaking backgrounds, 352 858 (about 21.8 per cent) say they speak nothing but English, 792 452 (53.1 per cent) -- although they use one or more other languages -- consider they speak this language very well or well, while only 275 346 (18.5 per cent) say that their knowledge of English is poor or even non-existent. This percentage is rather high compared with that in European countries where those who have no knowledge at all of the official language of the country in which they have settled seem to be fewer in number.

Of the 323 136 residents of Australia who stated they did not know or were very weak in English (i.e. only 2.4 per cent of the total population), 29 381 (or almost 10 per cent) were born in Australia: this once again confirms the importance of the educational problems to be solved if all those not belonging to the main ethnic group although they were born in Australia are to learn English and thus have a minimum possibility of becoming fully integrated in Australian society (Table 4).

Table 4

Population Aged over 5, Broken Down by Place of Birth and Knowledge of English

	Speak English Only	In Addition to One or More Languages, Speak English Very Well or Well	Not Well or Not at All	No Answer Given	Total
Born in Australia	9 767 614	386 617	29 381	139 569	10 323 179
Born outside Australia	1 717 843	878 132	292 203	83 809	2 971 987
In an English-speaking country	1 364 984	85 683	16 858	13 175	1 480 700
In a non English-speaking country	352 858	792 452	275 346	70 631	1 491 287
Not stated	13 492	4 531	1 552	149 640	169 216
Total population over 5 years old	11 498 949	1 269 280	323 136	373 018	13 464 385

Source: Australian Bureau of Statistics. 1981 Census of Population and Housing.

d) The Population of Immigrant Origin in the State of Victoria

As statistics broken down by educational level and also by ethnicity (or place of birth) are difficult to obtain for Australia as a whole but not for some States such as Victoria, it seems useful to take this into account in the rest of our study on schoolchildren from foreign backgrounds.

We shall thus give a brief review of the population in the State of Victoria as an introduction to the study on children of foreign descent in Australian schools.

i) Total population and population of immigrant descent

In 1981 the State of Victoria had 3 832 443 inhabitants of whom 917 347, or 23.9 per cent of the total population, were born outside Australia. This is a very high percentage compared with European norms and is slightly higher than for Australia as a whole (21.8 per cent).

However, the breakdown of residents by place of birth is not quite the same in the State of Victoria as in the rest of the country, for of the 146 625 Greek immigrants in Australia, 72 270, or 49.3 per cent of the "Greek" immigrant population, have settled in Victoria; the "Italians" and "Yugoslavs" are also concentrated in this State (41.8 per cent and 39.8 per cent of the respective populations settled in Australia). Thus, excluding those born in the United Kingdom and Ireland (6.8 per cent of Victoria's residents), almost 17.8 per cent of Victoria's inhabitants were born in Europe (3 per cent in Italy, 1.9 per cent in Greece and 1.6 per cent in Yugoslavia), and 2.8 per cent in Asia, whereas 7.8 per cent of Australia's total population was born in the United Kingdom, 7.5 per cent in the rest of Europe and 2.2 per cent in Asia.

Some differences are also to be noted with regard to nationality: 76.1 per cent of Victoria's population was born in Australia, while this is the case of 78.2 per cent of the total population; but those born abroad who have become naturalized Australians represent 12.1 per cent of Victoria's population but only 10.5 per cent of the country's total population.

The proportion of residents of ethnic minority membership (5) is not insignificant and even exceeds that for Australia as a whole: of the 3 832 443 inhabitants of Victoria, both parents of 2 088 513 residents were born in Australia (or 54.5 per cent against 57.9 per cent), whereas at least one parent of 1 743 930 residents was born outside Australia (45.5 per cent as against 41.1 per cent). Of the latter group of residents, 826 583 were born in Australia (or 21.6 per cent of the population resident in the State of Victoria).

Ethnic pluralism has thus developed even more in the State of Victoria than in Australia as a whole, a fact that has contributed to the spread of "ethnic schools".

ii) English in the State of Victoria

Since English is one of the common denominators in Australian society, it is essential for residents of members of ethnic minorities -- particularly

Table 5

Population Aged Over 5 Resident in the State of Victoria
Broken Down by Place of Birth and Knowledge of English

Place of Birth	Speak English Only nb.	%	In Addition to One or More Languages, Speak English Very Well or Well nb.	%	Not Well or Not at All nb.	% (1)	No Answer Given nb.	% (1)	Total
Total population aged over 5	2 857 360	80.6	458 217	12.9	123 085	3.5	108 194	3.1	3 546 858
Born in Australia	2 448 748	92.8	143 420	5.4	5 920	0.2	41 424	1.6	2 639 509
Born outside Australia	405 448	44.7	31 335	34.5	116 627	12.9	30 901	3.4	907 349 (2)
In an English-speaking country	295 476	97.7	4 935	1.6	303	0.1	1 569	0.5	302 279
In a non English-speaking country	109 972	19.5	308 400	54.7	116 325	20.6	29 334	5.2	564 032
Of whom those born in									
Greece	2 557	3.5	39 877	55.3	25 091	34.8	4 572	6.3	72 103
Italy	9 566	8.3	66 256	57.5	32 993	28.6	6 478	5.6	115 291
Yugoslavia	4 544	7.7	35 992	60.7	14 251	24.1	4 502	7.6	59 288

1. The percentages are calculated in relation to the total population concerned.

2. Of whom 41 014 persons did not state their place of birth.

Source: Australian Bureau of Statistics. 1981 Census of Population and Housing.

those from non-English speaking countries -- to have a good knowledge of this language if they are to be better integrated with the other Australians.

As shown by Table 5, the proportion of those who speak no or little English is higher because of the larger number of immigrants from non-English speaking countries in the State of Victoria than in Australia as a whole; this is especially true of those born in Greece, Italy or Yugoslavia for, although only 3.5 per cent of Victoria's population aged at least 5 cannot speak English, almost 35 per cent of Greek, 29 per cent of Italian and 24 per cent of Yugoslav immigrants are unable to use this language, and it is also in these three groups that most children attend ethnic schools.

CHILDREN OF IMMIGRANT DESCENT IN SCHOOLS IN THE STATE OF VICTORIA

According to the latest statistics recorded (in 1982) by the Education Department of Victoria, there are 141 562 pupils of immigrant descent ("ethnic students") (6) among the 584 781 in State schools, which means that almost one pupil out of four is of foreign descent, a percentage that is very high compared with Europe.

An even more interesting fact is that of the 141 562 "ethnic students", only 30 937 (21.8 per cent) were born outside Australia and 109 531 in Australia (over three-quarters of the ethnic school population) (7).

Table 6 shows that while the government/State school population in the State of Victoria decreased in the 1980-82 period, the number of "ethnic students" rose, as did the number of the latter born in Australia.

Table 6

Trend in the Government School Population in the State of Victoria, 1980 to 1982

	1980	1981	1982
Trend in school population in Australia	606 147	595 042	584 781
Numbers of ethnic students	140 337	142 881	141 562
Percentage of ethnic students	23.2	24.1	24.2
Of whom:			
Those born in Australia	17.6	18.4	18.7
Those born abroad	5.4	5.4	5.3
Don't know	0.2	0.3	0.2

Source: Planning Report of Ethnic Census, Education Department of Victoria.

These figures are very revealing concerning the trend in the number of second-generation immigrants or rather for a generation of Australians whose parents were born abroad and educated in countries other than the one in which they work.

a) **Analysis by Educational Level**

A comparison between the distribution by level of schooling of ethnic students and the total government school population of Victoria reveals that for the first there are relatively more primary and technical schools students and relatively fewer secondary school students.

An examination of the breakdown of ethnic students in the various types of school in relation to the total school population (Table 7) shows that they are slightly over-represented in secondary schools. The reason might be that ethnic students might include those who were born outside Australia and had already started their schooling in their countries of birth in addition to those born in Australia; but this is simply an assumption that has still to be proved for we know that relatively few of those under 15 were born outside Australia.

b) **Analysis by Mother Tongue**

Of the 141 562 pupils from non-English speaking countries in 1982, almost 31 000 had English as their mother tongue and used it at home (about 22 per cent of the population of ethnic origin other than British).

Table 7

Breakdown of the School Population in the State of Victoria
by Educational Level, 1982

Educational Level	Total School Population (1) nb.	%	Ethnic Student Population (2) nb.	%	(2) as % of (1)
Primary	344 848	58.9	77 486	54.7	22.5
Secondary	167 784	28.7	50 839	35.9	30.3
Technical	66 919	11.4	12 269	8.7	18.3
Special	5 230	0.9	968	0.7	18.5
Total	584 781	100.0	141 562	100.0	24.2

Source: Education Department of Victoria, 1982.

The other languages used most in Victoria are Greek (32 897 pupils speak this language, or 23 per cent), Italian (spoken by 21 818 pupils, or 15.4 per cent), one of the Slavonic languages (spoken by 13 422 pupils, or 9.5 per cent) and, to a lesser extent, German, Dutch, Turkish, Maltese and Chinese.

Many pupils of the second group attend ethnic schools which are reserved for quite specific communities (Greek ethnic schools, Lutheran ethnic schools) and stand apart from other schools whether they come under the government system or not. The ethnic schools are after-hours schools which receive financial assistance from the government but do not "come under" either the government or the private system. In addition to these part-time schools, some ethnic communities have set up private independent full-day schools.

c) <u>Ethnic Students in Non-government Schools</u> (8)

In 1981, 595 042 pupils were attending 2 149 government schools and 121 611 pupils 632 non-government schools most of which come under the Catholic teaching system (where the ethnic minority pupils are mostly of Italian origin) (9).

Table 8 shows that more ethnic students attend private schools than government schools -- whatever the educational level -- and that this applies even more in the State of Victoria than in Australia as a whole.

d) <u>Ethnic Students in Ethnic Schools</u>

In any case, the ethnic student, whether attending government or a private school, must know English or learn it as a second language. Knowledge of English is a practical necessity in Australian schools as English (either alone or occasionally as part of a bilingual programme) is the medium of instruction in all schools. But some parents who want their children to be taught the language and culture of their native country send them to ethnic schools (also known as community schools or Saturday schools) for two to eight hours of lessons a week on their language and culture in addition to normal schooling, as in the system of non-integrated classes in Europe for immigrants' children. These provisions apply especially to primary school children.

The number of ethnic schools has risen considerably since the 1970s, particularly among the Greeks and Italians: in 1980, Greek was the mother tongue of 11 000 children and Italian of some 6 000 children out of the 25 444 ethnic school students in Victoria (10). The success of this system in the Greek community in Victoria is partly due to the concentration of the population of Greek descent in this State, and partly to the cultural drive shown by the Greek community.

e) <u>Conclusion</u>

Australia -- as an immigration country -- is increasingly a multicultural society in which the function of the English language is changing: after being a language of the community which founded the State, English is becoming an inter-community language making it possible to integrate the different community groups.

This very interesting development gives rise to two important issues that will be central factors in Australian life in the coming years: the first concerns non-discriminatory access to the job market for members of all communities so as to give everyone an equal opportunity for social and cultural advancement (today this equality of opportunity has by no means been

Table 8

Breakdown of Schoolchildren by Origin and by Type of School, 1980

	Australia			Victoria		
Educational Level and Type of School	Total School-children nb.	Non English-speaking Schoolchildren nb.	%	Total School-children nb.	Non English-speaking Schoolchildren nb.	%
Primary						
Government	1 508 000	243 100	16.1	374 700	81 000	21.6
Private	376 100	110 300	29.3	117 400	44 500	37.9
of which Catholic	322 000	101 300	31.5	97 700	41 000	42.1
Total	1 884 100	353 400	18.8	492 100	125 500	25.5
Secondary						
Government	810 000	157 000	19.4	231 500	58 600	25.3
Private	290 400	65 500	22.6	98 800	27 700	27.9
of which Catholic	200 200	55 600	27.8	63 300	22 900	36.2
Total	1 100 400	222 500	20.2	330 300	86 300	26.1
Total						
Government	2 318 000	400 100	17.3	606 200	139 500	23.1
Private	666 500	175 800	26.4	216 200	72 300	33.4
of which Catholic	522 200	156 900	30.1	161 000	63 900	39.7
Total	2 984 500	575 900	19.3	822 400	211 800	25.8

Note: As these data are from two different sources, they must be carefully interpreted.

Sources: For schoolchildren as a whole, Australian Bureau of Statistics, 1980.
For the non English-speaking population, National Survey of Students from non English-speaking backgrounds, 1980.

achieved since those from English-speaking backgrounds hold most of the key posts in political and economic life); the second concerns the place of cultures and languages other than those of the English-speaking world in a multicultural society where different cultures and races would coexist on a basis of equality.

NOTES

1. As has already been stressed, any person born in Australia is considered to be an Australian citizen even if he/she is of migrant descent.

2. The figures are from the ABS (Australia Bureau of Statistics).

3. However, it is not possible to give the date of birth for 84 141 of them.

4. This breakdown is not by nationality.

5. Born abroad or born in Australia of parents at least one of whom was born abroad.

6. Pupils born in a non-English speaking country or born in Australia of parents at least one of whom is from a non-English-speaking country are considered to be "ethnic students" in the report on the 1982 census on "ethnic education" published by the Education Department of Victoria.

7. 1 094 pupils were unable to state their places of birth at the time of the survey conducted in 1982 by the Education Department of Victoria.

8. The statistics available on this subject are from various sources and do not necessarily concern the same year.

9. The figures are from the section on Education in the 1983 Yearbook of Australia. Unfortunately, no distinction has been made between those born in Australia and those born abroad, and those with at least one parent from a non-English speaking country.

10. These figures are from the Review of Multicultural and Migrant Education published by the Australian Institute of Multicultural Affairs.

II. CANADA'S GROWING CULTURAL DIVERSITY: SOME PRELIMINARY OBSERVATIONS

CANADA'S RESIDENT POPULATION: SOME BASIC FACTS AND FIGURES

Canada, like other countries that have developed as a result of immigration, has a population which is ethnically and linguistically extremely diverse. Cultural pluralism therefore is inherent in the very nature of the country.

The numerous and successive waves of immigration that have continued right up to the present day have profoundly changed the country's initial cultural make-up in which the predominant influence was the presence of descendants of the two founder nations: the British and the French. The principal ethnic group -- the British -- is no longer in the majority, its share of the population having declined from 60 per cent at the end of the last century to 40 per cent in 1981, whereas the French ethnic group has kept its share of about 30 per cent and that of the remaining ethnic groups has tripled from 10 per cent in 1867 to over 30 per cent in 1981.

This change in the ethnic structure of Canada's population has been accompanied by a diversification of the origins of this immigration: the number of immigrants from Asian and Caribbean countries has increased to such an extent that they are beginning to outnumber those from southern and western Europe.

This rapid change in the ethnic make-up of Canada's population has brought with it problems of a linguistic, cultural and educational character: how, for instance, can the country's national identity be preserved, or even enhanced, in the face of the radical changes brought about by these continuing population movements? How can national unity be maintained during the transition from a dual-culture society, haunted by the spectre of the separatist movement in Quebec, to a multicultural society? What policy should be adopted with regard to language and to what extent should bilingualism be developed, or should it on the contrary be abandoned? Should the children of "immigrants" study their mother tongue or learn the official language of the region in which they live? These and many other questions continue to be subjects of keen political debate in Canada.

a) Ethnic Origins

More than 40 different ethnic origins were recorded by the official population statistics services in the last Census in 1981. The term "ethnic origin" is used by the census services to mean "the cultural or ethnic group to which the respondent or his ancestors belonged when they first arrived on the continent". The fact is that the vast majority of the population were originally immigrants to the country -- the indigenous population of Inuits and Indians represent only 2 per cent of the total.

It is necessary therefore to differentiate between ethnic origin and nationality or citizenship, and it should be said that in the previous censuses (prior to 1981) respondents were asked to state their ethnic or cultural antecedents solely on their father's side (which meant that each respondent gave only one ethnic origin), whereas in 1981 this restriction was dropped and the respondent could therefore give more than one ethnic origin. It is interesting to note that in a country like Canada the obsession with origins, roots however remote, is so strong that it is apparent even in the statistical classifications of a census.

Of Canada's resident population of 24 083 500 in 1981, 40.2 per cent claimed to be of British origin, 3.6 per cent of another origin in addition to British, 1.8 per cent of French as well as British origin, and 0.4 per cent of British, French and other origins, while 26.7 per cent claimed to be of French origin, 4.7 per cent German, 3.1 per cent Italian, 2.2 per cent Ukrainian, 1.7 per cent Dutch, 1.2 per cent Chinese, 1.2 per cent Scandinavian, etc.

The pattern, however, differs from one province to another: in Quebec, for example, 80.2 per cent are of French origin, only 7.7 per cent of British origin and 11 per cent of other origins, whereas in Ontario 52.6 per cent are of British origin, 7.7 per cent of French origin and close to 40 per cent of other origins. Ontario, moreover, has the largest proportion of "immigrants": virtually four out of every ten people living in Toronto are immigrants (1).

But in view of the fact that these census figures take little account of respondents' nationality, what does the term "immigrant" signify? Criteria other than ethnic origin ought perhaps to be taken into consideration, e.g. place of birth, mother tongue, whether the person has Canadian or other citizenship, period of immigration, etc.

b) Place of Birth

Of Canada's population of 24 083 500 in 1981, 3 867 160 or just over 16 per cent, were born abroad. Of these, the vast majority were Europeans, who accounted for 67 per cent (23 per cent from the United Kingdom), followed by those who were born in the Americas (15.6 per cent), Asia (14.1 per cent), Africa (2.7 per cent) and Oceania (0.9 per cent). This global figure of 16 per cent for those born abroad is high (although it is even higher in Australia, the figure for most European countries is less than 10 per cent).

Table 1 shows that, of persons born in Canada, one out of four is less than 15 years old, whereas only 7 per cent of those born abroad are under 15. There are, however, substantial differences depending on the country of origin: for example, those born in South America, South-East Asia, the United States, Vietnam or the Philippines are relatively young (with the under-15s accounting for between 14 and 25 per cent); family immigration is far more common in the case of these population groups. However, in the case of the British, the Poles, the Germans, the Greeks and the Italians the pattern is the reverse, i.e. the under-15s are very few in number, which suggests that second generation migrants are an important although "hidden"

Table 1

The Population of Canada by Age and Place of Birth (1981)

Place of Birth	Total Population nb.	%	Population under 15 nb.	%	Under 15 as Proportion of Total Population %
Canada	20 216 340	83.9	5 202 465	94.9	25.7
Abroad	3 867 160	16.1	271 745	5.1	7.1
Total	24 083 500	100.0	5 474 210	100.0	22.7

Source: Statistics Canada, 1981 Census.

factor in the case of these groups. Take the case of the Italians, for example: 10 per cent of them were born in Italy, but only 1.6 per cent of these were under 15; which means that family immigration from Italy has dwindled although the number of children under 15 and born in Canada of at least one Italian parent could well be relatively large.

c) Citizenship

Only three categories of citizenship can be extracted from the census data: "Canadian citizenship", "citizenship other than Canadian, namely that of the country of birth" and "citizenship other than Canadian but not that of the country of birth".

This is significant as far as calling in question the territoriality principle is concerned, particularly since, of the 3 867 160 persons born abroad, just over 68 per cent have adopted Canadian nationality (2) and slightly less than 31 per cent have kept their original nationality while only 1 per cent said they were Canadian by birth. Nonetheless, the number of those who have retained their nationality is high, although it would be interesting to know whether the fact that a person is allowed to possess dual nationality (which is not the case in the United States, for example) is an important factor in this respect.

Under Canadian law any person born on Canadian territory, whatever his parents' nationality, automatically has Canadian citizenship. To judge by these figures, Canada would appear to have considerable success in integrating its foreign population.

That said, it is not very meaningful for the purposes of this analysis to use this particular parameter. Cultural problems, as Canadians well know, cannot be settled by issuing passports but by paying special attention to language problems.

d) <u>Periods of immigration</u>

A few figures will suffice to illustrate the pattern of immigration into Canada during this century. The ten years from 1901 to 1911 witnessed the highest level of immigration in Canadian history with a total of 1.7 million new arrivals; the peak year, however, was 1913 when there were 400 000 immigrants. Between 1919 and 1930 immigration generally stayed at a figure of over 100 000 a year. Between 1931 and 1941 many Canadians, who had emigrated to the United States, returned to Canada. Between 1946 and 1981 a total of some 5 million immigrants were allowed into Canada at average annual rates of 150 000 during the 1950s, 141 000 during the 1960s and 144 000 during the 1970s.

At the time of the 1981 Census, of the 3 867 160 persons born outside Canada, 540 475 (14 per cent) had come to Canada prior to 1945, 572 570 (17.4 per cent) between 1945 and 1954, 135 555 (35.1 per cent) between 1954 and 1959, 920 520 (23.8 per cent) between 1970 and 1977 and 338 395 (8.8 per cent) between 1978 and 1981 (3).

The age of those emigrating to Canada is rising: of the 338 400 persons born outside Canada who had immigrated between 1978 and 1981, 9.9 per cent had been under 4 years old, 26.8 per cent between 15 and 19 and 63.3 per cent 20 or over, whereas of the 540 475 who had immigrated prior to 1945, 30.4 per cent had been under 5 years old, 44.1 per cent between 5 and 19 and only 25.5 per cent 20 or over. These figures bear out a comment made earlier, i.e. most of the younger people who said they were of foreign origin were born in Canada, and a particularly large number of them to parents who were born abroad and who emigrated to Canada at a relatively young age. These are what in Europe might be termed second-generation immigrants, though it must be remembered that these young people are all Canadian citizens.

e) <u>The Labour Market</u>

At the time of the 1981 Census there were 12 054 155 persons in the labour force (i.e. 50 per cent of Canada's total resident population); of these 4 874 125 (40.4 per cent) said they were of British origin, 3 111 670 (25.8 per cent) of French origin, 648 425 (5.4 per cent) of German origin, 410 275 (3.4 per cent) of Italian origin, 302 315 (2.5 per cent) of Ukrainian origin, 227 025 (1.9 per cent) of Dutch origin and only 123 310 (1 per cent) said they were of indigenous origin.

Table 2 gives a breakdown of the labour force by place of birth and occupation. The ratio of "foreigners", i.e. those born outside Canada, is larger in industry than it is in the service sector.

However, it is interesting to note that the ratios change according to the place of birth: a greater proportion of those born in the United Kingdom and the United States are in finance, insurance and public administration,

Table 2

Canada's Labour Force in 1981 by Selected Occupations and Place of Birth (%)

	Total Population	Born in Canada	Total	United States	United Kingdom	Southern Europe	Asia
Total labour force	100.0	100.0	100.0	100.0	100.0	100.0	100.0
Managerial, administrative	8.8	8.7	9.2	11.7	13.2	4.7	7.6
Clerical staff	18.6	19.3	15.4	16.2	20.6	9.4	15.9
Processing workers	4.1	4.1	4.2	2.2	2.1	6.8	5.1
Construction workers	6.5	6.4	6.8	4.3	4.9	13.7	2.1

(Population Born Abroad spans Total, United States, United Kingdom, Southern Europe, Asia)

Source: Statistics Canada, 1981 Census.

Table 3

Percentage of the Population Able to Speak One or Both of the Official Languages (1981)

	Canada	Ontario	Quebec
English only	66.9	86.7	6.7
French only	16.6	0.7	60.1
English and French	15.3	10.8	32.4
Neither English nor French	1.2	1.7	0.8
Total	100.0	100.0	100.0

Source: Statistics Canada, 1981 Census.

whereas more of those born in southern Europe are employed in manufacturing and construction.

This breakdown of the labour force would suggest that there is a hierarchy of nationalities amongst immigrants: those whose mother tongue is English tend to be at the top of the social scale and in the higher grade positions, whereas the others tend more to be in the manual worker category.

This situation is one of the underlying causes of the ethnic tensions that Canada is having to contend with, i.e. the dominant position of the English-speaking population. We are back once again with the language problem.

THE LANGUAGE SITUATION IN CANADA

The language situation is a complex one in Canada for several reasons: firstly, the fact that there are two official languages, English and French, causes problems particularly since the situation varies from one province to another; and, secondly, the existence of many different immigrant groups means that a variety of mother tongues are spoken other than English or French.

It is interesting to note from the figures in Table 3 that, taking the two official languages, the ability to speak English is much more common than the ability to speak French: although 15.3 per cent of Canadians are able to speak both English and French, 66.9 per cent are able to speak only English and 16.6 per cent only French. This means that 82.2 per cent of the population can speak English compared with 31.9 per cent who can speak French.

In the Province of Ontario, where English is the official language, 86.7 per cent of the population are able to speak only English and less than 1 per cent only French, although 10.8 per cent speak both English and French.

Moreover, in Quebec where French is the official language, 60.1 per cent are able to speak only French and 6.7 per cent only English, although 32.4 per cent of the population are able to speak both languages.

These figures clearly show the predominance of English speakers throughout Canada as a whole.

Table 4 shows the language situation in 1981 for Canada as whole and the two provinces of Ontario and Quebec where the dominant language is respectively English and French.

It will be seen from this table that there are more persons whose mother tongue is a language other than English or French in Ontario (17.2 per cent) than in Quebec (6.7 per cent); this highlights once again the scale of immigration in Ontario 23.7 per cent of whose population were born outside Canada (4).

Taking each language category separately, i.e. English, French or other, it is interesting to note the differences between the numbers speaking a particular language as their mother tongue and those for whom it is the language most often spoken at home. Thus for Canada as a whole, and also for

Table 4

Population by Mother Tongue and Language Most Often Spoken at Home for Canada and the Provinces of Ontario and Quebec (1981) (%)

	English	French	Other	Total
Canada				
Mother tongue	61.2	25.6	13.1	100.0
Most often spoken at home	68.2	24.6	7.2	100.0
Ontario (official language: English)				
Mother tongue	77.3	5.5	17.2	100.0
Most often spoken at home	86.1	3.9	10.1	100.0
Quebec (official language: French)				
Mother tongue	10.9	82.4	6.7	100.0
Most often spoken at home	12.7	82.5	4.8	100.0

Source: Statistics Canada, 1981 Census.

Table 5

The Population of Canada by Mother Tongue and by Place of Birth (1981)

Mother Tongue	Total Population nb.	%	Born in Canada nb.	%	Born Abroad nb.	%
English	14 750 490	61.2	13 101 325	64.8	1 649 165	42.6
French	6 176 215	25.6	6 024 775	29.8	151 440	3.9
Other	3 156 785	13.1	1 090 235	5.4	2 066 550	53.4
Total	24 083 500	100.0	20 216 340	100.0	3 867 160	100.0

Source: Statistics Canada, 1981 Census.

Ontario and even Quebec, the proportion of those who speak English at home is larger than the proportion for whom English is their mother tongue. Similarly, a substantial proportion of those whose mother tongue is a language other than English or French (13.1 per cent of the population of Canada as a whole and 17.2 per cent of the population of Ontario) prefer to use English in the home rather than their mother tongue (the figures for those who continue to use their mother tongue at home are much lower: 7.2 and 10.1 per cent respectively). In the Province of Ontario French is the mother tongue of 5.5 per cent of the population, but only 3.9 per cent speak it at home.

In Quebec, where the official language is French, there is no difference between the percentage for whom French is their mother tongue and the percentage who speak mainly French at home. On the other hand, of the 6.7 per cent whose mother tongue is a language other than French or English, 4.8 per cent speak their mother tongue at home and the rest English.

The figures in Table 5, giving a breakdown by place of birth, are extremely illuminating: the mother tongue of more than half of the "new arrivals" in Canada (i.e. those born outside Canada) is a language other than English or French whereas, in the case of persons born in Canada, this is true of only 5.4 per cent -- which means that a more or less essential prerequisite for satisfactory assimilation in Canadian society is a good command of English or French, (depending on the province) the more so since knowledge of one of these two official languages is required in order to obtain Canadian nationality.

Also striking is the small percentage of those born outside Canada who are French-speakers (not even 4 per cent): so if the French language is holding its own in Canada and more particularly in Quebec, this is due far more to its ability to resist than to its ability to attract. In Quebec, for instance, whereas only 26.9 per cent of those born outside Canada speak mainly French in the home, the figure for those born in Canada is 87.5 per cent.

This fact highlights the significance of Quebec's language policy and is proof of the inherent cultural dynamism of a community that is determined to retain its individuality.

Unlike French, however, the use of English is gaining ground even though, as was seen earlier, the relative size of the ethnic British population is declining: of the "new arrivals" in Canada, 63.2 per cent choose to speak English in the home compared with 4.3 per cent who choose French and 32.6 per cent another language (whether this be their mother tongue or some other language).

Thus the dual English and French language system in Canada is under increasing threat and Canadian society is going to have to contend not only with the dominance of the English language, but also with the growth of multiculturalism and linguistic pluralism.

NOTES

1. See M.S. Devereaux, <u>Immigrants au Canada</u>. Immigrants are defined as persons born outside Canada.

2. Note that in 1976 a new Act came into force reducing the minimum period of residence required for obtaining Canadian citizenship from five to three years with, however, certain provisos: e.g. three years of actual residence over the last four years. At the time of the 1981 Census, of the 3.5 million immigrants who had entered the country before 1978, 75 per cent had obtained Canadian citizenship.

3. The "remaining" 39 645 born outside Canada qualified for Canadian citizenship at birth.

4. Taking Canada as a whole, 16.1 per cent of the population were born abroad whereas for Quebec the figure was only 8.3 per cent.

Part Four

FACTORS OF INEQUALITY: A CAUSAL ANALYSIS

I. SOCIAL AND CULTURAL INEQUALITIES: AN OVERVIEW

A statistical study of the school careers of foreign children in seven OECD Member countries shows that a substantial proportion (varying according to their nationality or nationality group) experience difficulties in the school system of their host country. Proportionately, they are more often directed into special education, for example, or into the shorter secondary cycles, or vocational training. Conversely, they are less present, in relative terms, in upper secondary classes -- where the general education is given that is needed for going on to higher studies.

However accurate these statistics may be, they do not tell the full story. They are merely the first, necessary step in a wider inquiry into the causes and possible special character of what, for brevity, may be termed the "failure at school" of many foreign pupils.

It is a necessary step because the unassailable figures focus attention on the unremittingly dismal situation of a constantly growing (in relative and absolute terms) segment of the school population.

It is, however, no more than a step, of which the limitations are clearly recognised. The variable of "nationality" that serves as a basis for quantitative analysis (since it is the only one recorded in nationwide school statistics) provides a convenient approach to the problem under discussion. This does not make it into an explanatory factor, let alone the sole explanatory factor.

The notion of cumulative handicap, or combined disadvantage, used in describing the situation of numerous foreign pupils, expresses the role of multiple interacting variables in explaining these children's plight. Briefly mentioned at an early stage of the project, this concept now needs to be developed, clarified, and -- as far as available material permits -- verified.

THE STATED OBJECTIVE (1)

It is superficially tempting to round off the first, quantitative, phase of the investigation with a second, qualitative, phase. There are, however, at least two good reasons for rejecting this symmetrical terminology as inexact:

-- One, because numerical data are needed (even though they may be derived from other statistical materials) for determining the impact of certain variables, other than nationality, on the school careers of foreign pupils;

-- Two, because a number of factors, such as "cultural distance" from the norms of the host society, "heterophobia", and the value accorded by foreign pupils and parents to academic success, have had to be discounted. They probably play an active part in creating the general environment of schooling for foreigners but, since they are not amenable to "objective" assessment, they must remain outside the scope of the study.

In consequence, the term "causal analysis" seems best to sum up the method adopted for the second phase of the exercise.

Before laying out the main findings and setting them against those of the first phase of the study, a quick glance at the limitations imposed by the material is in order.

The first is common to both stages of the investigation and concerns the obligatory concept of "foreigner" used to distinguish the school careers of indigenous and exogenous pupils. The trouble with this term in designating the dividing-line between the two segments of the school population is that it leaves out of account the growing category of young nationals of foreign parentage who, despite their citizenship, may display the same socio-economic and socio-cultural traits as foreigners in the primary sense of the term. Moreover, the term may give the impression that the foreign population thus identified makes up a perfectly homogeneous group.

The variable of "nationality" thus appears to be too reductive and, at the same time, too all-embracing.

Two further limitations concern the second phase only, in which pupils panels and samples were called upon:

-- The numbers in question, with a few thousands of foreigners at most, mean that the sub-populations remaining after several variables have been applied are extremely small. Conclusions based on these sub-groups may therefore be devoid of mathematical significance and not generally applicable to all children of foreign nationality;

-- The field of investigation is restricted in advance to the variables decided upon at the time the panel is constituted. If a variable that might prove relevant to the study (say, the parents' familiarity with the language of the host country) has been omitted, it cannot be introduced afterwards when the explanatory factors are being sought.

This being so, the causal analysis that has been carried out applies to the findings of three surveys, each of a different kind:

-- In France, the data were derived from three samples (panels) of nationally representative pupils, assembled by the Ministry of Education. The pupils in these groups were followed throughout their school careers beginning with their first year in primary school (for the 1978 sample), or in secondary school (for the group formed in 1972-1973-1974 and the one formed in 1980).

-- In Switzerland, a sample of pupils was chosen on a territorial basis (the Canton of Geneva) and their school careers were observed, with special emphasis on two key junctures, i.e., retardation at the end of primary studies, and choice of stream at the beginning of secondary schooling. In order for the sample to be sufficiently large, it was composed of children who had attended the final year of primary education in Geneva's publicly-run schools during a five-year period (from 1980/81 to 1984/85).

-- For the United Kingdom, the data were taken from the Swann Report, published in March 1985 under the title <u>Education for All</u>, and its main conclusions were summarised. Taking as its starting-point the situation described by a large number of previous studies, this report seeks to elucidate why pupils of West Indian and Asian origin obtain dissimilar results at school, although they are all Commonwealth citizens.

The dossiers for these countries provide the substance of the next three chapters.

THE MAIN FINDINGS

Despite the varied nature of the situations under study and the analytical instruments used, the guiding theme of the investigation in the three countries appears to be the same.

What happens to the differences in school career observed between the children of minority groups (whether or not they are defined as foreigners) and those of the majority when variables -- demographic, socio-economic or socio-cultural other than that of "nationality" or "ethnic minority" -- are introduced.

The answers obtained for each country are set out in what follows.

i) <u>The case in France</u>

The mass of statistical material compiled by SIGES made it possible to test the overall differences recorded in school performance between national and foreign pupils in both primary and secondary schools against a wide range of variables.

Using indicators peculiar to each panel but which, for convenience, may be summed up in the single term "normal school performance", the researchers found that the differences associated with the sole criterion of national/foreigner decreased more or less markedly when other criteria were applied, although they did not disappear entirely.

One finding of the exercise was that the head of household's socio-economic category was a strong explanatory factor for some pupils' educational difficulties, with other variables (size of family, degree of education of the person having responsibility for the child and, to a lesser extent, the occupational status of the mother) also contributing.

Furthermore, when socio-economic category was crossed with one or the other of the above variables, the differences between French and foreign pupils became still less marked. On the other hand, the place of birth of young foreigners (France or the country of origin) appeared to have less of an effect except in secondary education and then only over a fairly long period of observation.

The extraordinary complexity of the problem comes from the close correlation of the variable of nationality with socio-economic category, family size, the degree of education of the person having responsibility for the child and the mother's occupational status. A refined analysis using crossed variables, and consequently involving very small samples, brings out this interweaving very clearly. As one example of this snowball effect, the proportion of foreigners in the 1980 group rises from 7.3 per cent (all criteria combined) to 37.9 per cent for children whose father is a manual labourer, and to 55 per cent when the father is a labourer and there are five or more siblings.

It may be asked whether studying the effects of socio-economic category and family size criteria is merely another way of reintroducing the variable of nationality.

ii) **The case in Geneva**

The computerised data base on education of the Canton of Geneva Sociological Research Service covers all of the school attenders in the Canton's public and private schools, from kindergarten up to university entrance. It enables the school performance and learning difficulties of children of Swiss nationality to be compared with those of children of foreign origin throughout their school careers.

The Geneva situation is interesting for several reasons. First, there is a very strong foreign presence -- some 32 per cent at the present time. Second, the cohorts of pupils are particularly large: according to the computer data base, total school attendance in 1985 in the Canton's publicly-run schools, from kindergarten to upper secondary level, amounted to 55 797 pupils, of whom 19 980 were of foreign nationality. Third, as Geneva is an important centre for international affairs, a not insignificant proportion of the foreign children belonged to the upper end of the social spectrum.

By means of data collected on 18 300 children (36 per cent of whom were of foreign nationality) in their final year of primary school, in the Geneva public school system between 1980/81 and 1984/85, it was possible to follow them at the crucial moment of transition to secondary education and to study their choice of secondary stream by nationality, date of arrival in Geneva, and the head of household's socio-economic category.

Two indicators of difficulties at school were selected:

-- The age-grade relation at the end of primary studies (6th year), which measures the difference between the "normal" age for that grade (11-12 years) and the pupil's actual age, making it possible to detect a repeated grade during the primary education cycle;

-- The choice of stream at the beginning of secondary education, and more particularly at the beginning of the "pre-gymnasium" courses (classics and science) which are the most highly regarded, academic avenues leading to university.

The main conclusions from the five years of observation are as follows:

-- The proportion of educationally retarded children at the end of the primary cycle is slightly higher for foreigners than for nationals, but is more sharply differentiated according to socio-economic category: 20 per cent of children from working-class families suffer from retardation compared with 5 per cent only of children from the upper reaches of society;

-- The proportion of retardees is also affected by place of birth (or age of arrival in Geneva): natives of Geneva and foreign children born there or immigrating there at a very early age (before the age of 4) suffer much less from retardation than children arriving in Geneva after their fourth birthday;

-- Lastly, when both variables, social origins and age of arrival in Geneva, are considered simultaneously, the nationality factor loses much of its power to explain the differences among categories of pupils handicapped by retardation;

-- As far as choice of stream is concerned, the differences are very striking between "normal" pupils (those whose age corresponds with or is lower than the standard age for the grade) and "retarded" pupils. A full 76 per cent of the former are admitted to "pre-gymnasium" classes, as against 26 per cent only of the retardees. These average percentages change according to the social origins of the parents (for example, the 76 per cent average includes a figure of 57 per cent for the children of unskilled and semi-skilled workers and 91 per cent for the children of professionals), somewhat less according to the age upon arrival in Geneva, and least of all according to national origins.

The findings produced by the data base seem to establish firmly the order of importance of the factors responsible for difficulties at school: first, social background, second, the age upon arrival in the Canton and, third, nationality -- which, in the case of the middle and upper socio-economic categories, sometimes has a negligible impact.

However important this clarification may be, it is irremediably tainted by a statistical vice: young foreigners make up 72 per cent of all pupils from an unskilled working background, and 64 per cent of those arriving in Geneva after the age of three. Such a heavy proportional representation in certain categories points up the limitations of multi-criteria analysis.

iii) <u>The case in the United Kingdom</u>

Many of the pupils residing in the United Kingdom who belong to ethnic minorities are of West Indian or Asian origin (in 1981, there were 604 000 West Indians and 1 114 000 Asians).

Despite the similar status of both of these minorities (British citizenship, identical socio-economic profiles) the school performance of children with an ethnic minority background varies greatly. That of West Indian pupils is significantly worse than that of Asian children, whose level tends to equal that of white pupils.

In the face of this situation, the United Kingdom Government set up a commission of enquiry into the education of minority groups. Two reports were produced: first, the Rampton Report which noted the poor school performance of West Indian as compared with other children; second, the Swann Report, published in 1985 under the title of Education for All, which attempted to elucidate the reasons for the situation described.

The Swann Report examined four types of possible causes for the differences in school performance observed between West Indians, Asians and whites:

- Although forms of unintentional racism (expressed through superior, paternalistic attitudes or disparaging, disappointed opinions about ethnic minority pupils) may exist, implied or overt racism at school cannot by itself fully account for unsatisfactory school performance; it is a contribution element, linked with other unfavourable social factors;

- Differences in IQ noted between West Indian and native British children diminish sharply when other, more discriminating, variables are introduced, such as skill-level of the head of household, income, family size. This being so, the differences in IQ are not in themselves an adequate explanation for poor academic performance;

- Social factors (income, employment, health, housing conditions, etc.) have a profound bearing on school careers: white and ethnic minority children living in the same socio-economic conditions have identical academic records. It would not, however, be correct to assume that adverse socio-economic conditions inevitably produce failure at school; some children have very successful school careers in spite of extremely adverse living conditions;

- Lastly, the residual difference not explained by socio-economic factors seems to be determined by other factors, notably cultural ones, located at the point where school and society interact. Pupils of West Indian origin suffer from a handicap in this respect that the young Asians do not encounter. This kind of factor cannot be evaluated satisfactorily at present.

In comparison with the studies carried out in France and Switzerland, the work done in the United Kingdom in connection with the Swann Report offers the advantage of taking a much wider range of factors into account at the investigatory stage, even though some of them cannot be quantitatively appraised.

A number of lessons may be drawn from the Report:

-- No single reasons can be advanced to explain why many West Indian and Bengali pupils perform poorly at school;

-- Socio-economic conditions are, in fact, not alone to blame for academic failure, important as they may be;

-- Other causes of a social, educational or cultural nature play a much larger part than is commonly assumed in the school careers of children from ethnic minorities.

Further studies are needed in order to refine this analysis and arrive at solutions that are apposite with respect to the difficulties encountered by these children.

CONCLUDING REMARKS

A first period of research governed by the question "What education do foreign children receive?" has been succeeded by a second phase in which the question has become "How does this situation come about?" In other words, an attempt has been made, drawing on the various sources of information available, to pinpoint the causes for the unsatisfactory school performance of pupils hitherto identified by no more than their foreign nationality.

The investigation thus took the form of seeing what happened to the disparity between the school performances of nationals and foreigners when other criteria, mainly economic and demographic, were introduced.

It was found that, out of all the variables tested, social background -- understood as the socio-economic category of the head of household, with all that that implied for the child's environment and quality of life -- was the most convincing explanatory factor. The effect of socio-economic category was, moreover, enhanced when combined with other, frequently related, characteristics, such as family size and the degree of education of the parents.

The findings of all the studies used point to social background as being the paramount factor. But does this mean that the case can be closed because socio-economic conditions totally blot out the effect of national origins? A number of considerations counsel prudence:

-- First, all of the calculations, in which the proportional distribution of nationals was weighted to equal that of foreigners while maintaining the success (or failure) rate corresponding to each variable treated (socio-economic category, family size, age on arrival in Geneva, etc), demonstrate that, even if the initial difference between nationals and foreigners narrows, it does not disappear entirely;

-- Second, the relative weight of foreigners in certain categories (children of manual workers with large families, children arriving in Geneva after the age of three, etc.) is so heavy (60-70 per cent and sometimes more) that it is well-nigh impossible to distinguish the effects of the chosen variable from what may be due to national origins;

-- Third, and more tangibly, the British report convincingly showed that, despite equivalent economic status and background, Asian pupils fared much better at school than the West Indian minority.

The main conclusion to be drawn is that the differences in school careers observed between pupils of varying nationality are due not to a single cause but rather to a set of causes resulting from a combination of factors.

Some of these factors, economic or demographic ones, lend themselves to quantitative assessment. Others, probably socio-cultural, are impossible to evaluate.

Foreign origin thus appears to be an aggravating circumstance coming on top of other inequalities common to various categories of pupils irrespective of nationality.

The fact of reaching such conclusions is not an admission of powerlessness. It rather comes as a timely reminder of the complexity of a problem which calls for further study. In any case, we should not forget -- and there are many examples to prove it -- that where academic achievement is concerned individual determination can always offset the harmful influence of collective factors.

NOTE

1. This section is based on studies carried out in France and Switzerland, which supplied the bulk of the material presented. The case of the United Kingdom is different, in that the analysis is more qualitative in nature. It is therefore possible to compare the lessons to be learnt from two complementary approaches that endeavour to elucidate the causes of the same problem: the differences in educational performance by foreign pupils (in France and Switzerland) and pupils belonging to ethnic minorities (in the United Kingdom).

II. COMPARISON OF FAMILY CHARACTERISTICS AND EDUCATIONAL CAREERS OF SCHOOLCHILDREN FROM INDIGENOUS POPULATIONS IN FRANCE

THE APPROACH

The Administrative and Statistical Data Processing Service (<u>Service de l'informatique de gestion et de statistique -- SIGES</u>) of the French Ministry of Education has been monitoring three successive samples (panels) of pupils (described in Annex 3):

-- A group of secondary stage pupils selected on their entry to the first class of secondary school (6th grade in the French system) in 1972, 1973 and 1974 (referred to below as the "1972-74 sample"). It comprises 37 437 children (including 2 496 of foreign nationality) and describes their educational performance to the end of their studies;

-- A group of primary stage pupils starting in the first grade of primary school (<u>cours préparatoire -- CP</u>) during the school year 1978/79 (known as the "1978 sample"). It comprises 17 438 children (including 1 431 of foreign nationality) who were observed throughout their passage through primary education;

-- Finally, a second group of secondary stage pupils grouping 20 321 children (including 1 483 of foreign nationality) who started in the first class of secondary school in 1980 (known as the "1980 sample").

There is an important difference between the figures obtained from the statistical surveys of school attendance which are produced annually at national level and the figures derived from these samples, a difference which must be borne in mind: the former case involves cross-sectional data (or, put in another way, a "photograph" of the situation at a given point in time) which cannot relate to the same individuals from one year to another because of input and output movements in the educational system. On the other hand, with the samples, we are concerned with the same individuals who are observed from the beginning to the end of the period of reference; the data relating to them are longitudinal. We use the terms "synchronous study" where we are concerned with statistical observation and "diachronous study" where we are concerned with a causal analysis.

These three samples have provided us with a body of information on the educational progress of French and foreign schoolchildren: for example, the percentage admitted to a particular class, the number of pupils showing a normal educational performance, successive streaming in various cycles and course alternatives during the progress of the child's education.

These sets of information are correlated with other data on the situation (mainly family circumstances) of the children by a consideration of several economic and socio-demographic variables, studied individually (simple variables) or in relation to one another (cross-linked variables).

Hence it becomes possible to show in respect of a given educational situation (for example, the percentage of adolescents with a normal educational performance) not only the nationality of the young people in question but also the socio-economic category (SEC) of the father and, more importantly, the SEC cross-linked with another variable which may be significant, such as the size of the family or the duration of the child's pre-school education.

It then becomes possible -- and this is the particular value of this supplementary investigation -- to explore the following aspects:

-- How the discrepancy observed in educational progress as between French and foreign pupils changes, whether the gap remains the same or widens and, if so, to what point;

-- Whether, apart from the French/foreign gap, similarities emerge in educational performance between children belonging to the same socio-economic category or having the same number of brothers and sisters, etc.

The plan followed in the conduct of this research was dictated by the nature of the material available and by the fact that it seemed more worthwhile to bring together the information contained in the three samples.

In the interests of clarity but without underestimating the risk of oversimplification that this presentation may involve -- since the variables are heavily interdependent -- we shall examine in turn:

-- The impact on educational progress of the simple variables;

-- The effect of the cross-linked variables;

-- Finally, in a conclusion setting out the main lessons drawn from the two preceding parts, we undertake a critical evaluation of the results obtained.

THE IMPACT OF THE SIMPLE VARIABLES

The relation between a particular indicator of educational progress and a particular variable is here ascertained with respect to:

-- Two indicators (the socio-economic category of the head of the household and the place of birth of the foreign children), for all three of the panels monitored by SIGES;

-- Four other indicators (the size of the family, the level of education of the person responsible for the child, whether the mother goes out to work and the duration of pre-school education), only for the 1978 sample (1).

i) The socio-economic category of the head of the household

In the 1978 sample

Table F (in the Annex) indicates the distribution of French and foreign children according to the SEC of the head of the household and highlights the important differences which exist between these two groups. Thus for 45 per cent of French children, the head of the household belongs to one of the following four socio-economic categories: middle management, clerical staff, shop-floor supervisory staff and skilled tradesmen, which is only the case for 23.7 per cent of the foreign children. On the other hand, 57 per cent of the latter live in a household the head of which is an unskilled worker, whereas only 12 per cent of French children are in this situation.

A link can be established between the nature of the SEC and the percentage of children showing a normal educational performance. Indeed Tables 1 and 2, which depict the educational situation at the end of four years of schooling through the primary stage [i.e. the proportion admitted to the cours moyen 1ère année (CM1: 1st year of the final grades at primary school) in 1981/82], show that, with identical SEC, the educational achievement of foreign pupils is not far behind that of indigenous children.

Table 1

Rates of Normal Schooling from Enrolment in CP in 1978 to Admission to CM1 in 1981/82 According to Nationality and SEC

	French		Foreigners	
	Numbers Entering CP	% Accepted in CM1	Numbers Entering CP	% Accepted in CM1
Farmers	827	79.4	3	66.7
Farm workers	158	61.4	33	45.5
Entrepreneurs and businessmen	1 411	82.1	35	65.7
Senior management	1 536	95.8	23	91.8
Middle management	2 226	88.7	24	91.7
Clerical staff	1 847	79.5	33	57.6
Shop-floor supervisors and skilled workers	3 137	74.9	281	58.7
Unskilled workers	2 892	63.2	817	51.9
Domestic staff	543	61.9	52	59.6
Other categories	461	84.8	4	100.0
Unemployed and various	934	63.3	125	52.1
Total	15 972	77.2	1 430	55.3

Source: SIGES, document 5311.

With a random mix of SECs the French/foreign discrepancy is 21.9 points (77.2 per cent of entrants in the first group, 55.3 per cent in the second), whereas it is only 16 points for the "shop-floor supervisory staff and skilled worker" category, about 11 points for unskilled workers and 4 points for senior management (a value which has to be approached with caution, having regard to the poor representation of foreigners among the staffs in question).

The information contained in Table 2 makes it possible to narrow down the analysis, on the one hand by breaking down the average rate of foreign entrants (55.3 per cent) by certain nationalities or nationality groups and on the other hand by focusing on the difference between the percentages obtained for all SECs together and those characterizing the numerically most important category: that of unskilled workers.

On the first point, the "Other Europeans" are found to achieve the best results (63.5 per cent of them show a normal educational performance), followed by the Portuguese (58.2 per cent) and the "Other Nationalities" group (55.6 per cent). Only half of the children in the Maghreb group show a normal educational performance, while over one third of them (36.9 per cent) are one year behind and 12.2 per cent are in a more difficult situation.

In relation to the second series of data it is interesting to note that the discrepancies between the results under the heading of "All SECs" and those under "Unskilled Workers" are very small for the North Africans and the Portuguese (1 point or less) but much higher for the other foreign nationals (over 10 points). However, this must be seen against the fact that three quarters of the North African and Portuguese children come from a working

Table 2

Educational Situation of the Pupils at the Start of Their 4th Year at School in 1981/82 After Enrolment in CP in 1978 According to Nationality and Certains SECs

	Foreigners		Maghreb		Portugal		Other Europe		Other Nat.	
	All SECs	Unsk. Work.	All SECs	Unsk. Work.	All SECs	Unsk. Work.	All SECs	Unsk. Work.	All SECs	Unsk. Work.
Normal schooling	55.3	51.8	50.9	50.6	58.2	57.1	63.5	51.9	55.6	33.6
One year behind	34.4	36.4	36.9	36.7	32.1	31.3	32.1	39.9	33.1	47.6
More than one year behind or remedial class	10.3	11.8	12.2	11.7	9.9	11.6	4.5	8.1	11.3	15.8
Total numbers entering CP in 1978	1 431	817	666	401	414	259	200	75	151	82

Source: SIGES, DT309.

class background, compared with only a third of the other foreign schoolchildren.

In the 1972-74 sample

Regarding the educational streaming of the schoolchildren who entered the first class of secondary school during this three-year period, Table 3 shows very clearly that within one and the same nationality group the incidence of SEC on educational performance is considerable: indeed 88.7 per cent of French schoolchildren belonging to the advantaged SECs reach the end of the first cycle and 71.7 per cent pass on to the 2nd long cycle, whereas only 54.7 per cent of the sons of manual workers manage to complete the first cycle and 27.5 per cent enter the long stream. A similar situation is to be observed among the foreign school population, but with lower proportions at each socio-economic level: for example, 77.8 per cent of the children of foreign executives and businessmen (compared with 88.7 per cent of their French counterparts) and 44.3 per cent of the children of foreign manual workers (compared with 54.7 per cent of the indigenous population) completed the first cycle of secondary education.

Looked at in terms of identical SECs, the discrepancies between French and foreign schoolchildren, as far as entry into the second cycle is concerned, become narrower as we go down the social ladder. Indeed, whereas the gap is 16.1 points for "all SECs together" (41.8 -- 25.7 per cent), it is 10.3 points for the senior management group, 7.2 points for middle management and only 4.7 points for manual workers.

In the 1980 sample

Three tables put together from the data for the 1980 panel supply much the same kind of information.

With regard to the age of entry to the first grade of secondary school (Table 4) and educational performance during the preceding primary phase (Table 5), it emerges that, although considerable gaps exist between the French and foreign schoolchildren, they seem to narrow when the comparison is made within the same SEC (see Table M in the Annex, which shows the distribution of pupils in this panel according to nationality and SEC of the head of the household).

Indeed for "all SECs together", there is a gap of over 30 points (63.6 -- 33 per cent) between the percentage of French children who are at least one year behind on starting secondary school (i.e. aged 12 years and over) and the percentage of foreign children with the same handicap. But in the category of "Manual Workers" (taken as a whole) the difference is only about 23 points (65.8 -- 42.4 per cent).

Similarly, close on 31 per cent of French children (all SECs together) but 39 per cent of those from a working class background have repeated at least one class in primary school, whereas the rates of repeat-years among the foreign children are 43.4 and 44.2 per cent respectively (Table 5).

With regard to the school careers of the adolescents who started secondary school in 1980, Table 6 shows the differences which emerge after one year in the first class.

Table 3

Course Selection of Pupils Enrolled in Secondary Education in 1972-74 According to Nationality and SEC of Head of Household

	French							Foreigners						
	Enrolled in First Class	Reaching End of First Cycle		Enrolled in 2nd Long Cycle		Rate of Transfer (1)	Enrolled in First Class	Reaching End of First Cycle		Enrolled in 2nd Long Cycle		Rate of Transfer (*)
		nb.	%	nb.	%	%		nb.	%	nb.	%	%
All SECs	34 676	22 955	66.2	14 501	41.8	63.2	2 501	1 189	47.5	644	25.7	54.2
Including:												
Advantaged SECs: Entrepreneurs, top businessmen, senior and middle management and other categories	8 529	7 569	88.7	6 118	71.7	80.8	158	123	77.8	97	61.4	78.9
Intermediate SECs: Self-employed tradesmen, small businessmen and clerical staff	6 501	4 623	71.1	2 908	44.7	62.9	192	119	61.9	72	37.5	60.5
Disadvantaged SECs: Manual workers	12 663	6 921	54.7	3 484	27.5	50.3	1 757	779	44.3	401	22.8	51.5
Farm workers, domestic staff, unemployed and others	3 627	1 753	48.3	866	23.9	49.4	362	155	42.8	69	19.1	44.5

1. Rate of transfer from the end of the first cycle (or troisième) to the 2nd long cycle.

Notes: No breakdown is given in this table for farmers' children, because of their very small numbers among the pupils of foreign nationality. There is some variation in the numbers presented in this table compared with the table in the Annex. But here we are concerned with the pupils enrolled in the first class of secondary school in 1972, 1973 and 1974, whereas the other tables are concerned with pupils actually entering the first class in 1972, 1973 and 1974.

Source: Data from the 1972-74 secondary sample.

Table 4

Age on Enrolment in First Class of Secondary Education in the 1980 Panel

	French				Foreigners			
	All SECs		Manual Workers		All SECs		Manual Workers	
	nb.	%	nb.	%	nb.	%	nb.	%
Age 10 and under	861	4.6	117	1.8	17	1.1	3	0.3
Age 11	11 765	62.5	3 665	55.7	522	35.2	364	33.9
Age 12	4 561	24.2	2 037	30.9	542	36.5	401	37.3
Age 13 and over	1 651	8.8	757	11.5	402	27.1	306	28.5
Total	18 838	100.0	6 576	100.0	1 483	100.0	1 074	100.0

Source: SIGES, DT297.

Table 5

Previous Educational Performance of Pupils Enrolled at Secondary School in 1980

	French				Foreigners			
	All SECs		Manual Workers		All SECs		Manual Workers	
	nb.	%	nb.	%	nb.	%	nb.	%
Normal primary schooling	12 355	65.6	3 780	57.5	554	37.4	396	36.9
One repeat year	4 526	23.9	2 026	30.8	459	30.9	359	33.4
At least two repeat years	1 288	6.8	544	8.3	186	12.5	116	10.8
Other courses (a)	669	3.6	226	3.4	284	19.2	203	18.9
Total	18 838	100.0	6 576	100.0	1 483	100.0	1 074	100.0

a) Pupils who have attented initiation classes or who have had schooling abroad (including 188 foreigners, all SECs together).

Source: SIGES, DT297.

The percentages of pupils going up from the first to the second class (from sixième to cinquième) are 82.6 per cent for French children and 76.9 per cent for foreign children, in other words a difference of 5.7 points, all SECs included; the difference is less than 3 points if only the "Manual Workers" categories, both skilled and unskilled, are considered. On the other hand, the rate of repeats is lower among the foreigners, whatever their socio-economic category. This is mainly due to the fact that the proportion of them leaving the normal educational cycle to pursue alternative courses of education (transfer to pre-vocational courses [classe pré-professionnelle de niveau -- CPPN], apprenticeship preparation courses [classe préparatoire à l'apprentissage -- CPA] or preparation for the vocational aptitude certificate [certificat d'aptitude professionnelle -- CAP]).

ii) Size of family

In the 1978 sample

The fact that over half the French schoolchildren belong to families with fewer than three children, compared with only a quarter of the foreign children (see Table I in the Annex), must not be overlooked, since there is a link between educational performance and family size: generally speaking, the greater the number of children in a family, the poorer the educational performance.

Graph 1 illustrates these results, showing in addition that the gaps between rates of normal educational performance narrow as family size increases. Moreover, in families with at least six children, the foreigners seem to show a slightly higher rate of success than the French children (but the size of the groups in question is very small).

Moreover the same observations apply irrespective of the specific nationality of the schoolchildren in question. In families with six or more children, school results -- albeit poorer than those recorded for smaller families -- seem better for the North Africans than for the Portuguese. (However, the relative preponderance of the North Africans in this family category -- about seven times higher than their representation in the sample as a whole -- suggests the need to approach this indication with some caution).

In the 1972-74 sample

Table B in the Annex confirms this characteristic of the foreign schoolchildren, i.e. the fact that a majority of them belong to large families: over 60 per cent have at least three brothers or sisters, nearly 45 per cent have at least four (a situation only found for 40 per cent and 24 per cent of the French children).

Graph 2 shows very clearly the influence of family size on the educational streaming of children entering the first class of secondary school, regardless of their nationality: all the curves show the same trend, differing only in their starting level and slope.

Thus the proportion of pupils selected for CPPN or CAP courses increases with family size and, conversely, that of pupils having completed the first cycle or having reached terminale (i.e. the final grade of the second cycle of secondary education) decreases considerably.

Table 6

First Year of Observation in 1981/82 for Pupils Entering Secondary School in 1980 According to Nationality and SEC of Head of Household

	French								Foreigners (All)							
	All SECs		Sk. Work.		Unsk.Work.		All SECs		Sk.Work.		Unsk.Work.	
	nb.	%	nb.	%	nb.	%	nb.	%	nb.	%	nb.	%
Entering 2nd class	15 562	82.6	2 956	80.7	2 238	76.8	1 140	76.9	280	77.8	258	73.9
Repeating 1st class	2 442	13.1	560	15.3	477	16.4	171	11.5	40	11.1	94	13.2
Entering CPPN	475	2.5	93	2.5	139	4.8	82	5.5	16	4.4	54	7.6
Other courses (a)	359	1.9	52	1.4	61	2.1	90	6.1	24	6.7	38	5.3
Total	18 838	100.0	3 661	100.0	2 915	100.0	1 483	100.0	360	100.0	714	100.0

a) Pupils entering CPA, entering CAP, entering other classes, leaving the country, lost.

Source: SIGES, DT297.

Graph 1.
**RATES OF NORMAL SCHOOLING FROM CP TO CM1
ACCORDING TO NATIONALITY AND SIZE OF FAMILY,
ALL SEC TOGETHER**

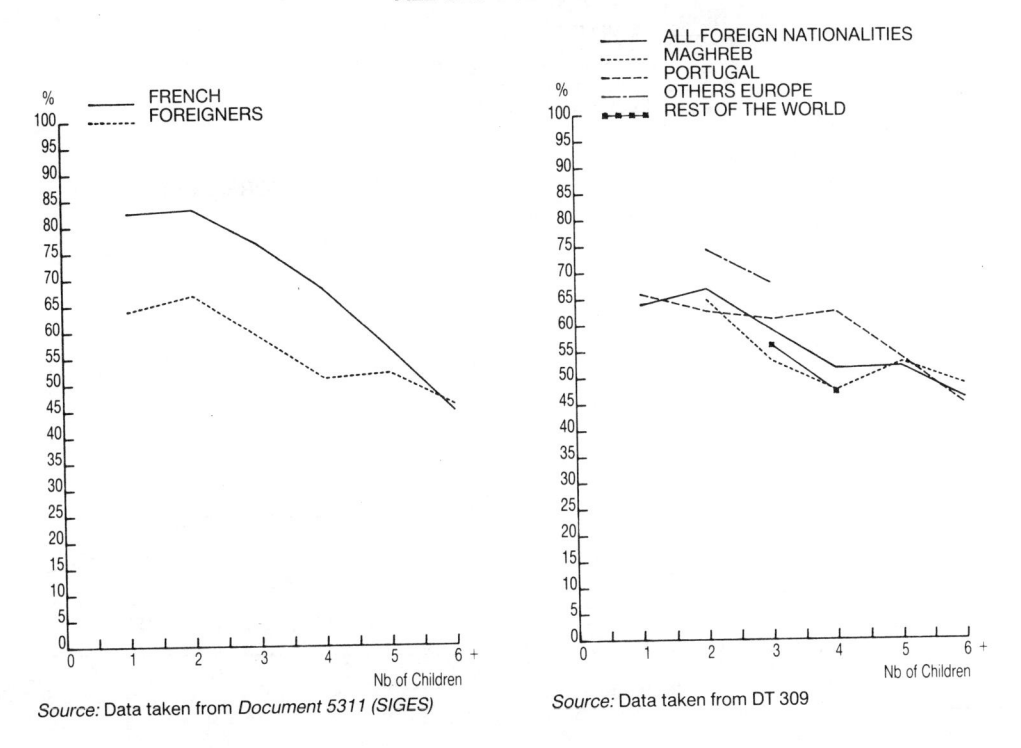

Source: Data taken from *Document 5311 (SIGES)*

Source: Data taken from DT 309

iii) Place of birth of the foreign children

In the 1978 sample

This sample supplies a number of indicators that make it possible to evaluate the influence of the place of birth of the foreign pupils (see Table H in the Annex) on their progress through primary education.

Table 7 shows that almost 10 per cent of children of foreign nationality enter the <u>cours préparatoire</u> after the age of seven (less than 1.5 per cent of the French children) and that the average rate of 9.2 per cent alters dramatically, depending on whether the children were born in France (3.9 per cent) or outside France (18.4 per cent).

On the other hand, with regard to the subsequent progress of these children through the educational system, it is difficult to assess the effect of this variable (Tables 8a and 8b). The foreign children born in France are only ahead of the average rate of normal schooling of 55.3 per cent by one point (56.2 per cent), while the immigrant children fall short of it by less than 2 points (53.6 per cent).

Graph 2.

**STREAMING OF PUPILS ENROLLED
AT SECONDARY SCHOOL IN 1972,73,74**

——— COMPLETING 1st CYCLE
········ ENTERING CPPN
– – – STARTING 1st YEAR OF CAP
–·–·– ENROLLED IN 2nd LONG CYCLE
■–■–■ REACHING TERMINALE

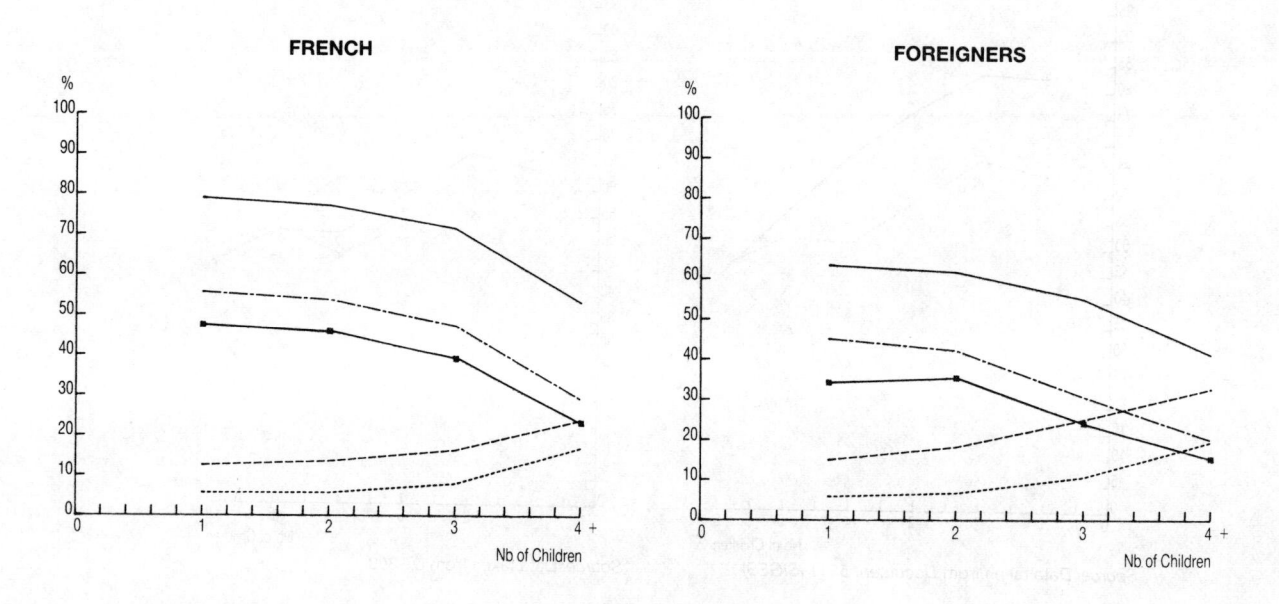

FRENCH

FOREIGNERS

FRENCH AND FOREIGNERS

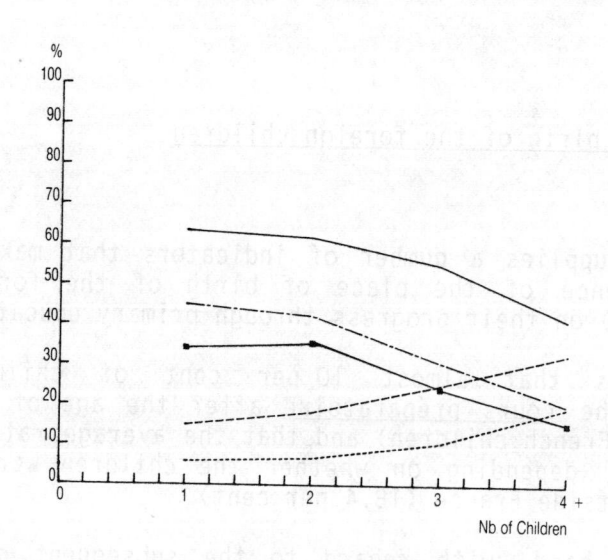

Source: Data from the 1972-74 Secondary Sample

Table 7

Age on Entering CP of Pupils in the 1978 Intake

	French		Foreigners		Foreigners Born in France		Foreigners Born Abroad	
Age	nb.	%	nb.	%	nb.	%	nb.	%
Less than 6	445	2.8	5	0.3	3	0.3	2	0.4
Between 6 and 7	15 317	95.8	1 292	90.5	876	95.7	416	81.2
Over 7	227	1.4	131	9.2	37	3.9	94	18.4
Total	15 989	100.0	1 428 (a)	100.0	916	100.0	512	100.0

a) The age on entry to CP of three pupils is not known.

Source: SIGES, DT309.

Table 8 (a)

Educational Performance of Pupils According to Nationality and Place of Birth from Enrolment in CP in 1978 to the 4th Year of School in 1981/82
(percentages)

	French	Foreigners	Foreigners Born in France	Foreigners Born Abroad
Normal schooling from CP to enrolment in CM1	77.1	55.3	56.2	53.6
Pupils falling behind including:	22.9	44.7	43.8	46.4
One repeat year	18.8	34.4	..	..
More than one repeat year or remedial class	4.1	10.3	..	..

Source: SIGES, DT309.

Table 8(b)

Educational performance of pupils by individual nationalities and place of birth from enrolment in CP in 1978 to the 4th year of schooling in 1981/82 (%)

	Maghreb		Portugal		Other Europe		Rest of the world	
	(1)	(2)	(1)	(2)	(1)	(2)	(1)	(2)
Normal schooling	50.8	51.1	60.1	52.5	61.5	68.4	..	52.3
1 repeat year	36.4	38.1	30.5	36.6	33.6	28.1	..	35.4
More than 1 rep. year or remedial school.	12.8	10.9	9.5	10.9	4.9	3.5	..	12.3
Total (Numbers)	437	229	313	101	143	57	21	130
(%)	100.0	100.0	100.0	100.0	100.0	100.0	..	100.0

Notes: (1) Born in France
(2) Born abroad

Source: SIGES, DT 309.

In terms of specific nationalities -- taking only the two largest groups, the North Africans and the Portuguese -- a clear difference emerges between them. In the case of the former, place of birth has almost no effect on educational progress (same rate of normal schooling, percentage of pupils repeating classes slightly higher among those born in the country of origin); in the case of the latter, on the other hand, those born in France show a higher rate of success than the others: 60.1 and 52.5 per cent respectively, entered CM1 in 1981/82.

In the 1972-74 sample

As Table 9 shows, the foreign children surveyed in this sample are fairly evenly divided among those born in France (52.7 per cent) and those born abroad (47.3 per cent). A careful examination of the educational progress of these two groups reveals some differences with regard to the course options for which they were successively selected during their passage through secondary education.

To begin with, 55 per cent of those born in France completed the first cycle of secondary education and almost a quarter (24.5 per cent) got as far as terminale. These proportions are only 40 per cent and 17 per cent for those who entered the country as immigrants during their childhood.

Table 9

Streaming in the 1st and 2nd Cycles of Pupils Enrolled in
First Year Secondary School in 1972-74

	French nb.	%	All Foreigners nb.	%	Born in France nb.	%	Born Abroad nb.	%
Pupils entering the first class in 1972-74	34 941	100.0	2 496	100.0	1 315	100.0	1 181	100.0
Including:								
Entering CPPN or 4e pratique	3 805	10.9	379	15.2	189	14.4	190	16.1
Entering CPA or 3e pratique	2 891	8.3	242	9.7	115	8.7	127	10.7
Entering CAP 1st year in 3 years (excluding agriculture course)	6 440	18.4	702	28.1	359	27.3	343	29.1
Completing the 1st cycle	23 066	65.9	1 196	47.9	723	55.1	473	39.9
Enrolled in the 2nd long cycle (including agriculture course)	14 743	42.2	666	26.7	403	30.6	263	22.3
Enrolled in the 2nd short cycle (including agriculture course)	7 563	21.6	457	18.3	288	21.9	169	14.3
Reaching terminale	12 265	35.1	526	21.1	322	24.5	204	17.3

Source: Statistical tables produced by SIGES.

Conversely the numbers of foreign children selected for CPPN, CPA and first year CAP courses were proportionally higher among those born abroad than among those born on French territory (CPPN: 16.1 per cent compared with 14.4 per cent, CPA: 10.7 per cent compared with 8.7 per cent, CAP: 29.1 per cent compared with 27.3 per cent). In particular, the percentage of foreigners admitted to the long second cycle varies significantly depending on whether or not they were born in France (30.6 and 22.3 per cent respectively).

In the 1980 sample

A more comprehensive body of data (see Table 14) supplies some indications which appear to contradict the above.

Let us first look at the facts: the pupils who entered the first class of secondary school in 1980 are in the following situation in 1981/82:

	French		Foreigners		Foreigners born in France		Foreigners born abroad	
	nb.	%	nb.	%	nb.	%	nb.	%
Entering 2nd class	15 562	82.6	1 140	76.9	573	76.4	567	77.4
Repeating 1st class	2 442	12.9	171	11.5	109	14.5	62	8.4
Entering CPPN	475	2.5	82	5.5	37	4.9	45	6.1
Other courses	359	1.9	90	6.1	31	4.1	59	8.1
Totals	18 838	100.0	1 483	100.0	750	100.0	733	100.0

After one year at secondary school -- and the short duration of the period of observation perhaps explains the results obtained -- the number of foreign pupils born outside France who moved up into the second class was proportionally higher than that of the pupils born in France (77.4 and 76.4 per cent respectively) and those who stayed down in the first class proportionally smaller (8.4 and 14.5 per cent respectively), smaller even than the number of French children experiencing that handicap (13 per cent).

The fact remains that the percentage of those moving out of the normal educational cycle -- selected for CPPN or another branch of the system -- is 14 per cent among the immigrant children compared with 9 per cent for the other foreigners, and only 4.4 per cent for the indigenous French children. Furthermore on the date to which the information refers, the selection process had not yet had time to take full effect.

iv) The other simple variables

Three different variables are grouped under the same heading (the educational level of the person responsible for the child, the situation of the mother with regard to occupational activity and the duration of pre-school education) because the data which would make it possible to link any of these variables with educational options are all drawn from the 1978 sample which comprises children undergoing primary schooling.

a) <u>The education level of the person responsible for the child</u>

In this area the differences between the French and foreign groups are very marked (see Table G in the Annex): 40.7 per cent of those in charge of indigenous children have a level of education beyond primary school, which is only the case for 7.6 per cent of the foreign children (3.4 per cent for the Portuguese and 3.6 per cent for the North Africans).

When these data are cross-referred to those relating to the percentages of children admitted to the CM1 grade (i.e. fourth year of a normal primary cycle) it is noted (Table 10):

-- On the one hand that the proportion increases significantly (by over 20 points) when the person responsible for the child has a standard of education higher than primary, whatever the person's nationality (from 65.7 to 87.6 per cent for the French; and from 52.3 to 75.2 per cent for the foreigners);

-- On the other hand that, with equal levels of education, there is a significant gap (of the order of 12-13 points) if the "nationality" variable is reintroduced to the analysis. For example, when the person responsible for the child has a level of education higher than primary, 88 per cent of the French children enter CM1 normally, compared with only 75 per cent of the foreign children.

Table 10

Rates of Schooling from CP in 1978 to Enrolment in CM1 in 1981/82
According to Nationality and Level of Education of
the Person Responsible for the Child

	French		Foreigners	
	Primary	Better than Primary	Primary	Better than Primary
Numbers entering CP	5 637	6 493	675	109
Percent enrolled in CM1	65.7	87.6	52.3	75.2

Source: SIGES, group of primary school pupils sampled in 1978.

Whether the mother works or not

The situation of the mother with regard to employment may be not without its influence on the educational progress of the children. Indeed the fact that a mother works often correlates with a higher level of education.

At the same time, the French and foreign children are often in a very different situation with regard to their mothers' occupational status: almost 43 per cent of the former have a mother pursuing an occupation, compared with 16 per cent of the latter, and even greater contrasts emerge when the observation is narrowed further to take account of differences in nationality (see Table J in the Annex).

The influence of the mother's occupational status on rates of normal schooling emerges from Table 11: the percentages of children admitted to CM1 whose mother works and whose mother does not work show a gap of 8 points among the French children and 13 points among the foreign children.

The fact remains however that, given equal status, the overall gap between the indigenous and immigrant children, i.e. 21.9 points (77.2 -- 55.3 per cent) is only substantially narrowed when the mother goes out to work. The gap is then only 15.9 points (82.3 -- 66.4 per cent).

Table 11

Rates of Normal Schooling from CP in 1978 to Enrolment in CM1 in 1981/82
According to Nationality and Whether the Mother Works or Not

	French		Foreigners	
	Entering CP	Enrolled in CM1	Entering CP	Enrolled in CM1
Mother works	6 720	82.3	220	66.4
Mother does not work	8 577	73.8	1 138	53.3
Status unknown	675	68.7	72	52.8
Total	15 972	77.2	1 430	55.3

Source: SIGES, document 5311.

The duration of pre-school education

Foreign children generally undergo a shorter period of pre-school education than their French counterparts (an average of 2.2 years compared with 2.6 years), and only 42 per cent (compared with 60 per cent of indigenous children) attended nursery school for 3 years or more (see Table K in the Annex). The difference is even more marked in the case of foreigners who entered the country in the course of immigration as a family: some 44 per cent of them had no pre-school education at all or only attended nursery school for one year.

To allow for this handicap, which is peculiar to the children of immigrants, Graph 3 only presents the educational situation of the 914 foreign children born in France (of a total in the sample of 1 431). It shows that, regardless of nationality, children who underwent three or four years of pre-school education tend to be more successful than children whose pre-school education did not exceed two years.

Moreover, the extension of pre-primary education seems to be beneficial to children from the Maghreb, since their results improve according to its duration, and even slightly surpass those of foreigners in general. On the other hand, the educational results of the Portuguese remain the same whatever the duration of pre-primary education, which is generally short.

Graph 3.

**RATES OF NORMAL SCHOOLING FROM CP TO CM1
ALL SEC TOGETHER**

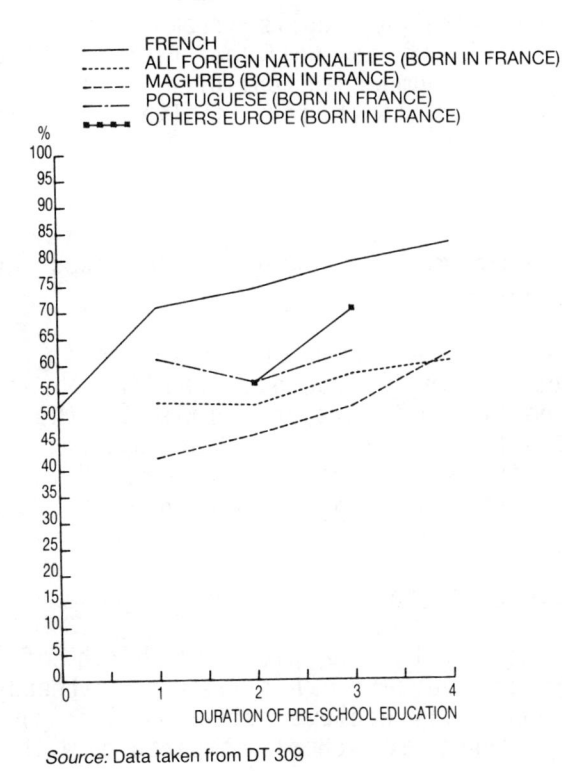

Source: Data taken from DT 309

THE EFFECT OF CROSS-LINKED VARIABLES

The reality is infinitely more complex than is suggested by the first stage in the search for explanatory factors, in the course of which each variable was analysed as though it acted alone. There is, for example, a correlation between the level of education and socio-economic category (SEC) of the head of the household or between SEC and size of family. Table P, collated for the 1980 sample (see Annex), shows the interrelationships which arise in this connection.

The investigation now pursued rests upon the cross-linking of socio-economic category with most of the variables previously observed individually (i.e. size of family, place of birth of the foreign children, level of education of the person responsible for the child and duration of pre-school education), wherever possible making use of the information supplied by the three samples.

i) <u>SEC and family size</u>

Graph 1, plotted from the data for the 1978 sample, showed the role of family size in the rate of normal schooling of the children since, the greater the number of brothers and sisters, the poorer the results achieved by the pupil.

Graph 4 takes this indicator a stage further by considering in addition the SEC of the head of the household. It thus emerges that:

-- (Graph below) foreign pupils from the "lower" socio-economic categories do almost as well as French children from the same background as the number of children in the family increases and, where there are at least four siblings, do even better than the indigenous children;

-- (Graph on the right) among the children of immigrants, the educational profiles are fairly similar whatever the SEC of the head of the household may be, whereas the gaps are wider among the indigenous children.

Clearly the over-representation of foreigners in certain socio-economic groups and family sizes has an influence on the two phenomena just described. For example, the proportion of foreign pupils in the sample for the 1978 sample overall (all SECs and family sizes taken together) is 7.3 per cent; it rises to 20.6 per cent in families with 5 or more children as a whole and to 55 per cent in families with 5 or more children whose father is an unskilled worker.

ii) <u>SEC and place of birth</u>

The influence exerted by the place of birth of foreign children on their progress through the educational system has already been highlighted: those born in France generally achieve better results than the others, which tends to make their progress at school comparable with that of indigenous pupils.

Graph 4.

**RATES OF NORMAL SCHOOLING FROM CP TO CM1
ACCORDING TO NATIONALITY, SEC AND SIZE OF FAMILY**

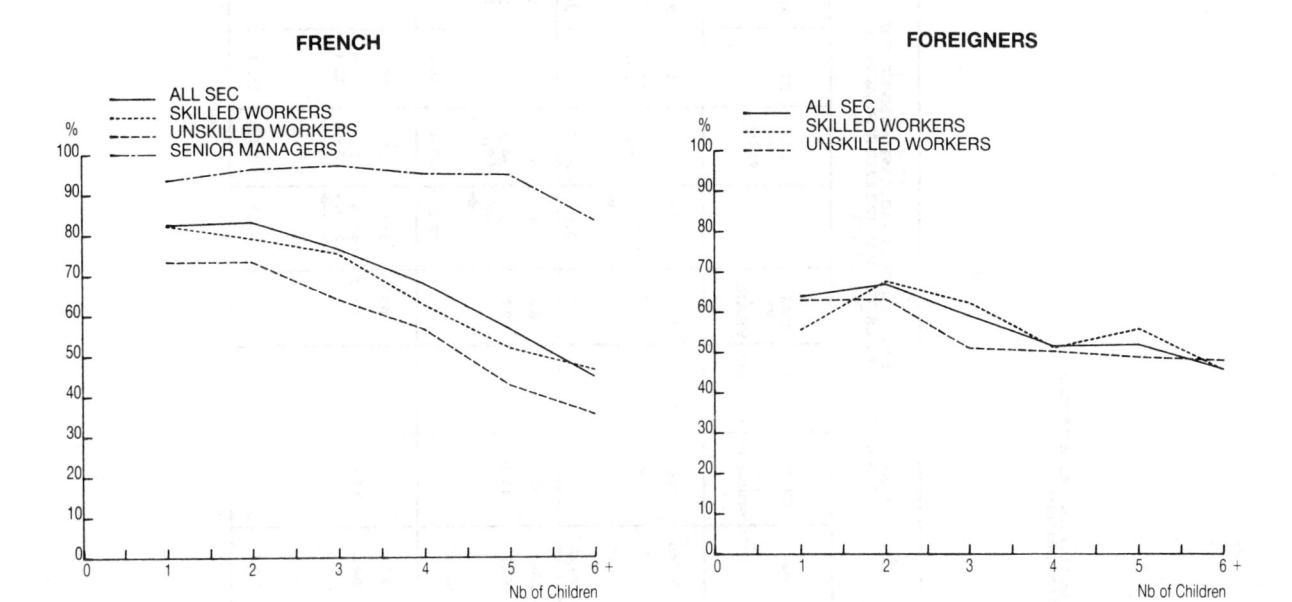

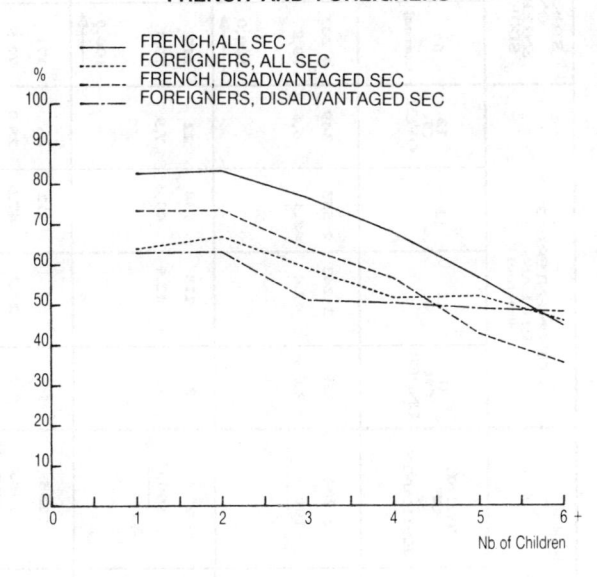

Source: Data taken from *Document 5311 (SIGES)*

TABLE 12

EDUCATIONAL PERFORMANCE AT SECONDARY SCHOOL OF PUPILS WHOSE FATHERS ARE SKILLED WORKERS

		TOTAL OF 6e ENTRANTS	AGE ON ENTERING 1st CLASS (sixième)				STREAM ON ENTERING SIXIEME			PUPILS REACHING THESE LEVELS, WHATEVER THE EDUCATIONAL ROUTE BY WHICH THEY REACHED THE LEVEL								
			10 OR UNDER	11	12	13 OR OVER	6e normal	6e "allégée"	4e	CPPN or 4e pratique	CPA or 3e pratique	CAP in 3 YEARS	3e	2nd long cycle	BEP	Première	Terminale
PUPILS OF FRENCH NATIONALITY	BORN IN FRANCE	5 284 100,0 ↑	139 2,6	2 243 42,4	2 553 48,3	349 6,6	4 203 79,5 100,0 ↑	1 081 20,5	3 346 63,3 79,6	718 13,6	557 10,5	1 360 25,7	3 074 58,2 100,0 ↑ 73,1	1 617 30,6 52,6 38,5	1 156 21,9 37,6 27,5	1 429 27,0 46,5 34,0	1 303 24,7 42,4 31,0
		277 100,0 ↑	3 1,1	118 42,6	134 48,4	22 7,9	219 79,1 100,0 ↑	58 20,9	186 67,1 84,9	32 11,6	28 10,1	63 22,7	169 61,0 100,0 ↑ 77,2	95 34,3 56,2 43,4	67 24,2 39,6 30,6	90 32,5 53,3 41,1	80 28,9 47,3 36,5
FOREIGN PUPILS	BORN ABROAD	236 100,0 ↑	1 0,4	57 24,2	112 47,5	66 28,0	171 72,5 100,0 ↑	65 27,5	128 54,2 74,9	33 14,0	20 8,5	63 26,7	112 47,5 100,0 ↑ 65,5	66 28,0 58,9 38,6	36 15,3 32,1 21,1	59 25,0 52,7 34,5	55 23,3 49,1 32,2

SOURCE: SIGES DT 308

TABLE 13

EDUCATIONAL PERFORMANCE AT SECONDARY SCHOOL OF PUPILS WHOSE FATHERS ARE UNSKILLED WORKERS

	TOTAL OF 6e ENTRANTS	AGE ON ENTERING 1st CLASS (SIXIEME)				STREAM ON ENTERING SIXIEME			PUPILS REACHING THESE LEVELS, WHATEVER THE EDUCATIONAL ROUTE BY WHICH THEY REACHED THE LEVEL								
		10 OR UNDER	11	12	13 OR OVER	6e normal	6e "allégée"	4e	CPPN or 4e pratique	CPA or 3e pratique	CAP in 3 YEARS	3e	2nd long cycle	BEP	Première	Terminale
PUPILS OF FRENCH NATIONALITY — BORN IN FRANCE	5 755 100,0 →	98 1,7	1 949 33,9	3 214 55,8	494 8,6	4 003 69,6 100,0 →	1 752 30,4	3 026 52,6 75,6	1 165 20,2	860 14,9	1 665 28,9	2 677 46,5 100,0 ↑ 66,9	1 202 20,9 44,9 30,0	1 137 19,8 42,5 28,4	1 035 18,0 38,7 25,9	930 16,2 34,7 23,2
BORN ABROAD	548 100,0 →	6 1,1	158 28,8	333 60,8	51 9,3	358 65,3 100,0 →	190 34,7	287 52,4 80,2	96 17,5	42 7,7	192 35,0	261 47,6 100,0 ↑ 72,9	129 23,5 49,4 36,0	126 23,0 48,3 35,2	116 21,2 44,4 32,4	99 18,1 37,9 27,7
FOREIGN PUPILS	611 100,0 →	2 0,3	68 11,1	330 54,0	211 34,5	320 52,4 100,0 →	291 47,6	230 37,6 71,9	122 20,0	84 13,7	213 34,9	187 30,6 100,00 ↑ 58,4	92 15,1 49,2 28,8	77 12,6 41,2 24,1	78 12,8 41,7 24,4	68 11,1 36,4 21,3

SOURCE : SIGES DT 308

207

The cross-linking of the variable "place of birth" with the socio-economic category (SEC) of the head of the household makes it possible to extend the observation.

As far as the 1972-74 sample is concerned, for one and the same SEC (skilled worker in Table 12, unskilled worker in Table 13), the scores of foreign children born on French territory turn out to be higher than those of children who entered the country in order to join their parents, and this is found at all stages of progress through the educational system. Thus, for example:

-- (Table 12): 79 per cent of foreign schoolchildren born in France whose father is a skilled worker are enrolled in the normal first class of secondary school (sixième normale), 34 per cent enter the long second cycle and 29 per cent reach the final grade of secondary school (terminale). The percentages for those entering as immigrants from their home countries are 72.5, 28 and 23 per cent respectively;

-- (Table 13): when the father is an unskilled worker, the scores recorded at the same stages reveal gaps of the same order, intensified further by the "place of birth" factor: among those born in France, 65 per cent are enrolled in sixième normale, 23.5 per cent enter the long second cycle and 18 per cent reach terminale; for the others the proportions are only 52, 15 and 11 per cent.

These tables also show that, within the same SEC, foreign schoolchildren born in France achieve results as good as (unskilled workers') or even better than (skilled workers') indigenous children.

Thus, among the children of skilled workers starting in the first class, less than a quarter (24.7 per cent) of those with French nationality reach the terminale grade, while almost 29 per cent of the foreign children born in France do so. Among the children of unskilled workers, the proportions of those achieving the same educational performance are, respectively, 16 per cent for the indigenous children and 18 per cent for the foreign children born in France.

Nevertheless there are two facts which suggest that these observations should be approached with some caution: on the one hand, the meagre representation of the group of foreigners on the sample at the end of secondary education (less than 100 for each SEC studied), which amounts in practice to the observation of individual cases only; on the other hand, the fact that the survey does not take account of "accidents in transit" (notably repeat years), centring its observations on the point of arrival.

With regard to the data obtained from the 1980 sample (Table 14), the results are evidently more uncertain.

In terms of the "Skilled Worker" SEC the same phenomenon is observed as before, i.e. that the foreign schoolchildren born in France achieve better results than the others: 79.5 per cent for the former (compared with 75.2 per cent) move up into the second grade after one year at secondary school. On the other hand, for the children of unskilled workers, the rates are reversed: normal educational progress appears in 70 per cent of children born in France, whereas this same rate is 77 per cent for children who entered the country as part of an immigrant family.

Similarly, a smaller proportion of the latter do repeat years than the indigenous children and foreign children born in France -- regardless of the SEC of the head of the household -- but they are more likely to be selected for CPPN streaming (on average twice as likely as the French children, foreigners born in France occupying an intermediate position).

Thus the data summarized in Table 14 highlight two important facts: on the one hand, for one and the same SEC the rates of normal schooling of the foreign children, whether born in France or abroad, are comparable with those of the French children; on the other hand, foreign children are more likely than indigenous children to be selected for short courses of vocational education -- a higher proportion of them are streamed in CPPN, CPA or CAP courses.

Even so it is true that, in the case of this panel, only the results after one year of enrolment have been analysed (from 1980 to 1981/82); the situations may thus alter, with gaps opening up as the children feed through the education system.

iii) SEC and the level of education of the person responsible for the child

In the 1978 sample, the rate of admission to CM1 in 1981/82, i.e. the fourth year of a normal pattern of schooling, is found to be heavily dependent on the level of education of the person responsible for the child. Indeed there is a gap of over 20 points (21.9 for the French children, 22.9 for the foreigners) between the pupils, depending on whether the person responsible is of a primary or better than primary standard of education.

The data in Table 15 moreover show that, apart from the "Clerical Staff" category (a very imprecise designation), this gap narrows as we go up the social ladder: 20 points for the children of domestic staff, 17 when the person responsible is an unskilled worker, 10 when he is a shop-floor supervisor or a skilled worker. These observations were only recorded for the French pupils, as the numerical distribution between the two levels of education was too unbalanced where the foreigners were concerned.

A very pertinent study conducted by Guy Truchot (2) on the basis of rates of normal schooling at primary level according to SEC and the level of education of the person responsible for the child shows that, for one and the same SEC, the better educated the parents, the better is the child's educational performance, but that, conversely, for one and the same level of education, the gaps in educational results between the skilled and unskilled SECs are less wide. Thus the children whose parents are unskilled workers and are of a primary educational standard are in the least favoured position.

That is the position of a great many foreign schoolchildren.

Table 14

First Year of Observation in 1981/82 of Pupils Entering Secondary School in 1980 According to Nationality, Place of Birth (for Foreigners) and SEC of Head of Household

French

	All SECs nb.	%	Skilled Workers nb.	%	Unskilled Workers nb.	%	Foreigners (All) All SECs nb.	%	Skilled Workers nb.	%	Unskilled Workers nb.	%
Entering 2nd class	15 562	82.6	2 956	80.7	2 238	76.8	1 140	76.9	280	77.8	258	73.9
Repeating 1st class	2 442	13.1	560	15.3	477	16.4	171	11.5	40	11.1	94	13.2
Entering CPPN	475	2.5	93	2.5	139	4.8	82	5.5	16	4.4	54	7.6
Other courses (1)	359	1.9	52	1.4	61	2.1	90	6.1	24	6.7	38	5.3
Total	18 838	100.0	3 661	100.0	2 915	100.0	1 483	100.0	360	100.0	714	100.0

Foreigners Born in France / Foreigners Born Abroad

	All SECs nb.	%	Skilled Workers nb.	%	Unskilled Workers nb.	%	All SECs nb.	%	Skilled Workers nb.	%	Unskilled Workers nb.	%
Entering 2nd class	573	76.4	167	79.5	236	70.2	567	77.4	113	75.2	292	77.2
Repeating 1st class	109	14.5	29	13.8	61	18.2	62	8.4	11	7.3	33	8.7
Entering CPPN	37	4.9	7	3.3	22	6.5	45	6.1	9	6.1	32	8.5
Other coures (1)	31	4.1	7	3.3	17	5.1	59	8.1	17	11.3	21	5.6
Total	750	100.0	210	100.0	336	100.0	733	100.0	150	100.0	378	100.0

1. Pupils entering CPA, CAP or other classes, leaving the country, lost.
Source: SIGES, DT 297.

Table 15

Rates of **Normal** Schooling from CP in 1978 to Enrolment in CM1 in 1981/82 According to Nationality, Certain SECs and Level of Education of the Person Responsible for the Child

	French					Foreigners				
	Primary		Better than Primary			Primary		Better than Primary	
	Entering CP	Enrolled in CM1	Entering CP	Enrolled in CM1		Entering CP	Enrolled in CM1	Entering CP	Enrolled in CM1	
	nb.	%	nb.	%		nb.	%	nb.	%	
All SECs	5 637	65.7	6 493	87.6		675	52.3	109	75.2	
Including:										
Senior management	..	..	1 240	95.9		..	..	16	93.7	
Clerical staff	542	68.1	796	86.6		13	53.8	7	100.0	
Shop-floor supervisors and skilled workers	1 268	71.1	1 213	81.6		147	58.5	29	65.6	
Unskilled workers	1 910	59.9	391	77.1		432	51.4	24	50.1	
Domestic staff	306	56.5	103	76.7		21	42.9	..	..	

Source: SIGES, primary school group sampled in 1978.

211

Graph 5.

RATES OF NORMAL SCHOOLING FROM CP TO CM1 ACCORDING TO NATIONALITY AND DURATION OF PRE-SCHOOL EDUCATION

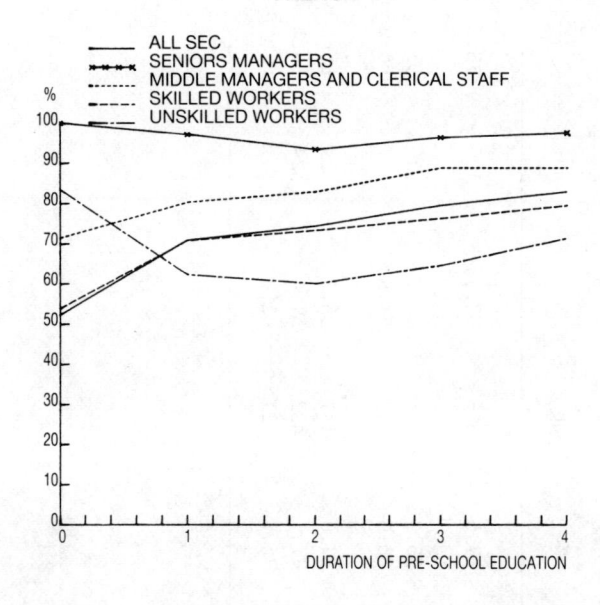

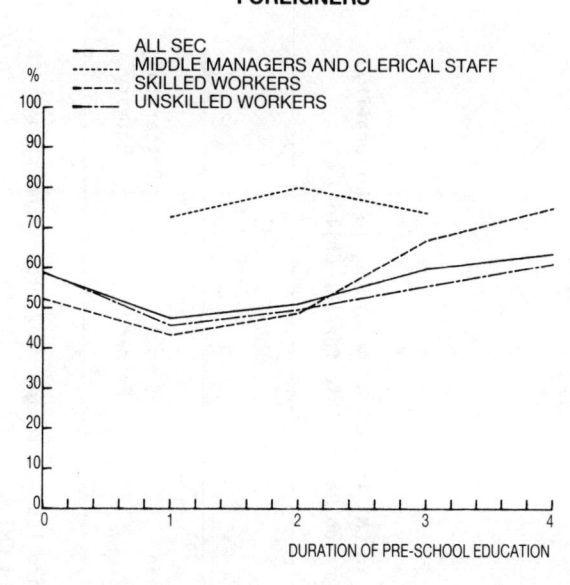

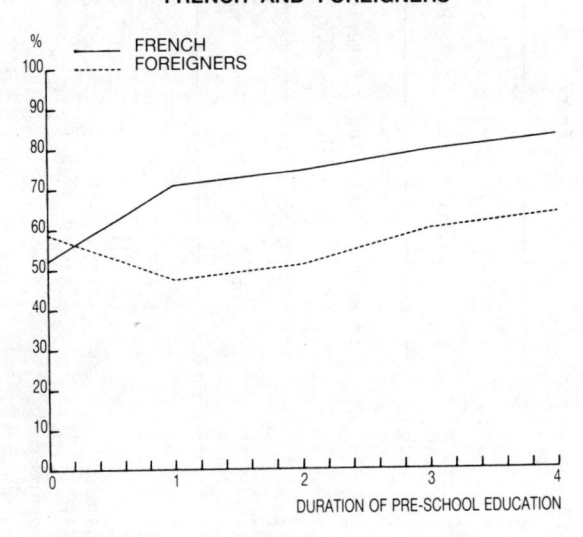

Source: Data taken from *Document 5311 (SIGES)*

iv) SEC and the duration of pre-school education

Graph 3 showed the correlation which exists between the duration of pre-school education and educational performance, regardless of the nationality of the pupils (indigenous children on the one hand and foreign children born in France on the other).

When we round off the observation by introducing the SEC variable, we are no longer dealing with the same statistical material, in the sense that the comparison is made between French schoolchildren and all the foreign children, whatever their place of birth. Hence in their case, there is a difference in slope between the curve in Graph 3 and that plotted in the lower part of Graph 5.

When the SEC is taken into account, it is found that the improvement in rates of normal schooling -- linked to longer periods of pre-school education -- varies according to the socio-economic and socio-cultural context in which the pupils live:

- In the case of the highly placed SECs, the increase in quality of results turns out to be more limited because it is more difficult to progress from a high starting level (the curve for the French children of senior executives offers a typical example of this mechanical effect);

- In the case of the intermediate and least favoured SECs, on the other hand, the progression is very marked: the curves illustrating the educational performance differential of pupils (French and foreign) whose father is an unskilled worker, in relation to duration of attendance at nursery school, are very revealing.

While Graph 5 does not permit any conclusion as to the influence of nationality (since the duration of pre-school education is correlated with the time of arrival in France -- by birth or by immigration), it does indicate clearly that a longer period of pre-school education is more beneficial, the more humble is the socio-economic background of the children.

CONCLUSIONS

This very detailed study reveals that the overall differences between the educational careers of the French and foreign children narrow to a greater or lesser extent when factors other than the pupils' nationality are taken into account.

But this interesting point revealed by the study still does not tell us why the school careers of children of different nationalities are so dissimilar. This is borne out by the essays in "theoretical reconstruction" at the end of this paper, which are intended to provide a basis for further consideration of the subject.

The synoptic presentation below sets out some of the findings on the three samples studied, taking in each case:

-- A single indicator of normal educational performance (although in fact each sample could have provided several indicators);

-- A single type of information, chosen from all the data available, so as to measure (in numbers of points) French and foreign children's educational achievement when certain variables are taken into account.

The extent to which certain variables explain differences in the educational achievement of French and foreign pupils is the following:

I. **1978 Sample**

Indicator of normal educational performance: percentage of pupils admitted to grade CM1 in 1981/82 after having entered the CP in 1978. When nationality alone is considered, the difference between French and foreign children is 21.9 points. When other simple or cross-linked variables are introduced, that difference changes in the following manner (points):

Head of family's SEC

-- Business or industrial entrepreneur,
    manager: 11.0

-- Clerical or sales worker, foreman
    or supervisor, skilled worker: 18.0

-- Unskilled worker: 11.3

Size of family

-- 3 or fewer children: 18.1
-- 4 or more children: 10.0

Mother's occupation

-- Mother does not work outside the home: 20.5

Level of education of the person responsible for the child

-- Primary education: 13.4

Duration of pre-school education

-- 3 years (this applies only to
    foreign children born in France):   21.3

Place of birth of the foreign children

-- In France: 21.0
-- Abroad: 23.6

SEC x size of family

-- Unskilled worker with 4 or more
   children: -3.1

SEC x level of education

-- Unskilled worker and primary education: 8.5

II. **1972/73/74 Sample**

Indicator of normal educational performance: percentage of pupils admitted to the 6th grade in 1972, 1973 and 1974 and having successfully completed the 1st cycle of secondary education. On average, there is an 18.1 point difference between the French and the foreign children. When other variables are taken into account, this difference changes as follows (points):

Head of family's SEC

-- Skilled worker: 3.7
-- Unskilled worker: 7.8

Size of family

-- 3 or fewer children: 16.1
-- 4 or more children: 10.8

Place of birth of the foreign children

-- In France: 11.0
-- Abroad: 19.0

III. **1980 Sample**

Indicator of normal educational performance: percentage of pupils admitted to the 5th grade in 1981/82 after entering the 6th grade in 1980. On the basis of nationality alone, the difference between the French and foreign children is 5.7 points. When other variables are introduced, it changes as follows:

Head of family's SEC

-- Skilled worker: 3.0
-- Unskilled worker: 2.9

Place of birth of the foreign children

-- In France: 6.2
-- Abroad: 5.2

It should be noted that the difference (in points) is calculated by subtracting the percentage figure for the foreign pupils from that for the nationals. For instance, the 21.9 point difference noted for the 1978 Sample was calculated as follows: 77.2 - 55.3 per cent.

While this synoptic presentation does not, of course, allow for methodological precautions or for the refinement of interpretation described earlier, it does have the advantage of being clear, since by setting out the changes in the overall difference due to the variables observed it makes it possible to rank those variables according to the extent to which they contribute to explaining the differences in educational achievement between the French and foreign pupils.

If, for instance, we look at the data for the 1978 sample (the one in which the greatest number of simple and cross-linked variables are taken into consideration), it can be seen quite clearly that:

-- The head of family's SEC and the size of the family are major factors, since when the children are grouped according to social class the overall difference falls from almost 22 points to 11 (regardless of whether the class considered is advantaged or disadvantaged) and to 10 points in the case of pupils belonging to large families (four or more children);

-- Moreover, when these two variables are cross-linked, the difference between the French and foreign pupils whose fathers are unskilled workers and who have at least three brothers or sisters is wiped out completely and indeed swings the other way, to the advantage of the foreign pupils;

-- On the other hand, two other factors -- whether the mother goes out to work or not, and whether the foreign child was born in France or abroad -- seem to have very little effect on the initial difference in educational performance, changing the figures by no more than one or two points in either direction;

-- As for the level of education of the person responsible for the child, the effect of this lies somewhere between that of the factors already mentioned: for a given level (primary), the difference in percentage points between the French and foreign pupils showing a normal educational performance is reduced from 21.9 to 13.4 points.

In looking at these findings, it has to be remembered that where the difference in average performance disappears, this does not necessarily mean that the performance of the foreign pupils has improved. While there may be upward levelling, as for instance in the case of managers' children (whatever their nationality), there may also be downward levelling (as for all the children of unskilled workers with large families, where the French pupils fare just as badly as the others).

We could, of course, leave the matter there and conclude with S. Boulot and D. Fradet that "rather than blaming cultural deprivation and linguistic handicap, as is usually done, we must look for the causes of underachievement by immigrants' children in the accumulation of unfavourable educational and socio-economic conditions" (3).

Without disagreeing with this view, backed up as it is by the information obtained by studying the three samples, it may be worth while mentioning one last line of investigation which yet again highlights the complexity of the problem and shows how impossible it is to find any single solution.

The general idea of the "theoretical reconstruction" attempted here may be described as follows: where the socio-economic or socio-demographic situation of the French nationals and the foreign pupils is the same, is the percentage of educational success the same for both groups, or is there a difference between the two? and if so, of what order of magnitude?

Table 16 sets out the findings of such a simulation, constructed on the basis of the "socio-economic category" variable (though it could equally well have been based on that of the level of education of the person responsible for the child, or of whether the mother goes out to work, or any other of the factors taken into consideration in studying the samples). The Table, which uses raw data obtained on the 1978 sample, is set out in three columns:

-- (1): "theoretical" enrolment of French nationals for each SEC, applying the proportional distribution observed for the foreign pupils;

-- (2): actual success rate recorded for nationals in each SEC;

-- (3): "notional" number of pupils admitted to CM1 after four years schooling, obtained by applying the Column 2 percentages to the numbers noted in Column 1.

The simulation effected in this way indicates that of the 15 972 French pupils who began their schooling in the CP in 1978, 10 751 would have been admitted to grade CM1 in 1981/82, i.e. a 67.3 per cent success rate, against:

-- On the one hand, the rate actually observed for nationals (77.2 per cent);

-- On the other, the rate actually observed for foreigners (55.3 per cent).

The theoretical percentage thus falls half-way between the two actual rates; in other words, the initial difference is cut by half, but still subsists.

When the same exercise was repeated, but using other variables, similar findings were obtained, i.e. although the the "scores" of the two categories of pupil came closer to each other, they were never exactly the same. No factor, however influential, automatically abolished the difference in educational achievement.

In the end, it proves extremely difficult to answer once and for all the question: "Is there or is there not an underachievement that is specific to foreign pupils?" In the present state of research -- and the studies of the samples have helped increase the sum of knowledge on the subject -- two hypotheses can be put forward. First, the sole fact of being foreign is not in itself an explanation of underachievement at school; secondly, the

Table 16

**Changes in the Number of French Pupils Admitted to CM1 in 1981/82
(1978 Sample) (Notional Breakdown by SEC)**

SEC	Theoretical Enrolment of French Nationals if Breakdown Were the Same as for Foreigners (1)	Percent of Nationals Admitted to CM1 (2)	Notional Number of Pupils Admitted to CM1 on the Basis of the Theoretical Enrolment (3)=(1)/(2)
Farmers	33	79.4	26
Farm workers	369	61.4	227
Business and independent entrepeneurs	391	82.1	321
Senior management	257	95.8	246
Middle management	268	88.7	239
Clerical staff	369	79.5	293
Supervisory staff and skilled workers	3 138	74.9	2 350
Unskilled workers	9 125	63.2	5 767
Domestic staff	581	61.9	360
Other categories	45	84.8	38
Unemployed and various	1 396	63.3	884
Total	15 972		10 751

1. The breakdown of the foreign pupils by SEC is shown in Table F of Annex 3. The percentage relating to each category (0.2 per cent farmers, 2.3 per cent farm workers, and so on) has been applied to the total French enrolment (15 972 pupils) in order to obtain a theoretical national enrolment for each SEC (e.g. farmers: 15 972/0.2 per cent = 33, etc.).

2. Rates of admission to CM1 are shown in Table 1.

explanation must lie in the interrelation of a whole range of factors, some of which it is impossible to assess quantitatively. There is a very fine dividing line between what is measurable and what is not, and above all imperceptible oscillation between one and the other. For instance, the overrepresentation of foreigners in the disadvantaged classes -- with all the consequences that this entails from the point of view of housing, living conditions, and so on -- creates a particular cultural situation that increases the chances of underachievement.

NOTES

1. Although there is a description of the pupils according to one or another of these criteria for the other two samples.

   Referring to the document included as an Annex, it will in fact be seen that:

   -- In the 1972-74 sample, there is a distribution of the pupils according to size of family (Table B) and duration of pre-school education (Table C);

   -- In the 1980 sample, there is a distribution of the pupils according to family size (Table N), whether or not the mother works (Table R) and duration of pre-school education (Table S).

2. Guy Truchot, "Niveau d'études des parents et scolarité primaire des enfants" (Level of education of parents and primary schooling of children), in Etudes et formation, SIGES, June 1984.

3. Serge Boulot et Danielle Boyzon-Fradet, "L'échec scolaire des enfants de travailleurs immigrés (un problème mal posé)", in Les Temps Modernes, March-April-May 1984.

III. PASSPORT OR SOCIAL POSITION?

SOME FACTS AND FIGURES ON THE SUCCESS AND EDUCATIONAL CAREERS OF SWISS AND FOREIGN CHILDREN IN THE LIGHT OF THEIR FAMILIES' SOCIAL CLASS

by Walo HUTMACHER
Head of Department of Education of the Sociological Research Unit,
Canton of Geneva (Switzerland)

The research described here was undertaken at the invitation of the OECD as a contribution to the CERI project "Education and cultural and linguistic pluralism". The question asked seems relatively simple: how do foreign children (first- and second-generation) fare in their schooling, given the social class of their families? It is generally taken for granted that immigration and foreign status are both detrimental to a "normal" school career because of insufficient command of the language of the host country, patchy information about its education system and other factors besides. In the context of social inequality in schooling, we ask here whether and to what extent the "educational handicaps" associated with immigration and foreign status compound the already frequently observed differences in educational success due to position on the social ladder.

The canton of Geneva is a particularly interesting case in this respect because it is the meeting point for migratory flows from a number of origins involving the entire social hierarchy and not only the poorest categories. It is thus possible to compare the educational scores of Swiss children and foreign children, born in Geneva or abroad, right across the social spectrum.

The statistical data used in this report are available thanks to the existence for the last 15 years of an "educational data bank" covering all State and private schools, from the pre-school to university entrance. It is possible to refer to this data bank, but within the limits of the information available, of course, for statistics that are fairly closely relevant to a research subject such as this. We would like to thank Mr. Bernard Lambert for his active collaboration in producing the statistical tables required.

INTRODUCTION

The extensive transmigratory movements of the last 30 years have brought education policy-makers face to face with the special problems of schooling for immigrants' children (second generation) or immigrant pupils (first generation). More or less large-scale programmes and action tailored to the situation and special problems of these children have been launched in many places. Often based on American doctrine and practices in this area, these programmes endeavour notably to overcome their linguistic "handicap" and, more broadly, those which are considered to be due to the distance separating these children's original cultural world from the norms and values prevailing in the immigration society and its schools.

There has been a considerable migratory inflow into the canton of Geneva, too, since 1950, and perhaps proportionally more than elsewhere. That year, 17 per cent of the population of some 200 000 were foreigners. They now account for 32 per cent of the present population of 360 000. Since about 40 000 naturalisations were registered during this period (foreigners acquiring Swiss nationality) it may be claimed that, all in all, three-quarters of the canton's demographic growth over the last 30 years has been due to foreign immigration (migratory and natural increases combined). Immigration has also contributed a great deal to the rising birth rate in the canton (nearly half of the children born in 1970 were foreign).

Some 42 per cent of the children attending State primary schools in 1974-77 were foreigners, mostly born in Geneva (second generation). However, educational policy as far as foreign children are concerned remained for a long time implicit rather than explicit, it being understood that various general measures also benefited the children of foreign workers. For instance, the enrolment in nursery classes open to all children (two years before compulsory schooling) also helped foreigners to learn French early, enabling them to follow the usual school curriculum later on.

Side by side the children of resident immigrants, the canton recorded regular arrivals of school-age children for whom reception classes incorporating intensive French language teaching were introduced as early as the mid-1970s, the prime aim being integration in normal classes.

In Geneva, as elsewhere in the world, most of the groups of foreigners regarded as facing or raising an educational problem are from the socially deprived classes, manual workers who take the jobs spurned by nationals in the secondary sector (building, industry) and in hotels and catering. Their immigration follows the tradition of geographical mobility which began with industrialisation and urban concentration with immigration from relatively declining to economically thriving regions, within national borders at first (the flight from the land) and thereafter across these borders, peopling the economically prosperous regions and at the same time facilitating the immigrants' social mobility, i.e. the elevation of native-born citizens from the poorest social classes to middle and higher status (Hutmacher, 1981). For Geneva, this flow has for many years come from three Latin countries in Southern Europe: first Italy, later Spain and more recently Portugal. These "immigrant workers", as they are called, have usually left their home countries under pressure from the precarious economic situation there, hoping to find a job and better pay in the receiving country. Often socialised in a rural and traditional environment or in poor urban districts, they generally have no occupational training recognised in the urban-industrial world to which they have emigrated. Their schooling was of short duration. Unversed in the knowledge, tactics, beliefs, standards and values that are typical of modern urban life, they bring with them, in addition to their difference of language, ways of seeing, thinking and doing which mark them off sharply from nationals in many areas of existence: family life, male/female roles, nutrition, attitudes to work and children's upbringing. These foreigners therefore leap to the eye in every circumstance of daily life.

Since the majority of these "traditional" immigrants are starting from the bottom of the social ladder with little or no recognised skills, the concomitant long-term result is that the poorest urban classes, and notably unskilled workers, will include a large proportion of immigrants who are estranged from the urban and industrialised context by their socialisation if not necessarily by their nationality.

At the same time, since it has been established by many studies that working-class children, of whatever national origin, on the whole have less chance of a problem-free schooling than children of middle- and upper-class social origins, we may ask how these inequalities tie in with each other. Very broadly speaking, we have to decide which of two assumptions is correct:

a) The smaller educational success of working-class children as a whole, of whatever national origin, is due to the fact that a large proportion of them are foreign (first- or second-generation immigrants); in the Geneva context, this means that only foreign workers' children would be less successful, while the children of Swiss workers would be significantly more successful than these foreigners and in appreciably the same proportions as the children of middle- and upper-class families.

b) The smaller success of immigrant children is due to the fact that their parents mostly have poorer social status; in that event, social origin being equal, foreign pupils would have much the same success rates as Swiss pupils.

Reality has little chance of being so simple and clearcut. But empirical evidence of the predominance of either assumption will be useful both for practical reasons and for research:

-- When questioned about the reasons for some of their pupils' poor performance, teachers often give the impression that they regard foreign status as a very important explanatory factor; whether they refer to problems of language or culture in general, assumption (a) seems to predominate in their view. There is, of course, no question of doubting the reality of certain special difficulties for immigrant children, notably the foreign language. But is there not a risk of attaching excessive importance to the most visible aspects of their difference and of orienting action (or inaction) relating to problem pupils in the light of factors which, though plausible, are not necessarily the most pertinent?

-- If assumption (a) were to prove more probable than assumption (b), this would be regarded as a further reason for introducing special curricula for immigrants' children and migrant pupils. It would also provide a promising path in the search for knowledge and practices likely to favour greater social equality in school and hence to improve the success of the educational project as a whole.

-- If, on the contrary, the social status of the parents proved to be the dominant factor in determining the probabilities of educational success [assumption (b)], there could, of course, be no question of denying the special difficulties that may confront foreign pupils, if only for linguistic reasons. But the theoretical framework guiding the search for knowledge and practices to make the school socially equal must then be extended to explain the difficulties experienced by native children as well as foreigners in doing well in class and adapting to school.

The present chapter takes an essentially quantitative approach to the study of this problem; it has no other pretension than to provide empirical evidence which might be used to decide between the two assumptions. Using reasonably reliable indicators of educational problems, we intend to compare native and immigrant children on the basis of equal social status (1).

However, in the case of Geneva, it is possible to approach the problem in a broader framework. We have shown elsewhere (Hutmacher, 1981) that another immigration flow exists, one which from the point of view of socio-economic and cultural realities is quite different. This second flow is linked with the growth of the activities of international organisations and recently above all of foreign and/or multinational firms, bringing to Geneva people with a middle and high level of qualifications and corresponding social status (lower and middle-level management, senior managers, managing directors) from all over the world. Coming from the middle and upper social classes of highly developed countries (notably the United States, France, Germany, Sweden and the United Kingdom) or the modern sectors of less developed countries, these immigrants are well able to take a full part in urban and industrialised society. Because of their often high educational level, not to speak of their initial socialisation, their ways of seeing, thinking and doing are modern. Their professional skills are relevant to modern society. A good knowledge of French was often one of the criteria which pointed their way to Geneva. Their immigration was usually decided by themselves in the context of a career plan which they control, at least in part. They are quite easily assimilated into the working world and society in Geneva, either because they are not very different from the natives or because their difference is regarded as a positive value at professional level and/or an exotic attribute.

While the first flow consists mainly of individual immigrants, possibly married but usually young and childless, the second more often involves the movement of families, with the children taken along as part of their parents' immigration. On immigrating to Geneva, these senior managers' and managing directors' families often turn (60 per cent) to the private schools, which offer a wide range of foreign education systems and curricula (American, British, French, German, Swedish, etc.) (2). However, a proportion of these white-collar immigrants (40 per cent) does use the State system.

As opposed to other countries, it is therefore possible in Geneva's State schools to compare the educational careers of foreign children whose parents are from a very wide variety of social classes, from the "traditional" immigrants with low occupational skills and social status to those in senior managerial and directorial positions who are, on average, highly educated and thoroughly trained professionally.

However, not all foreign adults are immigrants; the population of Geneva was already 17 per cent foreign in 1950. Conversely, not all the Swiss residents are natives born in the urban and tertiary context of Geneva: over the last 30 years there have also been constant flows of immigration to Geneva from the rest of Switzerland. Even though the migratory balance shows that these exchanges with the rest of Switzerland have on the whole been negative for about 10 years now, they cannot be overlooked, since they bring adults and children from frequently very different socio-economic structures and education systems to the canton.

Unfortunately, the available sources of information do not show parents' place of birth. We are therefore obliged, in spite of these reservations, to treat the Swiss as native Genevans (which they mostly are) and foreigners as immigrants (same remark).

On the other hand, it is possible to distinguish among the children between those born in Geneva and consequently socialised in the local context since birth and those who immigrated there during their childhood. For the purposes of the present study, we shall subdivide the latter according to their age on arrival in Geneva:

-- Between 1 and 3 years old: before pre-school education;

-- Between 4 and 7 years old: first years at school;

-- Over 7 years old: primary schooling.

It is, of course, assumed that the older the child on arrival in Geneva, the greater the potential educational difficulties will be, notably as regards educational level (language problems, information for parents on the local school structures, different curricula or teaching methods, etc.). But we consider that these potential problems do not concern only foreign immigrants but also, particularly in the Swiss federal context, nationals migrating within their own country. Do Swiss migrant children differ in this respect from foreigners? We shall pay close attention to this question too (3).

Further details concerning the organisation of schools in Geneva will be given as our analysis proceeds. But a brief outline of the main socio-economic and political features of the Genevan community will give a clearer idea of how the facts fit into a general context which is perhaps unfamiliar to foreign readers. In its very small territory, the Genevan community is above all urban: 92 per cent of the population are grouped in a single conurbation. Its economy is predominantly tertiary: as early as in 1955 over half of all business activities were in the tertiary sector; today, service firms provide 75 per cent of the 200 000 or so jobs in the city. After a very brief period of recession following the first oil shock (in 1975-77), the Genevan economy began to grow again, at a rate admittedly much slower than during the 1960s, but showing real gains as compared with other Swiss regions and other European countries. Between 1976 and 1982, some 23 000 jobs were created (+ 11 per cent), while the rate of unemployment never exceeded 1 per cent of the labour force.

From this economic structure stems a particular type of social stratification. Broadly speaking, three out of every ten members of the labour force are manual workers; four are in clerical or lower- or middle-level supervisory or managerial jobs, one belongs to the traditional middle class (small self-employed) and two are senior managers or directors, or practise a profession. In several respects, the canton of Geneva has the post-industrial society characteristics defined by A. Touraine (1973) and

P. Heintz (1974): a heavy concentration of scientific research capacity, a tertiary sector whose thrust is towards controlling or piloting business in other parts of the world, and a leading-edge secondary sector. The importance attached for the last quarter of a century to the development and modernisation of the training system has a great deal to do with the canton's own particular socio-economic development. A few figures will give an idea of the high educational enrolment rate in Genevan society: this rate has for several years stood at 90 per cent at the age of 4 (two years before compulsory school age); only 5 to 7 per cent of the young people completing compulsory education undertake no further training; at the age of 20, about a third of each cohort leaving the local education system have a <u>certificat de maturité</u> giving access to higher studies, only 13 per cent have no training, while the remainder have completed some form of occupational training. (For further details, see in particular Hutmacher, 1982, 1985.)

Some further methodological details now follow before the analysis itself:

a) The study concerns pupil cohorts completing their primary schooling, the curriculum of which covers six years. In view of the small size of the Genevan community (a generation currently numbers 3 500-4 000 births), we have combined the data for the last five years (1980-1984) during which the educational institutions functioned in a relatively homogeneous fashion and in a fairly stable environment.

b) The available indicators of educational difficulties are:

-- The age-grade ratio (AGR) in the final year of primary schooling (6th grade). The normal formal age for enrolment in this grade is 11; we refer to lost educational ground when speaking of older pupils who have usually had to repeat a year of the curriculum during primary schooling;

-- Streaming on entrance to secondary education, which in this case is a differentiated comprehensive school (streaming cycle) covering the last three years of compulsory schooling; we distinguish between pupils going into the "pre-gymnasial" streams (Latin and science) and those directed to the general or practical sections; for the former, all paths are still open, including higher education, while the latter can expect little besides occupational training, usually via an in-house apprenticeship.

c) As regards social stratification, the educational data bank distinguishes 15 socio-economic categories, specified hereafter. Only eight have been chosen for the purposes of this study:

-- Unskilled and semi-skilled workers (1);

-- Skilled workers and subordinate personnel (2, 3, 7);

-- Small self-employed (4, 5, 6);

-- Qualified white-collar workers (8);

-- Lower and middle-level supervisory and managerial personnel (9, 10);

-- Senior managers (11);

-- Professionals and general managers (12, 13);

-- Miscellaneous and not gainfully employed (14, 15).

These categories encompass all dimensions: economic (access to material resources, consumption); social (position in the hierarchy of production organisations and on the ladder of social prestige, access to decision-making and power positions, etc.); and cultural (distance from the knowledge, know-how, experience, standards which denote excellence in the modern urban world). They have a twofold link with schooling, in terms of:

-- Difference of educational experience on the parents' side: length and level of education and training, familiarity with and accessibility of the educational world, information on teaching, evaluation and selection methods, and, more broadly, attitude towards the school and towards the academic knowledge it provides and values;

-- Differences in the educationally profitable cultural capital that children bring to the school, which, as a result of the preceding, places the pupils further from or nearer to the norms of educational excellence both as regards academic learning and, more broadly, ways of behaving, speaking and working, dedication or otherwise to school work, etc.

SOCIO-ECONOMIC CLASSIFICATION IN GENEVA

1. <u>Unskilled and semi-skilled workers</u>

   Manual workers whose apprenticeship, generally less than six months, is not regulated by the OFIAMT.

2. <u>Skilled workers</u>

   Manual dependent workers in occupations which usually require an apprenticeship regulated by the OFIAMT. This category includes people who although not in possession of a federal apprenticeship certificate nevertheless have or say they have a job of this type.

3. <u>Foremen and workshop, shift or site supervisors</u>

   Dependent workers who directly supervise a group of workers belonging to categories 1 and 2. The "maîtrise fédérale" is a frequent but not essential level of training.

4. <u>Independent manual workers</u> (craftsmen, etc.)

   Category 1 and 2 workers working on their own account in a small way.

5. <u>Non-manual independent workers</u>

   Owners and tenant managers of small distribution and service enterprises (small shops, restaurants, cafés and the like).

6. <u>Farmers</u>

   Owners or tenant farmers of farms, vineyards, horticultural and market gardening enterprises or the like.

7. <u>Subordinate personnel</u>

   Dependent workers, particularly in businesses concerned with security, surveillance, control, handling of stocks, etc., whose work does not usually require an apprenticeship regulated by the OFIAMT (gendarmes, security guards, local government officials, ushers, railway inspectors, firemen, porters, office storemen and the like).

8. <u>Qualified white-collar workers</u>

   Dependent workers in non-manual occupations which usually require an apprenticeship regulated by the OFIAMT (clerical, secretarial and commercial personnel, correspondence clerks, salesmen and the like).

9. <u>Lower management</u>

   Category 8 workers either directly responsible for supervising a group of workers in categories 7 and 8 or completely in charge of particular activities (office head, chief clerk, etc.).

10. <u>Middle management</u>

    Dependent non-manual workers who are usually assumed to have had a comprehensive training in a full-time vocational school (higher technical school, teacher training college, school of social studies, etc.).

11. <u>Senior management</u>

    Dependent employees who direct category 10 personnel or non-manual dependent personnel and whose work requires university education (manager, engineer, etc.).

12. <u>Professionals</u>

    Independent workers whose profession generally implies a university education, or those practising the following professions, even as dependent workers: judge, doctor, lawyer, clergyman.

13. <u>Industrialists, managing directors, managers of large firms</u>

   Dependent or, more usually, independent non-manual workers in positions of general authority over large firms or offices (managing director, industrialist, company director, State counsellor, etc.).

14. <u>Housewives</u>

   Housewives not in gainful employment.

15. <u>Miscellaneous and non-working</u>

   Students, pensioners, disabled people, persons with private means.knowledge, know-how, experience, standards which denote excellence in the modern urban world). They have a twofold link with schooling, in terms of:

   -- Difference of educational experience on the parents' side: length and level of education and training, familiarity with and accessibility of the educational world, information on teaching, evaluation and selection methods, and, more broadly, attitude towards the school and towards the academic knowledge it provides and values;

   -- Differences in the educationally profitable cultural capital that children bring to the school, which, as a result of the preceding, places the pupils further from or nearer to the norms of educational excellence both as regards academic learning and, more broadly, ways of behaving, speaking and working, dedication or otherwise to school work, etc.

BRIEF DESCRIPTION OF THE GROUP STUDIED

Between 1980/81 and 1984/85, some 18 300 children were enrolled in primary 6th grade (6P) in the Genevan State schools. About 80 per cent of them were born in Geneva, either of parents who were themselves natives of the canton or of immigrant parents. One out of every five of these 18 000 children had therefore himself immigrated:

   -- 6 per cent under 4 years of age;

   -- 8 per cent between 4 and 7 years old (school entrance age);

   -- 6 per cent over that age, i.e. at some time during the primary school years.

Slightly under two-thirds (64 per cent) of these pupils were Swiss, 80 per cent of whom were born in Geneva. The foreigners comprise two groups:

   -- Pupils from the three Southern European countries in which Genevan firms traditionally recruit extra manual labour (Italy, Spain,

Portugal); they formed 23 per cent of the 6P pupils from 1980 to 1984 and 80 per cent of them were born in Geneva;

-- Pupils of other national origins, representing nearly every country in the world, who formed 13 per cent of the group studied, less than half (47 per cent) of them born in Geneva.

The three groups of nationalities are highly contrasted as regards social stratification, as shown in Table 1.

Roughly speaking, about a third of the children are of working class origin and as many come from new middle-class homes (qualified white-collar workers, lower and middle supervisory and managerial staff), while a fifth belong to the families of senior managers or managing directors and a twelfth to the traditional middle class (small self-employed: craftsmen, small tradesmen, farmers). Over half (54 per cent) of the pupils of Swiss origin belong to middle-class families and about a quarter to working-class or managerial families. Over three-quarters of the pupils from the Southern European countries, on the other hand, are from working-class homes. Lastly, the group of "other foreigners" comprises relatively few manual workers (19 per cent), a large proportion of the new middle class (40 per cent) and one third are the children of senior managers and managing directors(!).

Table 1

6P Pupils According to Social Origin and Nationality, 1980-84

Social Origin	Total	Switzerland	Italy, Spain, Portugal	Other Countries
Unskilled and semi-skilled	11	5	32	5
Skilled workers and subordinate personnel	23	17	45	14
Small self-employed	8	10	7	5
Qualified white collar	18	21	7	20
Lower and middle managerial	18	23	5	20
Senior managers	14	15	2	27
Professionals and managing directors	6	7	1	6
Miscellaneous and not gainfully employed	2	2	1	3
Total = 100%	18 311	11 635	4 206	2 470
Manual workers	34	22	77	19
Traditional middle class	8	10	7	5
New middle class	36	44	12	40
Senior managers and managing directors	20	22	3	33

These contrasts reflect the major migratory trends over the last 20 years: on the one hand, mass recruitment of manual workers in the Latin Southern European countries; on the other, rapid turnover (immigration-emigration) of qualified and highly-qualified white-collar workers, notably in connection with the activities of international organisations and multinational enterprises. At the same time, the Swiss tend to reject manual jobs and to join the middle class as senior managers or professionals and managing directors.

The various national and social groups differ appreciably as regards the proportion of immigrant pupils, which indicates the frequency of family immigration with young children. Among the Swiss, it amounts to about 13 per cent; it is much lower for manual workers (8 per cent) and much higher for management (16-20 per cent). Among the pupils of Italian, Spanish or Portuguese origin, one out of every five in 6th primary arrived in Geneva after birth; the proportion is particularly low for the families of the small self-employed (probably longer-established) and much higher for senior management. The magnitudes change when we turn to the group of other foreigners: half of the 6P pupils in this group were not born in Geneva; the proportion is even as high as two-thirds for the children of senior managers and managing directors [Table 2(a)].

Table 2(a)

**Proportion of 6P Pupils Not Born in Geneva
According to Social Origin and Nationality, 1980-84**
(as percentages)

Social Origin	Total	Switzerland	Italy, Spain, Portugal	Other Countries
Unskilled and semi-skilled	20	8	22	52
Skilled workers and subordinate personnel	17	10	21	37
Small self-employed	7	6	3	26
Qualified white collar	19	13	21	53
Lower and middle managerial	19	13	21	48
Senior managers	32	20	40	62
Professionals and managing directors	24	16	58 (1)	68
Total	20	13	21	53

1. Reference group less than 50.

Table 2(b)

Resident 6P Pupils According to Social Origin, Nationality and Age on Arrival in Geneva, 1980-84

					Arrived in Geneva at age:		
Social Origin	Nationality	Total = 100%	Born in Geneva	Total	0-3 years	4-7 years	8 years or over
Unskilled and semi-skilled	Swiss	561	92	8	2	4	2
	ISP	1355	78	22	6	8	8
	Other	129	48	52	9	20	23
	Total	2045	80	20	5	8	7
Skilled & subordinate personnel	Swiss	2014	90	10	4	4	2
	ISP	1899	79	21	5	8	8
	Other	349	63	37	7	13	17
	Total	4262	83	17	5	7	5
Small self-employed	Swiss	1104	94	6	3	3	-- (1)
	ISP	301	97	3	1	1	1
	Other	122	74	26	8	9	9
	Total	1527	93	7	3	3	1
Qualified white collar	Swiss	2462	87	13	4	6	3
	ISP	307	79	21	7	8	6
	Other	471	47	53	10	18	25
	Total	3240	81	19	5	8	6
Lower and middle management	Swiss	2607	87	13	6	5	2
	ISP	219	79	21	6	8	7
	Other	481	52	48	15	17	16
	Total	3307	81	19	7	7	5
Senior management	Swiss	1716	80	20	8	8	4
	ISP	72	60	40	11	17	12
	Other	674	38	62	15	18	28
	Total	2462	68	32	10	11	11
Professionals & managing directors	Swiss	857	84	16	7	6	3
	ISP	12	42 (2)	58 (2)	8 (2)	25 (2)	25 (2)
	Other	148	32	68	15	23	30
	Total	1017	76	24	8	9	7

1. Fraction less than 0.01

2. Reference group less than 50.

Table 2(b) gives more details concerning age on arrival in Geneva while retaining the distribution according to social and national origin.

The high proportion of recently immigrated pupils (in Geneva for three years at most before the time of observation) from countries other than Latin Southern Europe is partly explained by the inflow during the last few years of refugees, notably from Latin America, South-East Asia and Africa -- but partly only, and mainly in the lower and middle social classes. The large proportion of recent immigrants among the children of senior managers and managing directors is above all due to the frequent movements during their careers of professionals of this category attached to international organisations and multinational enterprises.

IMMIGRATION AND EDUCATIONAL GROUND LOST AT THE END OF PRIMARY SCHOOLING

School organisation provides for annual teaching cycles, grade by grade; each grade corresponds to a curriculum and a particular age for the pupils concerned. In Geneva, entry to primary school (first compulsory grade) is normally at the age of six (sometimes five under the legally possible age derogations (birthday up to four months after the age limit). In 1984, 99 per cent of all six-year-olds in State schools were either in 1st grade (69 per cent) or 2nd grade (30 per cent). Only 0.5 per cent of children of this age still attended a pre-school 2nd grade; an equal number were in "special" classes. On the whole, therefore, entrance to school is at the theoretical age (2/3) or earlier (1/3).

A pupil cohort does not, however, progress uniformly through the grades. Repeating a grade is, in Geneva as elsewhere, one of the signs that differentiates pupils in difficulties. According to a survey carried out in 1961, such repeats concerned some 9 to 11 per cent of the pupils in each grade every year (Roller and Haramein, 1961). These repeat rates fell appreciably and steadily during the 1960s and 1970s to an average of about 2.5 per cent by 1979. A slight rise has been noted since 1980: on average, the repeat rate is now between 3 and 4 per cent per year according to grade. This is still much lower than in the early 1960s in Geneva, lower, too, than in other education systems.

Repeating a grade modifies the ratio between the theoretical age for that grade and the real age of the pupils concerned. Those whose age previously corresponded to the grade attended fall behind, while pupils younger than that theoretical age become "normal". The proportion of pupils who have fallen behind by the end of the primary cycle does not therefore reflect the total number of repeats recorded between the beginning and the end of primary schooling. Requests for age exemptions for entry into the primary cycle are more or less automatic, however, and are the general practice in every social class, so that in all groups the proportion of repeaters in terms of age/end-of-primary studies is probably proportional to the sum of previous repeats. We shall use this proportion of repeaters to measure the differences between groups in terms of success and at school adaptation. For the sake of simplicity, we distinguish only between:

-- "Normal" pupils, those whose age is equal to or lower than the theoretical age of the grade attended;

-- Repeaters, those who are older than the theoretical age for the grade (rarely by more than one year).

This is of course a very rough indicator which tells nothing about the specific nature of educational difficulties, nor about the distance separating the pupils (either repeaters or normal pupils) from the standard of excellence in the different subjects. We take the commonly-accepted view that in a cohort of pupils some are very bright and others not at all, while a majority between these two extremes are moderately successful. In view of the relative rarity of repeats in Geneva, they certainly indicate the pupils who for various reasons perform badly at a particular point in their schooling. The "normal pupils/repeaters" divide therefore distinguishes between pupils in each group according to whether they have or have not experienced this situation. We must, however, remember the weight in such situations of the opinion of teachers and parents (and sometimes the pupil) concerning the nature of their problems, and hence consider the social relations background to the "production" of that opinion (Perrenoud, 1984). The inherently random, arbitrary and vague nature of the process is such that a repeat is proposed for some pupils and not for others, although their deviation from the mean may be comparable, and the same pupil might have to repeat a grade or not according to whether his path crosses that of one particular teacher or another. However, repeats are on the whole imposed on pupils regarded as weak, floundering, immature, etc., and not on moderately good or brighter pupils.

But we shall refrain from drawing any too hard and fast conclusions. A high proportion of "repeaters" in a given group is only a sign of the higher frequency of educational difficulties within this group and not an exact measurement of the proportion of poor performers and, above all, not the equivalent of an average mark for the group.

We shall see later that when a pupil moves on to secondary education, his "repeater" status plays a decisive part in his assignment to one or other stream. If only because of the importance attaching to it at that time, it is impossible not to consider this indicator, which is admittedly rough and ready, but which the actors involved in the educational process seem to regard as significant.

On the whole, of the 18 300 pupils who attended 6th primary between 1980 and 1984, 12 per cent were older than the normal age for that grade. As in every known observation in this area, boys repeated more often (14 per cent) than girls (9 per cent). These proportions also vary according to nationality [Table 3(a)].

Among the Swiss there are only half as many repeaters as among the children from the Latin Southern European countries. Pupils from other countries fall between the two.

But the differences in the proportion of repeaters are much greater when the different socio-economic categories are compared [Table 3(b)].

Table 3(a)

Proportion of Repeaters in 6P According to Sex and Nationality
(as percentages)

Country of Origin	Total	Male	Female
Switzerland	9	11	7
Italy, Spain, Portugal	18	21	15
Other countries	12	15	10
Total	12	14	9

Table 3(b)

Proportion of Repeaters in 6P According to Sex and Social Origin
(as percentages)

Social Origin	Total	Male	Female
Unskilled and semi-skilled	21	24	18
Skilled and subordinate personnel	16	8	14
Small self-employed	11	15	7
Qualified white collar	12	14	10
Lower and middle management	7	9	4
Senior management	5	6	3
Professionals and managing directors	5	7	3
Miscellaneous and not working	22	25	20

Table 3(c)

Proportion of Repeaters in 6P According to Sex and Age on Arrival in Geneva
(as percentages)

Age on Arrival in Geneva	Total	Male	Female
Born in Geneva	10	13	7
Between 1 and 3 years	11	12	10
Between 4 and 7 years	18	19	16
Over 7 years	26	27	24

This table confirms observations made over a thousand times in the widest variety of education systems. Educational backwardness is more frequent the lower the social status. Among the children of unskilled or semi-skilled workers, one out of five is a repeater (one out of four even for boys), but only one out of every 20 of those whose parents are in the managerial category. It will be noted in passing, although we shall not go into this matter, that the difference between boys and girls is particularly marked -- up to twice as many boys as girls -- for pupils from the families of small self-employed businessmen and managers.

Lastly, and still in a general context, children born in Geneva or who have immigrated during early childhood are much less often repeaters than those who arrived after the age of 4 and especially than those who were over seven [Table 3(c)].

But to turn to the crux of our question; since we know the differences between the three groups of nationalities in terms of social structure (Table 1) and in terms of immigration (Table 2) and since we know that these three variables all have a link with the frequency of educational ground lost, how do they combine? In order to find out, we have cross-examined the three variables in Table 4 which shows the proportions of repeaters for each of the groups identified by social origin, national origin and age on arrival in Geneva. This table can therefore be used to compare the frequency of educational backwardness, holding two variables constant.

To begin with, let us set aside the possible effects of immigration and compare the frequency of falling behind at school only as concerns pupils born in Geneva (2nd column in Table 4). The arrangement of the table first suggests a comparison between nationality groups of the same social origin. It will be noted in this connection that within each social class the differences between nationality groups are relatively small. But there are still some: in every case, the Swiss seem to be slightly better off than the two foreign groups. Between the latter, on the other hand, consideration of social origin removes any significant, systematic differentiation. But at no social level does the comparison between Swiss and foreigners show any difference relating to orders of magnitude of educational backwardness as compared with the mean. This differential structure is also borne out when checked against age on arrival in Geneva, the few exceptions arising from random variations due to the low numbers.

Let us now take the opposite approach by varying social origins within each group of nationalities, beginning with pupils born in Geneva. Here the differences are much greater and the same ranking is repeated in every national group:

-- For the Swiss, the proportion of repeaters varies between 3 per cent (children of senior and top managers) and 17 per cent (unskilled and semi-skilled workers);

-- In the Italian, Spanish and Portuguese group, the proportion of repeaters varies between 1 and 18 per cent;

-- For other foreigners, the variations range from 4 to 25 per cent.

Table 4

Proportion of Repeaters in 6P According to Social Origin, Nationality and Age on Arrival in Geneva, 1980–84

(as percentages)

Social Origin	Nationality	Total = 100%	Born in Geneva	Arrived in Geneva at age: 0-3 years	4-7 years	8 years or over
Unskilled and semi-skilled	Swiss	18	17	10 (1)	22 (1)	46 (1)
	ISP	22	18	22	42	46
	Other	23	25	17 (1)	15 (1)	48 (1)
	Total	21	18	20	35	46
Skilled and subordinate personnel	Swiss	13	12	13	18	41 (1)
	ISP	19	15	28	30	38
	Other	18	11	16 (1)	26 (1)	37
	Total	16	13	21	26	38
Small self-employed	Swiss	11	10	7 (1)	20 (1)	40 (1)
	ISP	13	13	-- (1)	-- (1)	33 (1)
	Other	15	14	20 (1)	-- (1)	27 (1)
	Total	11	11	9 (1)	14 (1)	32 (1)
Qualified white-collar	Swiss	11	10	13	15	25
	ISP	14	13	13 (1)	21 (1)	24 (1)
	Other	17	12	12 (1)	17	27
	Total	12	10	13	16	26
Lower and middle management	Swiss	6	5	8	12	13
	ISP	11	9	14 (1)	22 (1)	21 (1)
	Other	9	8	9	9	15
	Total	7	6	9	12	14
Senior management	Swiss	4	3	2	8	9
	ISP	1	-- (1)	13 (1)	-- (1)	-- (1)
	Other	6	4	2	7	12
	Total	5	3	3	7	11
Professional and managing directors	Swiss	4	4	3	7	20 (1)
	ISP	-- (1)	-- (1)	-- (1)	-- (1)	-- (1)
	Other	10	4 (1)	5 (1)	6 (1)	20 (1)
	Total	5	4	4	7	19

1. Reference group less than 50.

In line with assumption (b) in the introduction, we can conclude that social origin constitutes a more determinant set of educational problem factors than national origin, even though within each social class the frequency of such problems is slightly greater for foreigners than for the Swiss.

Regarding age on arrival in Geneva, the results are as expected: the older the age on arrival, the higher the proportion of repeaters. As Table 3c shows, this is borne out at each social level and for each nationality group. Within each social class, the rise in the proportion of repeats according to age on arrival in Geneva is about the same for Swiss and foreign pupils (Table 4).

For a simpler reading of this rather complicated table, it is possible to calculate on each line the rate of increase in the proportion of repeaters between the best situation (born in Geneva) and the worst (immigrated during primary schooling). As a rule, this rate of increase is by a factor of 2.6. It is similar for unskilled and semi-skilled workers, qualified white-collar personnel and lower and middle management. The pupil groups from skilled workers' families, on the one hand, and from senior managers' families, on the other, seem to be rather more susceptible to the effects of immigration during primary schooling: the rate of increase is by a factor of 3. But the group which is apparently most sensitive to these effects consists of pupils whose parents are professionals and top managers (a factor of 5.5). It is possible that parents in this group more frequently ask for their children to be put in a lower grade than that proposed or deliberately repeat a grade in order to facilitate school integration at a better level.

To conclude this initial general view of the statistical data, it seems that nationality plays only a secondary role in determining educational ground lost at the end of 6th grade primary. Social origin, on the contrary, emerges as the main factor of differentiation and within each group of nationalities. Lastly, the effect of immigration on the pupil himself is increasingly important the later it is in his school career. Consequently, it is possible, without discarding too much information, to drop the difference by nationality so as to find a statistically significant number in each subdivision. Table 5 corresponds to this reduction to two variables. Within this defined area, the frequency of educational ground lost at the end of the primary cycle varies by up to tenfold between the "best off" pupils (whose parents are managers or directors and who were born in Geneva) and the "worst off" pupils (children of unskilled or semi-skilled workers who have recently immigrated to Geneva: 46 per cent).

Tables 5, 5(a) and 5(b) reintroduce the differences between boys and girls and call for the following comments:

-- The lower frequency of educational ground lost for girls is found in every social class and for all immigration situations;

-- The trend seems to be that girls are slightly more sensitive to the impact of immigration than boys, judging by the rates of increase in the proportion of educational ground lost between pupils born in Geneva and recent immigrants.

Table 5
Proportion of Repeaters in 6P According to
Social Origin and Age on Arrival in Geneva, 1980-84
(as percentages)

| | | | Immigrant Pupils ||||
| | | Pupils Born in Geneva | | Arrived in Geneva at age: |||
Social Origin	Total		Total	1-3 years	4-7 years	8 years or over
Unskilled and semi-skilled	21	18	35	20	35	46
Skilled and subordinate personnel	16	13	29	21	26	38
Small self-employed	11	11	15	9	14	32
Qualified white-collar	12	10	18	13	16	26
Lower and middle management	7	6	11	9	12	14
Senior management	5	3	7	3	7	11
Professionals and top management	5	4	9	4	7	19
Miscellaneous and not gainfully-employed	22	21	26	24	29	25
Total	12	10	18	11	18	26

IMMIGRATION AND STREAMING ON ENTRY TO SECONDARY EDUCATION

Since the creation of the streaming cycle in 1962-64, it is standard practice to place pupils in the various secondary school sections on leaving 6th primary essentially on the basis of their results at that point in their career. Pupils going up and considered "bright" according to the academic assessment and passing-up standards are put in the Latin section (L) and/or science section (S), depending on their choice. The others are assigned to the general section (G) or, if they seem particularly "weak", to the practical section (P). These streaming decisions are all-important for the subsequent educational and occupational careers of young people. For the bright pupils, every educational channel remains open, and notably higher studies. For pupils in the general section, it is still possible to enter high school if their marks on completing 7th grade allow them to go into the modern section; otherwise, their future educational/training prospects are very limited (essentially occupational training for manual and clerical jobs). With the general rise in training standards, the chances of pupils in the general section (and even more in the practical section) finding a vocational training opening in an "interesting" job have also appreciably dwindled over the last 15 years (Amos, 1984).

Table 5(a)

Proportion of Repeaters in 6P According to Social Origin and Age on Arrival in Geneva

(as percentages, males)

			Immigrant Pupils			
				Arrived in Geneva at age:		
Social Origin	Total	Pupils Born in Geneva	Total	1-3 years	4-7 years	8 years or over
Unskilled and semi-skilled	24	22	36	19	39	48
Skilled and subordinate personnel	18	16	30	22	27	42
Small self-employed	15	15	18	17 (1)	18 (1)	18 (1)
Qualified white-collar	14	12	20	10	21	28
Lower and middle management	9	8	14	11	14	17
Senior management	6	5	8	3	8	12
Professionals and top management	7	6	11	7 (1)	4 (1)	25 (1)
Miscellaneous and not gainfully-employed	25	24	26	27 (1)	29 (1)	24 (1)
Total	14	13	20	12	19	27

1. References group less than 50.

    Streaming for pupils going up from 6P to 7CO (<u>Cycle d'Orientation</u>) is therefore practically automatic in the sense that it calls for no action on the part of parents. However, faced with the school's decisions of principle, the latter may decide to request a departure from the streaming rules: about one pupil out of every ten goes into a pre-high school section (L or S) as a result of such a request and one out of every twenty or so is assigned to a general section for the same reason even though his 6P results would have allowed him to try his luck in LS (Bain, 1979).

    This relative flexibility of the streaming rules on entry to secondary education combines with a certain permeability of the sections during the three years of the streaming cycle. But transfers are more usually down than up.

    Since the mid-1970s, three of the seventeen <u>cycle d'orientation</u> schools no longer operate the system of graded sections but differentiate their pupils according to a system of levels and options. A study of the careers of the

Table 5(b)

Proportion of Repeaters in 6P According to Social Origin and Age on Arrival in Geneva
(as percentages, females)

Social Origin	Total	Pupils Born in Geneva	Total	1-3 years	4-7 years	8 years or over
				Immigrant Pupils — Arrived in Geneva at age:		
Unskilled and semi-skilled	18	13	34	22 (1)	32	45
Skilled and subordinate personnel	14	11	27	20	25	34
Small self-employed	7	7	13	4 (1)	11 (1)	50 (1)
Qualified white-collar	10	8	17	14	11	25
Lower and middle management	4	3	9	7	10	10
Senior management	3	2	6	2	6	10
Professionals and top management	3	1	8	- (1)	9 (1)	14 (1)
Miscellaneous and not gainfully-employed	20	17	25	20 (1)	29 (1)	25 (1)
Total	9	7	17	10	16	24

1. Reference group less than 50.

pupils from these schools after the streaming cycle suggests that the distribution of level and option profiles quite closely matches that of the sections in the "traditional" schools. The educational data bank does not record these profiles, however, and the present study cannot therefore comment on pupils from the three reformed schools. As just mentioned, there is nonetheless no reason to believe that their pupils have an appreciably different career.

For our study of the relationship between immigration and streaming, we are concerned with the pupils who went up from 6th primary to 7th streaming cycle between 1980 and 1984. This is the group already observed in the preceding section, but without the pupils in the three reformed schools and those who left the canton after 6th primary or went to a private school (about 800 pupils for these last two groups).

This reduced group comprises some 13 800 pupils; of these, seven out of ten were put into a "pre-gymnasial" section (Latin or Science), three out of ten continuing their education in a lower section (mainly general, more rarely practical and very rarely a special class). Tables 6 and 7 show that these rates vary appreciably according to social and national origin. Skipping this comparison of one variable with another, we shall turn immediately to a multivariate analysis with cross-referencing of the variables. It must be noted first, however, that the age/grade ratio very appreciably modifies streaming conditions. Indeed, for normal pupils (88 per cent of the group), the proportion going into the "pre-gymnasial" section is 76 per cent, against only 26 per cent for backward pupils. Most of the possible reasons for this big difference still have to be found. In principle, repeating a grade is regarded by the school as a means of allowing weak or slow pupils to catch up. Judging by the streaming on entry to secondary education, this expected or desired remedial effect is only obtained for a (very small) fraction of the pupils. It is possible that while repeating a primary grade can offer problem pupils a chance of making up their educational leeway, it also has the effect of stigmatising, lowering self-esteem and reducing hopes and ambitions both in the view of the pupils themselves and of their parents and teachers.

Nonetheless, the streaming differences between repeaters and normal pupils are so great that there can be no question of neglecting this variable when studying streaming, especially as we know from the preceding that the frequency of educational backwardness itself varies according to the pupils' social class, sex and, to a lesser extent, national origin.

Table 6 shows the proportion of pupils placed in the "pre-gymnasial" section, as observed in standard groups, according to social and national origin, age/grade ratio (AGR) and age on arrival in Geneva.

First considering the differences between national groups with equal social origin, AGR and age on immigration, we note that on the whole the differences between natives and foreigners are very small and/or usually statistically insignificant.

This observation that national origin alone does not have an impact on school career duplicates what we have already shown in the last section. For equal social origin, chances of success and type of educational career do not differ, or not appreciably, between the Swiss and foreigners.

It is therefore possible, here too, without discarding much information, to continue the analysis without the differences according to national origin. Table 7 gives this simplified picture.

The ranking according to social positions keeps to the eye, whatever the age/grade ratio or age on arrival in Geneva. Not more than 57 per cent of the "normal" pupils who are children of unskilled and semi-skilled workers go into a "pre-gymnasial" section against 91 per cent of the children of senior managers and company directors.

The very sharp reduction in admissions to the pre-high school section that is due to educational backwardness may be observed for every social group. It amounts roughly to a factor of three (2.9). This factor of reduction, calculated in the last three columns of Table 7, seems to be little affected by social origin; but it is much lower for the children of senior managers and company directors (2.0). Here we probably measure the effects of

Table 6

Proportion of Pupils Placed in a Pre-high School Section According to
Social and National Origin, Age/Grade Ratio and Age
on Arrival in Geneva, 1980-84

		Normal Pupils			Repeaters		
Social Origin	Nationality	Total	Born in Geneva +1-3 years	Immigrated after 3 years	Total	Born in Geneva +1-3 years	Immigrated after 3 years
Unskilled and semi- skilled	Swiss	58	58	59 (1)	23	22	30 (1)
	ISP	57	59	47	20	19	22
	Other	46	54 (1)	28 (1)	33 (1)	20 (1)	43 (1)
	Total	57	58	47	22	20	25
Skilled and sub- ordinate personnel	Swiss	70	70	65	19	17	36 (1)
	ISP	61	62	52	24	26	22
	Other	66	69	57 (1)	22 (1)	13 (1)	32 (1)
	Total	66	67	56	22	21	24
Small self- employed	Swiss	76	76	79 (1)	23	23	2/8 (1)
	ISP	67	68	1/3 (1)	19 (1)	17 (1)	1/2 (1)
	Other	61	63	55 (1)	27 (1)	20 (1)	1/1 (1)
	Total	73	73	70 (1)	23	21	36 (1)
Qualified white- collar	Swiss	76	76	77	25	22	40 (1)
	ISP	62	61	72 (1)	25 (1)	9 (1)	5/5 (1)
	Other	77	76	76	45 (1)	25 (1)	65 (1)
	Total	75	74	75	28	21	55
Lower and middle manage- ment	Swiss	85	86	78	35	30	54 (1)
	ISP	75	69	77 (1)	12 (1)	7 (1)	1/5 (1)
	Other	86	89	82	32 (1)	25 (1)	36 (1)
	Total	85	85	79	32	27	47 (1)
Senior manage- ment and directors	Swiss	91	91	91	39	37	42 (1)
	ISP	81	83	76 (1)	2/3 (1)	1/2 (1)	1/1 (1)
	Other	89	91	88	63 (1)	67 (1)	61 (1)
	Total	91	91	89	46	42	53 (1)
Not gain- fully employed	Swiss	72	72	71 (1)	39 (1)	30 (1)	5/8 (1)
	ISP	63 (1)	69 (1)	4/5 (1)	3/9	18 (1)	1/2 (1)
	Other	68 (1)	74 (1)	62	40 (1)	1/2 (1)	3/8 (1)
	Total	70	71	68	38	31 (1)	50 (1)

1. Less than 50 (percentages).
(/) Less than 10 (absolute figures).

Table 7

Proportion of Pupils Placed in a Pre-high School Section According to
Social Origin, Age/Grade Ratio and Age on Arrival in Geneva, 1980-84

	Normal Pupils			Repeaters			% normal/% repeaters		
Social Origin	Total	Born in Geneva 1+3 years	Arr. after 3 years	Total	Born in Geneva 1+3 years	Arr. after 3 years	Total	Born in Geneva 1+3 years	Arr. after 3 years
Unskilled and semi-skilled	57	58	47	22	20	25	2.6	2.9	1.9
Skilled and subordinate personnel	66	67	56	22	21	24	3.0	3.2	2.3
Small self-employed	73	73	70 (1)	23	21	36 (1)	3.2	3.5	1.9 (1)
Qualified white-collar	75	74	75	28	21	55	2.7	3.5	1.4
Lower and middle management	85	85	79	32	27	47 (1)	2.7	3.1	1.7 (1)
Senior management	91	91	89	46	42	53 (1)	2.0	2.2	1.7 (1)
Miscellaneous and not gainfully employed	70	71	68	38	31 (1)	50 (1)	1.8	2.2 (1)	1.4 (1)
Total	76	76	73	26	23	35	2.9	3.3	2.1

1. Less than 50.

quasi-automatic streaming, on the one hand, and of variations in the propensity to request a different streaming on the other, which, as we saw before, is much higher for the families of senior managers and company directors (Bain, 1979).

The reduction in pre-high school streaming because of educational backwardness is much greater for pupils born in Geneva or who immigrated before going to school (3.3 on average) than for those who immigrated to Geneva later (2.1). This difference is found for every social status; but it is particularly marked for the children of qualified white-collar workers and lower and middle-level managers, and much less so for those of senior managers and company directors. It is as though parents and the school agreed, at the time of streaming, that earlier educational problems due to immigration during schooling more rarely justify poor streaming than when this cause does not apply (pupils born in Geneva or who arrived there before going to school).

DISCUSSION

These then are the main statistical facts. The answer to the initial question is finally less equivocal then we expected. As regards children born in Geneva, the school discriminates against foreigners rather because they come from socio-economically and culturally deprived homes than because they are foreigners. Admittedly, social origin being equal, the Swiss have a very slight advantage over the foreigners, but this is quite small against the inequalities revealed by a comparison between different social origins for the same nationality.

When considering social origin, the differences between foreign groups (South European, others), corresponding roughly to two migratory flows, lose all statistical significance. Where several migratory flows exist side by side, their differences within the State education system relate not so much to nationality as to the foreigners' social status in the host country.

It will be argued that, for pupils born in Geneva, the absence of any difference between Swiss and foreigners reflects the familiarity with Genevan culture and institutions of parents settled for at least eleven years and children who have had all their pre-school and school education in Geneva. Both have had the time to become assimilated and to acquire the linguistic and social skills that make them "as Swiss as the Swiss" (political rights apart). This is an important argument. Length of stay is in many cases at once the sign, effect and cause of better cultural and social assimilation. It probably explains why many foreign children get through their schooling without mishap and do well.

But if the difference were only due to length of contact with Swiss culture and institutions, then there ought to be significant discrepancies between Swiss and foreign immigrant children. It will be remembered that for every national and social group the frequency of educational backwardness is always higher for children who arrived during their schooling. But here again, for the same social origin, differences according to nationality disappear: both Swiss and foreigners come up against the same obstacles, which are all the harder to overcome when their social status is lower.

Yet differences of nationality are usually associated with an unequal mastery of the language of the host country and its school, and, more broadly, its habitual ways of thinking, doing and living, codes of conduct, inter-relationship, communication, etc. The differences in the extent of such mastery are precisely the factors, among others no doubt, that are responsible for differences in educational success. Our findings now give us reason to believe that they are significant at educational level less because of distance from the home country and its language or culture than because of the parents' place in the social hierarchy of the host country. This brings us back more or less to the problems of social inequality in education and to the question of the more fundamental attitudes which, varying according to place on the social ladder, also determine mastery of the linguistic, social and educational codes. We can do little more here than suggest a direction for discussion.

We saw above that manual workers immigrating to Geneva come largely from economically declining regions with (or because of) a more traditional type of culture than the host society. The attitudes acquired during their early socialisation did not in theory predispose them for emigration and life in a modern urban society; nor did their frequently patchy and short schooling prepare them for that life. On the other hand, immigrants who come to take up posts as managers and managing directors often arrive from an economically developed environment and even when this is not the case their education at least had direct links with modern Western culture. In the matter of educational problems, we are speaking of a set of attitudes which emphasize:

-- The pre-eminence of knowledge over faith and of technical and scientific rationality over mythical and magical/religious references;

-- A view of the individual as broadly independent or capable of being made independent of his home community (or communities), ancestors or family;

-- An ability to live and find one's bearings easily in a wide social area where a sharp line is drawn between public and private and where formal organisations predominate, organisations that function relatively impersonally on the basis of compliance with rules and norms by persons seen as holding hierarchical roles and status rather than as individuals in their own right;

-- Belief that the future is not only an important dimension of life but can be fashioned, constructed out of the present, coupled with:

-- Confidence in the ability to influence one's own destiny and environment.

The list is not exhaustive and merely tries to show the general orientation of the attitudes which the school emphasizes in its daily operation, in what it teaches and in what it values. Modernity as understood in this sense is a component part of the educational institution. In school life and work, while these attitudes are essential, they are never explicitly required nor taught.

There is every reason to believe that their importance in the tradition-modernity dimension influences the relationship with the school and with school work, making a difference for both parents and for pupils:

For parents:

-- Unequal familiarity/proximity with the knowledge, tactics, standards and values of the modern urban world in general and its schools in particular;

-- Unequal predisposition and ability to collect and assimilate information on the way schools operate, the strategies brought into play there and what is at stake;

-- Unequal predisposition/ability to work out and carry through the strategies that ensure the best chances of educational success and the best school places for their children (educational action at home), and successful handling of relations with the school, its rules and its personnel.

For children:

-- Unequal predisposition and ability to show the right skills and attitudes at school and to possess a cultural capital bringing the best returns (Perrenoud, 1984);

-- Unequal predisposition and ability to grasp the strategies brought into play at school and what is at stake;

-- Unequal predisposition and ability to use the rules to promote their hopes and plans.

In order to describe the cultural difference between social statuses, Bourdieu (1972) uses the concept of class "habitus" with its dual components:

-- A system of aptitudes to perceive, think, evaluate and act that is produced and assimilated in interaction with a social environment in the living conditions peculiar to a given social class and in given historical circumstances;

-- A "grammar" generating practices and strategies consistent with the conditions in which this is the behavioural pattern and tending to reproduce it.

Cultural heritage as reflected in behavioural patterns is not merely the sum of items of knowledge or skills; much more than that, it motivates the strategies and practices (which are bound to be selective) used in acquiring knowledge and skills, determining what it is desirable/undesirable, thinkable/unthinkable and possible/impossible to acquire and master. From the standpoint of the mastery of linguistic codes, for example, this means that the cultural heritage determines not only mother tongue but, much more than that, rapport with language and with the practices of communication through language (Bernstein, 1973) and hence the meaning, at once subjective and social, of the mastery of skills valued by the school.

The brief description of the traits characteristic of modernity emphasized the importance of the fundamental and general dispositions that determine the rapport with the world, oneself and others, and hence with school. Plainly, these dispositions are unevenly distributed and unequally valued according to social position. This is perhaps a clue to the way in which to interpret our observations. If, social status and conditions of immigration being equal, foreign pupils differ so little from the Swiss in success and career at school, it is because it is their parents' place in the social hierarchy of the modern urban world that is taken by that world's logic as a measure of their unequal distance towards the culture, ideas, standards and values of modernity that are its criteria of excellence. By the same token, if Swiss and foreign pupils of equal social status differ so little, it is because their place in the social hierarchy measures their distance towards the modern cultural components of the educational institution.

On this assumption, the inequality suffered by Swiss and foreigners is the same. But this would not be understood by looking only at the most immediately visible aspects of daily school life such as the mastery of linguistic and social codes or parents' educational level or ability to help their children with their school work. All these factors are important, in the same way as economic and social inequalities, but they are themselves sometimes produced by, sometimes the producers of, more fundamental attitudes which, reflecting/producing rapport with the world, oneself and others, as well as with institutions, determine life plans and strategies for acquiring/demonstrating knowledge and mastery of skills in daily life as well as at school.

This line of thought is perhaps particularly pertinent in a socio-economic context such as that of the canton of Geneva, since the inequalities observed in this chapter occur in a society which has a high standard of living (although there are still wide disparities) and where both State and private involvement in education is considerable, as proved by the high school enrolment and the general educational level of the new generations. Moreover, primary education at least is largely homogeneous. The same subjects are taught according to the same methods by teachers who have had the same training and use the same teaching aids in largely the same material environment; and the various social classes are distributed throughout the urban fabric, without the heavy concentration of working class and/or immigrant families or poverty found in other cities. In Geneva, more than elsewhere, it seems that social inequality at school results when social and cultural differences encounter or are opposed to broadly standardized educational treatment and that, as Bourdieu suggests (1966), it is by treating unequals equally that the school brings about unequal success.

Statistical studies similar to our own made in other socio-political contexts, such as the United Kingdom (Swann, 1985) or Zurich (Gurny et al., 1984), come to the same conclusions, at least for the lower social classes. If the analysis outlined in this paper is correct, there is an urgent need to find out what really makes the difference and at the same time to see what the schools are doing about it.

NOTES

1. In Geneva, such analyses are facilitated by the existence of an educational data bank covering all pupils in State and private schools (general or vocational), from pre-school to university entrance.

2. For reasons of comparability, private schools -- which recruit about 11 per cent of all the pupils in the canton -- are not considered in the present study.

3. Demographic data available elsewhere confirm that the majority of Swiss immigrants come from another canton and the majority of foreigners from abroad.

BIBLIOGRAPHY

AMOS, J. (1984): L'entrée en apprentissage. Capital scolaire et marché de l'apprentissage à Genève (1970-1981), Geneva, Service de la recherche sociologique, Cahier No. 20.

BAIN, D. (1979): Orientation scolaire et fonctionnement de l'école, Berne, Peter Lang.

BERNSTEIN, B. (ed.) (1973): Class, codes and control, Routledge and Kegan Paul, London.

BOURDIEU, P. (1966): "L'inégalité sociale devant l'école et devant la culture", in Revue française de sociologie, No. 3, pp. 325-347.

BOURDIEU P. (1972): Esquisse d'une théorie de la pratique, Droz, Geneva.

GURNY, R. et al. (1984): Karrieren und Sackgassen, Rüegger, Zurich.

HEINTZ, P. (1974): Die Zukunft der Entwicklung, Berne, Huber.

HUTMACHER, W. (1981): "Migrations, production et reproduction de la société", in Gretler, A., Perret, A.N., and Poglia, E. (ed.) Etre Migrant, Berne, Editions Lang, Collection Exploration.

HUTMACHER, W. (1982): "Ecole et société : Changements quantitatifs et structurels. Le cas du canton de Genève 1960-1978", in Réévaluation de la planification de l'éducation dans un pays fédéraliste : la Suisse. Contributions to an OECD project, "Bulletin d'information de la Conférence suisse des directeurs cantonaux de l'instruction publique", No. 33, July.

HUTMACHER, W. (1985): "Enjeux autour de l'école dans une collectivité de type post-industriel", in Plaisance, Eric (ed.) L'échec scolaire : Nouveaux débats, nouvelles approches sociologiques, Paris, Editions du CNRS, 26 pages.

PERRENOUD, Ph. (1984): La fabrication de l'excellence scolaire, Droz, Geneva.

ROLLER, S. and HARAMEIN, A. (1961): "Enquête sur les retards scolaires. Resultats concernant le 6e degré de la scolarité obligatoire", Education Department, Geneva, (mimeo, 65 pages).

SWANN, Lord (1985): Education for All. A brief guide to the main issues of the Report (Committee of inquiry into the education of children from ethnic groups) and Report, Department of Education and Science, London.

TOURAINE, A. (1973): Production de la société, Editions du Seuil, Paris.

IV. WEST INDIAN AND ASIAN CHILDREN IN ENGLAND AND WALES

INTRODUCTION

Although children from a range of different ethnic backgrounds have long been present in the United Kingdom it is only since the early 1950s that the implications for education have been seen as an issue, largely as a result of the sharp rise in immigration from Commonwealth countries. This immigration reached a peak during the 1960s and early 1970s. The scale of immigration is now much reduced and the great majority of ethnic minority children in the United Kingdom were born in that country. They are not "foreign" or "immigrants", as in many other EC countries, but British citizens, with the same rights and responsibilities as other citizens.

Attitudes towards the educational needs of ethnic minority pupils have changed over the years, moving from the early days of "assimilation", through "integration" and attempts to give at least some recognition in schools to the backgrounds of ethnic minority children, to more recent moves towards "education for a multi-ethnic society".

The initial response of the education service to the arrival of increasing numbers of ethnic minority pupils during the late 1950s and early 1960s was to focus on absorbing them into the majority school population as rapidly as possible. The emphasis was therefore on the teaching of English as a second language to immigrant children, often in specialist language or reception centres which also provides some basic pastoral support to counter the "culture shock" or disorientation which children were felt to experience on arrival in a new country. Once these initial problems had been remedied it was believed that children might then be subsumed within the overall school population.

This policy of "assimilation" was gradually overtaken during the late 1960s by a growing awareness that the education process should give some recognition to the differences in lifestyle and cultural and religious background of ethnic minority children. The emphasis remained, however, upon integrating ethnic minority pupils into the majority society and culture with as little disruption to the life of the majority community as possible.

In the last decade or so a new concept of education for a multi-ethnic society began to emerge. This was based on two distinct but interrelated themes; first, meeting the particular educational needs of ethnic minority children and second, the broader issue of preparing all pupils for life in a multi-racial society. The first theme derived from an increasing realisation that many ethnic minority pupils still had educational needs which existing policies were proving unable to meet; West Indian children in particular appeared to be under-achieving at school. At the same time the ethnic minority communities themselves began to voice their own concerns about their children's education.

In 1977 a report by the House of Commons Select Committee on Race Relations and Immigration on "The West Indian Community" (House of Commons HC180: I-II, February 1977) urged the Government to establish "A high level and independent inquiry into the causes of the under-achievement of children of West Indian origin". The Government accepted the need for an inquiry but believed that it should look at the needs of children from all ethnic minority groups, though with early and particular attention to the educational needs and attainments of pupils of West Indian origin. A Committee of Inquiry into the Education of Children from Ethnic Minority Groups was accordingly set up in March 1979.

In 1981, the Committee of Inquiry published an interim report on the education of West Indian children, called the Rampton Report after the name of the Chairman of the Committee (West Indian Children in our Schools, Cmnd. 8273, HMSO, June 1981), which noted the existence of considerable educational underachievement among West Indian children compared with other children's performance. The Committee continued its work after 1981 under a new Chairman, Lord Swann, and turned to the educational needs and achievement of pupils belonging to all minority groups. The Committee's final report, the Swann Report, was published in 1985 under the title Education for All (Cmnd. 9453, HMSO, March 1985).

Pupils belonging to ethnic groups living in the United Kingdom can be divided according to their countries of origin, the two main categories being West Indians (1) and Asians (2). Within this latter category, which is too broad, there are five subgroups:

-- Pupils of Indian origin;

-- Pupils of Pakistani origin;

-- Pupils from Bangladesh;

-- Asian pupils from East Africa;

-- Asian pupils of other origins.

To the two main categories must be added a series of smaller minority groups, including:

-- Pupils of Chinese origin;

-- Pupils of Cypriot origin;

-- Pupils of Italian origin;

-- Pupils of Ukrainian origin;

-- Pupils of Vietnamese origin.

The present chapter confines itself to the educational problems of the two main categories, i.e. West Indians and Asians.

The educational achievement of the two categories differs: the average level of the West Indians is distinctly lower than that of the Asians, in spite of the similar status of these two ethnic minorities. Compared with the performance of the white majority, West Indian pupils on average have very much lower examination results, whereas those of the Asians are on the contrary very similar to those of white pupils. Why do these two groups differ so surprisingly when similarity rather than divergence would seem to be more likely. These two categories do not differ much from each other as regards socio-economic status and material living conditions (housing, parents' employment and income), yet their educational performance is appreciably different. Where socio-economic status is equal, not only are the average educational achievements of the two categories not comparable, but that of Asian pupils is near or, still on average, similar to that of the white majority.

The Swann Committee's analysis of this situation is particularly interesting and we therefore summarise here its comments and explanations on the educational performance of West Indian and Asian children and the discussion of achievement in its Chapter 3 ("Achievement and Underachievement").

UNDERACHIEVEMENT OF WEST INDIAN CHILDREN

Preliminary research in six educational areas where about half of all the school-leavers belonging to ethnic minorities are concentrated was carried out by the Statistics Branch of the UK Department of Education and Science in 1978/79. In connection with the annual school-leavers' survey it clearly demonstrated that West Indian children were not at all successful at school. Their performance, measured by examination results at the end of their schooling, was far inferior to that of Asian and white pupils. Another survey carried out by A. Craft and M. Craft in an outer London borough and published in 1983 ("The participation of ethnic minority pupils in further and higher education", Education Research 25.1) showed that, irrespective of social class, West Indian pupils are markedly under-represented amongst high achievers and markedly over-represented amongst low achievers.

The Statistics Branch of the Department of Education and Science was asked by the Committee of Inquiry to repeat in 1981/82 the school-leavers' survey exercise to see whether the relative performance of the groups had altered in any way in the intervening three years. Once again, it was found that West Indian children were performing markedly less well than their fellows from other groups on all the measures used.

UNDERACHIEVEMENT OF ASIAN CHILDREN

Despite the lack of official statistics on children's achievement broken down by ethnic group, we do nonetheless have the findings of several studies on this subject. Their broad consensus is that Asian pupils generally perform as well in public examinations as their peers in the same schools and neighbourhood. The two DES school-leavers' surveys bear out this conclusion, i.e. that the educational achievement of Asians is quite comparable with that of white children among both middle-class and working-class children. The lack of a common approach does not permit any reliable conclusions regarding the different subgroups included in the Asian category. There are indications of differences in performance between some of the subgroups, but these differences are not great, except in the case of Bangladeshi children, who in some cases have been shown to be performing less well than their school fellows in other subgroups.

Annexed to the Swann Report is an Inner London Education Authority background paper on the education of Bangladeshi children in the London borough of Tower Hamlets, where there is a heavy concentration of Bangladeshi families.

This paper confirms the poor educational achievement of Bangladeshi pupils compared with other children in the Asian community. This is not surprising, as a substantial number of those factors which are generally accepted as adversely influencing educational performance are present in relatively extreme forms in Tower Hamlets, combined with other factors more specifically related to disruption of schooling. Some of these children arrive in the United Kingdom having never been to school, or have had their schooling disrupted by extended "holidays" in Bangladesh.

FACTORS EXPLAINING THE DIFFERENCES IN THE EDUCATIONAL ACHIEVEMENT OF ETHNIC MINORITY CHILDREN

As already pointed out in our causal analysis of the French and Genevan data, there are many difficulties in evaluating the factors behind educational achievement and underachievement. The Swann Report emphasizes the complexity of this evaluation and warns against the temptation of looking for a single explanatory cause when all the research shows that many interrelated causes are involved. It would therefore be a mistake to blame only social class, racism, family structure, ethnic group culture or the school for the underachievement of minority group children, just as it would also be a mistake to assume that the same factor has the same effect on children from culturally different groups.

After this warning, the Swann Report considers the influence of racism, intelligence quotient, the interrelationship of social factors, and educational factors.

The explanation which blames *racism* in the school for the failure or educational problems of ethnic minority children was particularly discussed in the interim report by the Committee of Inquiry, which concentrated on the education of West Indian children. It is interesting to note that this explanation, which looms large in the British analyses, is practically never considered in the studies on the educational problems of immigrant children in the countries of continental Europe.

The findings of the Interim Report had shown that claims that teachers were racist were often rejected out of hand by the teaching profession as unjustified. However, the report acknowledged that there must inevitably be a small minority of teachers who held explicitly racist views, and that there was evidence of unintentional racism by some other teachers which was shown by their behaviour, and their negative and patronising attitudes towards ethnic minority children. Having no illusions on their account and not expecting much in the way of achievement from most of them, the teachers do not encourage their work or support them, and get results which confirm their opinion.

Nevertheless, while admitting the impact of these vaguely racist attitudes on educational achievement and accepting the existence of this type of reaction among teachers, the Committee of Inquiry asserts that explicit or implicit racism in the school cannot alone be responsible for underachievement. It is not alone the more or less latent racism existing in schools, nor teachers' lower expectations or difficulties in allowing for cognitive approaches different to those of the white majority which may be responsible for this situation, but a combination of these factors with hostile or unfavourable conditions existing in the social environment and which often stem from a diffuse, more widespread and undercover racism pervading society.

A second argument, which too is now practically never mentioned in the debate on this subject in other European countries, attributes educational underachievement to the lower intelligence quotient (IQ) of the children belonging to certain ethnic groups compared with the majority IQ. Poor performance would thus only be the inevitable result of the inadequate intellectual development of certain groups. Some authors (Jensen, Eysenck) have even claimed that this difference was genetic, propounding a thesis which enjoyed a certain popularity for several years. This issue was especially discussed in the United States, where it was discovered that the black population scored lower averages in intelligence tests than whites. In the United Kingdom, a similar difference was also observed, although less marked, between West Indian and native children.

The UK Committee did not wish to side-step this argument and asked Professor Nicholas Mackintosh, of Cambridge University, to review the opposing positions in this debate. The main conclusion of this very balanced and comprehensive work is that the IQ differences between West Indian and native children are closely related to other discriminatory factors such as parents' occupation, income, size of family, degree of overcrowding, city and neighbourhood. All of these factors also have a bearing on the IQ of white children. Allowing for these variables considerably reduces the differences between West Indian and white children. It must therefore be concluded that IQ is not a significant factor of underachievement.

The third type of argument groups a series of social factors: socio-economic status (income, employment, health, quality of housing, etc.), social class, neighbourhood. The converging findings of dozens of research studies over the last 20 years prove without a shadow of doubt that there is a close relationship between educational underachievement and worsening socio-economic circumstances. As was also observed when examining the French surveys and the Genevan data, this factor overrides differences of race, culture or nationality and has a bearing on the educational performance of local majorities as well as ethnic minorities. Since socio-economic deprivation has a negative impact on the majority, it would be surprising, notes the report, if it did not influence the performance of ethnic minority children too. As we just saw, these factors affect IQ. The differences in the educational achievement of West Indian, Asian and white pupils can be largely put down to social deprivation. The Committee's report asserts that educational achievement is ruled more by socio-economic circumstances, social class and region than by educational conditions.

For equal socio-economic handicap, there should be no difference between the school performance of West Indian, Asian and white children. Basing itself on the findings of several studies, the Committee finds that minority groups in the United Kingdom are quite evidently at a much greater disadvantage than whites. Consequently, the impact of deprivation on the achievement of minority group pupils is greater, which explains the higher rates of problem pupils among minority groups than among whites. On the whole, the socio-economic circumstances of ethnic minorities are worse than those of whites: their unemployment rate is higher, wages are lower and housing conditions are not as good. The Committee also admits that these circumstances can be blamed on to various forms of racial discrimination.

However, as the Committee finally notes, it would be a mistake to consider that socio-economic handicaps inevitably generate educational underachievement. There are some children who, despite very poor living conditions, succeed at school. Educational underachievement is not fatalistically predetermined. The school has its measure of responsibility.

The fourth category considered is educational factors. Because of the many complaints made to it by members of the West Indian community about teachers' attitudes, the Committee commissioned a review of research of the influence of teacher stereotyping and expectations on the school performance of ethnic minority children. More broadly, it considered the effects of factors other than socio-economic status on these pupils' school performance. Present research evidence does not permit a clear view of this issue. Explanations that blame a single factor for the educational underachievement of West Indians are simplistic and have never been corroborated by scientific research, which has difficulty in producing clear findings owing to the complexity of the problem. Too many factors are involved (gender, parents' educational level, types of pre-school education, family background, parents' views on education, etc.) to weight their influence accurately. This is not impossible, but it remains to be done, as already pointed out in the comments on the French and Genevan data. The UK Committee proposed research into this area, and the Department of Education and Science is now considering various proposals.

Concluding its examination, the Committee gives the following interpretation of the performance of West Indian and Asian pupils:

i) <u>West Indian pupils</u>

-- The average achievement of West Indian pupils is undoubtedly not as good as that of the white majority. This fact is undeniable;

-- The Interim Report on the education of West Indian pupils said that stereotyped attitudes among teachers and their low expectations were likely to be an important factor in this state of affairs;

— The Interim Report was criticised because it did not pay enough attention to the influence of IQ, social class and socio-economic factors whose impact on the school performance of the white majority has long been recognised;

— Research carried out on behalf of the Committee demonstrated that the gap between the IQ of West Indian and white majority children narrows sharply when socio-economic factors are considered. IQ is in fact also related to these factors. Thus, lower IQ is not the main cause of West Indian pupils' underachievement;

— The effect of social class and socio-economic status on school performance has been proved beyond a doubt. Where conditions are adverse, West Indian pupils suffer in the same way as white majority pupils who belong to the most deprived social classes. But the Committee observes that the ethnic minorities are particularly disadvantaged in social and economic terms and are therefore inevitably over-represented among the pupils who do not do well at school. The Committee also points out that the underachievement of West Indian children is not entirely attributable to socio-economic factors. These factors play an important part, but they do not fully explain the differences between West Indian and white majority pupils' performances;

— This residual difference which is unexplained by socio-economic factors is determined by several other factors relating to the interaction of the school and society with the West Indian child, the West Indian family, and the West Indian community, etc., whose relative weight cannot at present be accurately assessed;

— For the immediate future, the Committee considers that the first thing to do to improve West Indian children's educational achievement is to reduce ethnocentrism and racism in the education system.

ii) Asian pupils

— The average performance of most Asian pupils is undoubtedly comparable on the whole with that of white majority pupils, the only exception being Bangladeshi children, whose performance is on the contrary very poor;

— It is difficult to explain the similarity between the performance of Asian and white majority pupils. We do not know why racism affects the achievement of West Indian children and not that of Asian children. It might be assumed that the latter are less susceptible to the impact of racism than the former, but this remains to be proved. Similarly, the socio-economic conditions of the Asian community are no better than those of the West Indian community. We would therefore expect these two groups to show similar results, but that is not the case. Average Asian pupil achievement is comparable with average white majority achievement;

-- It might be assumed that this difference is explained by the Asian pupils having a higher IQ than the West Indians. The studies carried out on behalf of the Committee do not support this assumption;

-- If it is accepted that the socio-economic factors are the same and have the same effects both for the Asian and the West Indian communities, then it must be recognised that the real difference observed between the educational achievement of the two groups of pupils must be attributed to the influence of other factors, in other words to educational and social factors in the broad sense. The Committee believes that the explanation could lie in the different attitudes adopted by the white majority towards Asians as compared with West Indians. These forms of racial prejudice and discrimination vary according to the groups subjected to them.

-- The Committee also wonders whether it is possible to find out what enables the Asian community to cope more successfully with socio-economic handicaps and hostile and discriminatory attitudes. For the time being Swann does not have any definite conclusions but tentatively suggests that cultural factors may help Asians to overcome deprivation more successfully than West Indians.

Some observers suppose that an explanation can lie in the fact that the white majority has different ideas of each of these groups, based on their history, beliefs, abilities and the good or bad qualities attributed to them. It is therefore probable that the white majority's view of the Asian community is different from its view of the West Indian community and that one of these views is more damning than the other. The majority's attitudes to each community vary and are perceived differently and prompt different reactions in each of the two.

CONCLUSION

The educational underachievement of a number of ethnic minority groups is a fact which cannot be denied, but no satisfactory explanation has so far been found. The difference in the performance of West Indian and Asian children obviously shows that underachievement is not due to socio-economic factors alone. In spite of belonging to socio-economically deprived groups, Asian children do as well as white majority. The Committee must therefore conclude that something exists which helps them to overcome their handicap and hold their own better than West Indian children. But the Committee cannot yet identify with certainty the factors which improve their school performance.

It could be due to a combination of factors involving both the values constituting community culture and the attitudes of the white majority towards the different communities of ethnic minorities.

Generally speaking, the CERI Secretariat notes that no explanation for the good educational performance of Asian pupils has yet been found. More detailed analyses must be made, particularly of the school careers and of the strategies employed by the families, to get the most out of the education system. The British Committee of Inquiry gives no information in this connection. It may be that these strategies differ considerably from those of the white majority and that the price the Asian children have to pay, for example, is higher than we can guess for the moment.

NOTES

1. The Swann report defines West Indian children as "children who are black and whose families came originally from the group of islands known as the West Indies".

2. In 1981, according to the data gathered by the Ethnic Statistics Unit of the Office of Population Censuses, the West Indian population in the United Kingdom numbered some 604 000 and the Asian population 1 114 000.

Part Five

EDUCATIONAL STRUCTURES FOR IMMIGRANTS' CHILDREN

EDUCATIONAL STRUCTURES FOR IMMIGRANTS' CHILDREN

I. BACKGROUND

In the 1970s, the education systems of the OECD countries began to take a systematic interest in the education of immigrants' children. The causes of this new interest in a school population which differed in nationality, language and domestic ways and customs from the majority of pupils are many: some are contingent, others historical. It is not possible to examine the whole complex of this phenomenon in the present study. What is important to stress as a starting point is the fact that a new phase began roughly in the 1970s when State education systems started integrating the schools and classes which had developed outside the system itself to teach immigrants' children their mother tongue, native culture and even their parents' religion.

Most of these private initiatives had been launched by associations of immigrants or their churches and occasionally by the governments of their home countries. As a rule, immigrants' children went to the State schools of the host countries, while at the same time attending classes in these community schools, usually for a few hours a week. Arrangements of this type may be found in practically every Member country, be it in the United States, Canada, Australia or Europe. Until quite recently the State education system had paid no particular attention either to these special pupils attending two schools or to this increasing activity at its periphery.

This attitude has suddenly changed over the last few years. In Europe, the host countries have begun to legislate on the organisation of these classes; in the United States, ethnic minority groups have demanded and partly succeeded in getting the public schools to include special language courses in their curricula; in Canada, the Provinces have increased the arrangements for heritage languages; while in Australia, somewhat belatedly, the States have begun to look for a compromise with the ethnic schools.

The pattern of decisions taken in the late 1960s and early 1970s in the OECD countries is eloquent. Although incomplete, the following list will suffice to show the new direction taken by education policies, resulting in the invention of a new specialist field of action: the education of immigrants' children (IMCs) and ethnic minority groups:

1968 United States   Bilingual Education Act.

1969 Spain   Ministerial Order setting up the first Spanish institution concerned with the education of immigrants.

1970	Council of Europe	Resolution (70)35 of the Committee of Ministers of the Council of Europe on school education for the children of immigrant workers.
1971	Germany	Resolution on the education of immigrants' children of the Standing Conference (KMK) of Ministers of Education and Cultural Affairs of the Länder of the Federal Republic of Germany.
	Australia	Educational programme for immigrants' children.
	Canada	Formulation of principles for a policy of multiculturalism.
	Italy	Adoption of Act 153 concerning aid for the education of immigrants' children abroad.
	United Kingdom	Publication by the Department of Education and Science of the first report on the educational needs of immigrants (The education of immigrants).
	United Kingdom	Publication by the Department of Education and Science of the second report on the educational needs of immigrants (The continuing needs of immigrants).
	Sweden	Formation of the joint Swedish-Yugoslav working party on the education of Yugoslav children in Sweden.
	Switzerland	First meeting of the ad hoc Italo-Swiss Commission on educational issues.
1973	Australia	First experiments in bilingual education with the Aborigines.
	Canada	Application of the first special initiatives in Quebec.
	France	First census of the foreign school population.
	Switzerland	First meeting of the ad hoc Hispano-Swiss Commission on educational issues.
1974	Council of Europe	Ad hoc Conference on immigrant education.
	United States	Amendment to the Bilingual Education Act extending it to all children having an inadequate command of English.
	Canada	Multicultural Act passed in Saskatchewan.
1975	Council of Europe	Resolution No. 2 on the education of immigrants' children adopted by the Standing Conference of European Ministers of Education meeting in Stockholm.

Sweden   Extension to all immigrants' children of the special curricula previously intended for Finnish children alone.

Canada   Creation of the Ministry of Culture and Recreation in Ontario.

What is the meaning of this change and how is the situation in which it is taking place evolving? Is it a change of mentality and the traditional categories for perceiving the immigrant and otherness? In other words, does it indicate a substantial shift in the migratory policies introduced by the immigration and emigration countries? And, if such is the case, what are the school's new tasks in this connection? At first glance, these questions reveal an apparently paradoxical factor: the surprising similarity, despite the wide variety of countries, of the educational policies adopted throughout the OECD area. Whether in Europe or elsewhere, both in immigration countries and the traditional emigration countries, the educational reforms adopted on behalf of immigrants' children are based, with one or two exceptions, on the same principles.

The similarities have partly dictated our own reading of the situation. It is customary in this particular area to emphasize the specific character and differences both of emigrant status and the education systems. We do not wish to deny that these differences exist, but we consider that in this particular case they are less significant than the similarities. We therefore feel it is important in the following pages to stress the parallel and converging trends and common points of Member countries' educational policies and curricula for IMCs.

The information used comes primarily from official sources: ministerial decisions, educational plans and reports, periodicals published by government or public agencies, reports of bilateral commissions representing immigration and emigration countries for the education of IMCs, documents of international agencies, and contributions to CERI's project on "Education and Cultural and Linguistic Pluralism" (ECALP).

We have considered two types of curriculum for IMCs in order to facilitate comparison between the different countries and reveal the constants underlying specific national characteristics: induction curricula and mother tongue and native culture tuition (MTNCT). Chapter I describes European experience and chapter II non-European experience, with some general conclusions based on the preceding description.

II. CHANGE BUT CONTINUITY: THE EUROPEAN MODEL

An outstanding event in educational policies for immigrants' children in Europe was the publication of the EEC Directive of 25th July 1977 (Directive 77/486). By laying down Community legislation, this text created a new de jure situation as regards the education of IMCs, with the following features:

   i) Host countries are obliged to provide a free reception education which includes teaching their official language or languages;

   ii) Host countries and immigrants' home countries must co-operate in appropriate MTNCT action.

The novel aspect of this Directive is that host countries were obliged to organise the educational reception of IMCs at no cost either to the pupils or to their home countries. This is, briefly put, the first clause of a Directive which is in itself quite vague, making no clear distinction between the obligations of the host and home countries since it generally refers only to member States, which could quite easily be either. The Directive merely sanctions the obligation placed on member States, whether host or home, to organise education for IMCs.

Secondly, the Directive recognises the legitimacy of MTNCT since it obliges the member countries to promote it. Lastly, in admitting the necessity to train specialist teachers for the reception of IMCs, the EEC Directive laid the foundations for the creation of a corps of specialist teachers for IMCs education.

It is difficult to evaluate the precise significance and scope of a text such as this whose most important aspect is legal in nature. Indeed, from the educational standpoint, the Directive says nothing new compared with the previous arrangements: reception of new arrivals, MTNCT for IMCs already settled. What is significant here is the role assigned to member States, which are invited to take responsibility for IMCs education, an activity which had formerly been in the hands of private groups. Obviously, we will inevitably compare this decision with countries' migratory policies. But it is difficult to draw any precise conclusion from this concerning countries' intentions since the wording is in itself too vague.

In certain respects, it could be claimed that, by inviting the host countries to do something for IMCs -- organising courses to help them learn their language, training specialist teachers for IMCs education -- the intentions of the Directive are integrationist. Others, on the contrary, consider that it is more isolationist because, by requiring countries to take responsibility for MTNCT, it regards educational actions from the viewpoint of the immigrants' return to their home countries. The Directive seeks to strengthen immigrants' linguistic and cultural ties with their home countries, as stated in its preamble, with a view to facilitating possible reintegration in the member State of origin.

This Directive is very dated in its ambiguity: it reflects the ambiguity of the migratory policies applied at the time of its promulgation when it was difficult to decide which solution to adopt. Migratory flows had been so impressive that countries were prompted to adopt a progressive policy of integration: the economic boom which occurred in the meantime suggested caution. Although unemployment was not yet as high at that time as it has since become, there was already some ground to fear for the stability of employment of an insecure labour force. It was therefore prudent not to exclude return policies and above all to plan educational measures which might facilitate the resettlement of children in their home countries.

It is hard to say whether this Directive is still appropriate today given the developments on the employment market and changes in migratory flows. The EEC report on implementation of the Directive published in 1984 is merely a description by member States of how it has been applied. The impression it leaves is mixed: on the one hand, a lot has been done since 1977, but at the same time it must be admitted that the Directive has not been fully implemented. Consequently, it is no easy matter to judge the effects of the measures proposed.

This lack of evaluation is in itself unfortunate for teaching purposes since it makes it hard to reach unequivocal conclusions from the educational standpoint. Apart from this inconvenience, the Directive must be credited with responsibility for a degree of standardization among the educational initiatives for IMCs adopted in Europe and thus for the establishment of a European educational network for these children which we will now endeavour to describe briefly.

Induction Measures

The introduction of induction measures is based on the idea that the integration of IMCs in host countries' educational systems will be quicker and raise fewer problems if it is facilitated and encouraged by special induction arrangements. It is clear from the intentions of the promoters of classes for IMCs that school integration is held to be one of the basic conditions for social integration. Successful school integration is an essential prerequisite if IMCs are to have the same social opportunities as native children. The justification for creating a special structure to acclimatise IMCs to host countries' schools therefore has social overtones. This emerges clearly from the resolutions on IMCs education adopted by the Council of Europe Conference of Ministers of Education.

In 1975, at the Stockholm meeting, Ministers agreed that it was necessary to guarantee and/or promote the access of immigrants to education and equal opportunity. In Dublin, in 1983, they recommended appropriate educational initiatives for immigrants to enable them to take part fully in the host country's social life and to give them the same opportunities for personal and occupational development as nationals.

The reception measures introduced in the various countries are a very mixed bag. They may be ranked as three alternatives:

i) "Preparatory" [or "initiation", "induction" or "special temporary" (IC)] classes. These are meant to be temporary, but they vary in length and are subject to controversy since there are no exact limits on the duration of induction and adjustment. They cater for a mixed school population as regards nationality, age and educational level. They are usually separate classes and are found both in the nursery school and secondary education;

ii) "Special classes" or "catch-up classes" (CC), which are provided during the usual school hours side by side with normal schooling and, as in the preceding case, also cater for a mixed public;

iii) Bilingual classes (BC), confined to youngsters from the same country, in which tuition is given in the home country's official language and also in that of the host country, which gradually becomes the language of instruction as and when the pupils' linguistic abilities improve (subtractive model). It may also be decided that teaching in the first language will not be phased out and will be retained side by side with teaching in the second language up to the end of compulsory schooling (compound model).

The last alternative is least widespread. Bilingual classes may be found in Germany, especially for Greek and Turkish pupils, and in Sweden for pupils of Finnish extraction. The other two alternatives are more common. It is difficult to say why this is so, but the reasons are probably more administrative, not to say financial, and political than educational. From the practical standpoint, it is obviously not easy to have bilingual classes unless there is a heavy concentration of pupils speaking the same language.

These induction arrangements are accompanied by some anomalies. In Belgium, induction is organised from the nursery school, which contains a "special temporary" class, but it is not clear whether the children taken into this class are new arrivals alone or also include IMCs born in Belgium. The "special temporary class" probably also serves the latter, since support measures are also available during the first few years of primary school for children who have already had three years of pre-school education.

In Germany, where the educational system varies from one Land to another, there are roughly four types of induction structure for immigrant children (see Table 1):

-- Induction and preparatory classes (IC);

-- Bilingual classes (BC);

-- Intensive German-teaching classes (ILC);

-- Catch-up classes (CC).

The induction classes take pupils of all nationalities, but the bilingual classes are reserved for pupils who have the same mother tongue and intensive language classes are offered when there are not enough pupils to make up an induction class (norms vary from one Land to another); lastly, the catch-up classes help pupils who can follow the tuition in the normal classes. In principle, these forms of tuition ought to be short in duration, but, as we have already seen, there is a strong tendency for the provisional to become permanent.

In general, induction is very specialised. Each method is accompanied by alternatives designed for a wide variety of changing situations. Most solutions are applied both in primary and secondary schools, but induction is less well-organised in the upper secondary streams (Gymnasien and Realschulen) because the number of foreign pupils enrolling is very small. It is disturbing to note that there is a tendency in some cases to exempt IMCs from the study of English, a compulsory subject for German pupils. The English lessons are replaced by additional German or by tuition of the mother tongue. It may be asked whether this practice, which might at most be justified in the

Table 1

Types of Induction in Germany

Types	IC	ILC	BC	CC
Bade-Wurtemberg	x 1-2 years 10-20 pupils	x 6h/week min. 4 pupils	x	x 2-4h/week min. 4 pupils
Bavaria	x 2 years 10-20 pupils	x	x	x 4h/week
Berlin	x (1) 2 years 15-24 pupils	x 10h/week 10 pupils		x
Bremen	x (2) 2 years 10-20 pupils	x 7-8h/week 5-12 pupils		x
Hamburg	x (3) 1 year 15 pupils	x 2h/day	x 20-25 pupils 15 pupils	x 1h/day
Hesse	x (4) 2-3 years 15-30 pupils	x 14h/week	x	x
Lower Saxony	x 1-2 years 10-24 pupils	x 6-8h/week 1 year	x (5)	x 4h/week 8 pupils
North Rhineland-Westphalia	x 2 years 15-24 pupils	x		x
Rhineland-Palatinate	x 15 pupils no fixed duration			
Saarland	x 6 months-2 years 15-24 pupils	x		x
Schleswig-Holstein	x 1-2 years 15-30 pupils	x 12h/week 10-30 pupils		x 3h/week

Source: EEC.

Notes to Table 1

1. With the following alternatives: induction groups for beginners; induction groups for advanced pupils; special induction classes for pupils aged 14 and 15; special classes for foreign pupils.

2. With the alternative of initial induction classes for those arriving during school year.

3. Two alternatives: i) in the first year, multinational classes for 10-20 children or national classes 20-25 strong, which can be changed into bilingual classes; ii) from the second to the sixth year, multinational classes.

4. Alternative: preparatory class for children who have not been to a nursery school and speak no German. The classes begin six months before compulsory schooling and operate during the first half of the first year.

5. One experimental class only.

induction phase, is not counterproductive, adding a subsequent backwardness factor to the schooling of IMCs as compared with native children. Bilingual classes (BC) are least common, for two reasons: the necessity for a sufficiently high concentration of pupils of the same nationality speaking the same language, and reluctance to adopt a model which might seem segregationist. A few Länder do not rule out the possibility of creating national bilingual classes at induction level. They are suspicious of bilingual education.

Denmark and Sweden also have ICs and ILCs for primary schoolchildren in the normal classes, CCs and ICs for new comers over 14, etc. In Sweden, BCs exist mainly, if not exclusively, for young Finns; they were introduced in 1962 in the primary schools and were extended in 1977 to the first and second cycles of secondary education. The language of instruction is in this case Finnish, but Swedish teaching is compulsory (SOU, 1983, 57, pp. 12 and 18). Summer school is another alternative adopted in this country.

In France, one-year multinational initiation classes (INC) and catch-up classes for 2 to 8 hours a week have been introduced at primary level; the secondary schools have a 1-year adaptation course (AC) for youngsters aged 12 to 16 and 2-hour support classes.

In Luxembourg, induction is patterned on the complex official language setup. Side by side with French and German, which were the languages of instruction, the schools have recently introduced the Luxembourg national language, which only became a medium of instruction in 1984. Two types of IC exist side by side in the primary schools: the old regime, based on learning one of the two official languages (French or German) for one year; the new regime, in which children are taken into the normal classes closest to their own culture (Portuguese, French and Italian pupils in the French-speaking classes, for example) and also go into ICs to improve both languages of instruction as well as Luxembourgian. When there are too few pupils to have ICs, IMCs go into the normal classes and are given additional support lessons and intensive language coaching.

ICs in which the language of instruction is English are also the usual structure in the <u>United Kingdom</u> and the teaching staff decide case by case when a child can go into a normal class. There are also induction centres for new arrivals aged 8 to 16, with the same linguistic aims. Special induction structures also exist in Scotland and Wales for IMCs to learn Gaelic or Welsh.

a) <u>Numbers involved</u>

How many pupils go into transition classes? How many of these classes exist? How have they evolved since first being set up? The statistical data to hand are insufficient to give a detailed picture of the distribution of IMCs between the different forms of induction and to follow the development of induction practices over the course of time. Precise information has been provided for Germany (Table 2), where it is striking to note the differences between the Länder in the percentage of immigrant children in ICs:

-- Baden-Wurtemberg	8.9
-- Bavaria	47.8
-- Berlin	10.6
-- Bremen	5.10
-- Hamburg	14.6
-- Lower Saxony	3.7
-- North Rhine-Westphalia	23.6
-- Rhineland-Palatinate	16.9
-- Saarland	7
-- Schleswig-Holstein	7

These figures cannot be interpreted without more detailed information on the pupils' status: How long have they been in Germany? Were they born in Germany? How long do they stay in these classes? What percentage of new arrivals go into these classes? However, certain Länder are evidently more integrationist than others. It is also probable that the high averages in certain Länder mean that immigrant children stay in these classes longer.

In <u>France</u>, in school year 1983/84, the number of IMCs in primary ICs was 7 880 (i.e. 1.75 per cent of the IMCs in primary education) and their number in secondary ICs was 2 142 (or 0.65 per cent of the IMCs in secondary education). In all, French ICs received 0.99 per cent of all IMCs. There is thus practically no special induction structure in this country. A similar remark may be made for <u>Luxembourg</u>. In <u>the Netherlands</u>, according to Ministry of Education and Science estimates, in 1980-81 26 per cent of primary IMCs were in primary ICs and 20 per cent of the secondary IMCs were in secondary ICs.

b) <u>Organisation: specialisation and standardization</u>

The organisation and funding of the induction structure are the responsibility of the host country's authorities. Up to the mid-1970s the teachers and didactic material were the same as for the normal classes. Since then there has been a perceptible shift towards a growing "specialisation" of induction: for instance, "teaching for foreign children" has emerged, native teachers have been trained to cater for "immigrants' needs", the host country's language has been taught as a "foreign language".

The mother tongue was initially taught as a first language, then as a "second language" and finally as a "foreign language", although no details are given of the bias and content of the teaching of the ambient language, as though this changed in character when taught to IMCs. This process was accompanied by the creation of special training structures for teachers going to schools that have a high concentration of immigrants. Teacher specialisation for IMCs raises a number of questions. The aim is indeed very vague: the official texts usually refer to special IMCs needs but do not give any details. If there are problems relating to this fringe of the school population, is its extraordinary variety considered in connection with specialisation? Are these special needs not more socio-economic than cultural and linguistic?

The training of a corps of specialist teachers for the reception of IMCs raises a problem, as the Berque Report (1985) points out concerning the education of immigrant children in France. These difficulties also emerge in the debate on the policies of the <u>CEFISEMs</u>, the training and information centres for staff concerned with the education of immigrants' children. In any case, observes Berque, the real problem is "the quite inadequate, not to say non-existent, training of all the teachers and other staff concerned".

<u>Mother Tongue and Native Culture Tuition (MTNCT)</u>

The EEC Directive on the education of IMCs associates this tuition with the "possible return" of the youngsters concerned to their parents' home countries. Only <u>Sweden</u> rules this possibility out and considers that the development of MTNCT is justified for different cultural, educational, social and even economic reasons. The whole country benefits from any increase in the population's linguistic skills (SOU, 1974: 64). Sweden has adopted a different terminology to reflect this difference of interpretation: it does not talk about courses in the mother tongue and native culture but home language courses, meaning the language the pupils speak at home. As MTNCT developed, the initial reasons have been joined by other considerations such as the multicultural transformation of society, increasing the child's self-confidence, or neutralising IMCs' feelings of inferiority.

<u>Sweden</u> refers in this connection to "the intellectual and emotional disturbance of the child deprived of his mother tongue at an abstract level, the problems created in families and society's duty to preserve the child's right to his mother tongue" (SOU, 1983, 57: 12). The introduction to an official <u>Greek</u> programme states that MTNCT can "help to increase pupils' self-confidence and relieve the feelings of inferiority which are often experienced by the members of a socially inferior minority" (Programma Optico-Acousticou, 1982-1983: 7).

Table 2

Germany: Foreign Pupils by Type of Induction
(School Year 1981/82)

	Induction Classes			Intensive Language Classes			Bilingual Classes			Catch-up Classes		
	Primary	Secondary	Total	Primary	Secondary	Total	Primary	Secondary	Total	Primary	Secondary	Total
Baden-Wurtemberg	2 801	3 491	6 292 (a)	4 336	2 417	6 753	2 161	712	2 873 (b)	34 553	18 892	53 445
Bavaria (d)	..	..	1 026	..	..	15 100	..	..	26 964 (c)	..	..	..
Berlin	2 616	1 828	4 444 (e)	7 833	1 617	9 450	..	..	..	..	..	..
Bremen	..	..	466 (f)	..	..	..	..	..	..	..	..	..
Hamburg	..	..	982 (h)	..	..	6 600	1 461	605	2 066 (g)	..	..	..
Hesse	..	..	5 186 (i)	..	..	..	..	..	..	..	..	..
Lower Saxony	..	..	2 650 (j)	1 028	767	1 815	..	..	..	9 428	5 078	14 936
North Rhine-Westphalia	33 615 (k)	15 179	48 794	..	..	36 046	..	..	..	..	..	..
Rhineland-Palatinate	2 469	1 330	3 799 (l)	..	..	..	..	..	..	..	..	..
Saarland	251	50	301 (m)	..	..	67	..	..	..	594	294	888
Schleswig-Holstein	..	..	909 (n)	..	..	..	..	..	..	..	..	..

a) Most pupils in ICs are of Turkish origin (67 per cent of the pupils in these classes). Percentage of IMCs in ICs: 8.9.
b) The majority of BCs concern Greek pupils (76.8 per cent of all pupils enrolled in BCs).
c) 74.1 per cent of BC pupils are Turkish, which means that most BCs are German/Turkish classes.
d) In Bavaria, in 1981/82, 47.8 per cent of all IMCs were in induction or bilingual classes.

e) IMCs in ICs: 10.6 per cent.
f) IMCs in ICs: 5.1 per cent.
g) 88.5 per cent of IMCs in BCs are of Turkish origin.
h) IMCs in ICs: 14.6 per cent.
i) IMCs in ICs: 7.3 per cent.
j) IMCs in ICs: 3.7 per cent.
k) IMCs in ICs: 23.6 per cent.
l) IMCs in ICsL 16.9 per cent.
m) IMCs in ICs: 7 per cent.
n) IMCs in ICs: 7 per cent.

For some Member countries of the Council of Europe (Austria, Belgium, France, Sweden and Switzerland), the major objective of MTNCT is not now to facilitate resettlement in the event of a return home, but to facilitate integration in the host country, starting from the observation that knowledge of one's origins and identification with one's own culture are conducive to faster integration and avoid a generation gap for immigrants (E. Egger, 1985: 7).

MTNCT is organised in two ways: one provides MTNC tuition in the school itself either during normal school hours (parallel courses) or after school hours (semi-integrated courses); the other provides tuition outside the framework of normal teaching, in which case it may be given either on school premises or elsewhere. The two methods are distinguished by referring to integrated and non-integrated tuition (meaning included in the curriculum or not). The integrated courses are generally organised by the host country's local education authorities, while non-integrated courses are usually the sole responsibility of emigration countries and their consular authorities. This pattern mainly concerns primary education; it is much less common in secondary education since the study of modern languages provided for in the curriculum creates different conditions for MTNCT.

In **Belgium**, a distinction must be made between the Flemish- and French-speaking regimes. In the first case, since 1982, the integrated model tested in an EEC pilot experiment in Limburg is now being generally applied; it provides 4h/week of MTNCT (mother tongue and native culture tuition) in the first and second years, 3h/week in the third and fourth years and 2h/week in the fifth and sixth years. There are no integrated courses at secondary level.

Table 3

Germany: Forms of MINCT According to Land

	Integrated or Semi-integrated Tuition	Integrated
Bade Würtemberg		x
Bavaria	x (1)	
Berlin		x
Bremen		x
Hamburg		x
Hesse		x
Lower Saxony	x (1)(2)	
North Rhineland-Westphalia	x	
Rhineland-Palatinate	x	
Saarland		x
Schleswig-Holstein		x

1. Partly in BCs.
2. MINCT is in most cases relegated to the afternoons, when there are no classes for native children.

Integrated tuition is also accompanied by extracurricular coaching, but we have no figures of the number of pupils given either. Classes are generally provided for 4h/week on school premises.

In the French-speaking region, the integrated model was practised in a dozen primary and secondary schools in 1983. Extracurricular coaching was the rule, comprising 4h/week of MTNCT.

In <u>Germany</u>, as in the case of ICs, the organisation of MTNCT varies from one Land to another (Table 3).

The proportion of pupils provided with MTNCT is usually high and averages a third of the total number of IMCs. In some cases (Rhineland-Palatinate), it is not possible to distinguish between MTNCT and IC pupils, who are in principle taught in their mother tongue (Table 4).

Most of the courses are not integrated and are organised by the consular authorities outside normal school hours, i.e. in the afternoons (in Germany, schools function only in the mornings) or on Saturday mornings.

Table 4

Germany: IMCs Receiving Extracurricular MTNC Coaching, 1981/82

	Total Number of Foreign Pupils	% Pupils
Bade Würtemberg	110 029 (1)	58.3
Bavaria	21 134 (2)	69.2 (3)
Berlin	10 233	49.3
Bremen	..	..
Hamburg	21 236	22.0
Hesse	55 947	32.2
Lower Saxony	39 735 (4)	39.3 (5)
North Rhineland-Westphalia	224 647 (6)	44.2 (primary)
		53.9 (secondary)
Rhineland-Palatinate	8 512	60.0 (7)
Saarland	8 190	41.0
Schleswig-Holstein	..	..

1. For pupils aged 6 to 15.
2. In primary education and the Hauptschulen.
3. Including private education.
4. Only in integrated tuition.
5. Compared with all foreign pupils.
6. Primary and first cycle secondary.
7. Including IC pupils.

Source: EEC.

However, these courses usually take place on school premises put at the disposal of the consular authorities by the local authorities.

One issue which must be mentioned in connection with the development of MTNCT is the secondary school possibility of replacing the study of English (the first foreign language in Germany) by the mother tongue. Given the problems of equal opportunity and integration in the employment market, this tendency might compromise IMCs' chances of success. It must be pointed out, however, that the languages of the main emigration countries are taught practically everywhere and offered to all pupils, whether foreign or not, as optional third languages.

Table 5

France: Mother Tongue and Native Culture Tuition
1981-82

Nationality	Number of Pupils: Primary and Secondary	Integrated Tuition, Primary Only	Extra-curricular Tuition, Primary and Secondary Combined	Total (%)
Algerians	191 168	10 293	27 199	19.6
Moroccons	96 708	3 775	4 718	8.8
Tunisians	37 403	3 419	3 639	19.0
Spaniards	30 59	996	7 400	27.5
Italians Source EEC	21 637	8 149	2 256	48.0
Italian estimate		11 939	3 012	69.0
Portuguese Source EEC	148 450	16 664	21 047	25.5
Portuguese estimate		21 303	32 767	36.5
Turks	36 674	4 832	4 453	25.4
Yugoslavs	9 991	143	3 363	34.1

Secondary Level -- no figures available on the first or second modern language taught to foreign children.

Source: EEC, 1984 (FR) 5.

In France (Table 5), the two forms of MTNCT exist side by side. The integrated method (3h/week included in the 27-hour weekly timetable) is provided for children from countries which have signed bilateral agreements with France (Portugal, Italy, Tunisia, Spain, Morocco, Yugoslavia, Turkey and Algeria). In other cases, classes are held outside school hours (3h/week or more) under the joint responsibility of the French education authorities and the consular authorities.

The most frequently spoken immigrant languages are in theory offered as an option to all secondary school pupils, both as a first and a second language. In practice, the choice is limited by the availability of teachers. Thus, in Paris, only one school (first cycle secondary) offers Portuguese as a first foreign language, despite the large number of Portuguese pupils in the capital's schools.

In Luxembourg, MTNCT is mainly extracurricular and organised by the consulates representing the nationals who make up most of the immigrants (Italy and Portugal).

In the Netherlands, both models exist side by side. The Dutch authorities estimate that some 80 per cent of all foreign primary pupils receive MTNCT.

In the United Kingdom, it is interesting to note that MTNCT is still organised by the immigrant communities with varying forms of help from the local authorities. This was formerly the general situation which has almost disappeared on the continent. According to the EEC (1984: UK6), integrated MTNC tuition is only provided for 2.2 per cent of the pupils whose first language is not English.

In Switzerland too (Table 6), MTNCT is mainly organised at primary level. Less is available at secondary level in spite of a limited number of optional modern languages (usually the three national languages plus English). Apart from Italian, the other main immigrant languages are not taught in schools. The figures provided by the Italian authorities (Italians in Switzerland form the largest of the foreign communities) show a respectable level of participation by IMCs in MTNCT (nowhere less than a third attending such classes, with an average of around 50 per cent).

It is evident that most MTNCT is peripheral to school (see Table 7, for example), but it must also be added that it is not easy to organise the normal curriculum to include such classes if the authorities are not prepared to change the structural model on which schools are based.

Most of the difficulties raised by MTNCT stem from the special status of this activity: barely-recognised and accepted and sometimes tolerated rather than really encouraged. The main problems are as follows:

-- The excessive workload for children who have educational difficulties and whose material working conditions at home are generally unstable;

-- The competence of the teachers who take these classes; in most cases they are recruited by the emigration countries, are sent abroad with no special training, do not speak the host country's language and have a very different vocational training from the teachers in charge of the classes attended by IMCs;

-- The teaching material, especially textbooks, which comes from the emigration countries and is often of doubtful quality;

-- Pedagogical collaboration between the host country's education authorities and the consular authorities is often the barest minimum

Table 6

Mother Tongue and Native Culture Tuition in Switzerland
Number of Courses in the Primary Sector, 1980/81

Italian Consular Districts	Integrated Tuition Nb. of Courses	Semi-integrated Tuition Nb. of Courses	Extracurricular Tuition Nb. of Courses	IMCs % (1)
Zürich	20	41	218	46
Bern	42	87	32	64
St-Gall	28	110	–	–
Basle	12	86	27	75
Baden	7	61	–	30
Lucerne	44	–	–	70
Chur	6	35	3	80
Others	13	–	3	
Total German-speaking	172	420	283	
Neuchâtel (2)	6.1	75.8	18.2	69.8 (1452 pupils)
Lausanne (2)	3.3	37.0	59.7	37.7 (154 pupils)
Geneva (2)		66.0	34.0	41 (1326 pupils)

1. Percentage of pupils enrolled for courses compared with the total number of Italian IMCs at school.

2. The figures show the percentage of pupils taking the different courses.

Source: Centro pedagogico-didattico per la Svizzera, 1981.

or even non-existent. In any case, apart from a few pilot experiments (e.g. in Limburg), there is no link between the curriculum and the methods employed in the schools attended by IMCs and those practised in MTNCT;

-- The mix in MTNC classes, which include a wide variety of children with very different backgrounds (born in the host country, newly immigrated, etc.) and above all children whose familiarity with the language taught in these classes is very dissimilar: for some, it is their mother tongue and currently spoken at home; for others, it is a foreign language and completely unfamiliar; for others again, it is the official language of their home country but not at all the same as the dialect spoken at home. Added to this, these classes necessarily include children who come from different parts of the home country and only have their nationality in common;

-- The uniformity of the curricula sent out by home countries, with no adjustment for the special circumstances reigning in each host country.

In spite of these difficulties it must be admitted that MTNCT is enjoying a measure of success. The percentage of enrolments for these classes, which are not compulsory, is high and even very high for certain nationalities in some countries (see the case of Greece, Table 8). But no hasty conclusions should be drawn from this observation: their success often depends on such chance variables as the presence of an energetic and enthusiastic consul, the exceptional quality of some teachers, the cultural uniformity and vitality of the immigrant community, and the support of particularly understanding local authorities.

It is difficult to assess the effects of MTNCT on the education of IMCs. Besides, any evaluation of these programmes poses a problem since their aims are so ambiguous and vague. It is not surprising, therefore, that no assessments have been made. In 1983, at the Urbino Symposium on the education

Table 7

Portuguese Language and Culture Tuition by Type of Class

	Integrated Classes	Extracurricular Classes
France	945	1 454
Germany	145	733
Belgium	6	31
Netherlands	46	51
United Kingdom	8	44
Luxembourg	6	147
Switzerland	..	23

Source: Maria J. Sa Machado Marçal Grilo, CERI 1984, p. 28 (mimeo).

of IMCs organised by the Italian Ministry of Foreign Affairs, there was no lack of criticism and scepticism concerning the effectiveness of MTNCT: "there have been no substantial improvements except in the case of a few marginal initiatives of an experimental type", said the representative of the Italian emigration associations (Ministero Affari Esteri, 1983: 113). These reservations and comments are significant as they are made by representatives of a country which has committed itself heavily to the development of MTNCT during the last decade.

In the absence of sufficient valid research (for example, comparing the educational achievement of IMCs taking MTNCT with those not doing so, assessing progress in the mother tongue due to attendance at MTNC classes and measuring the educational benefit obtained), it is impossible to give a calm and collected opinion of MTNCT.

The problems raised by the organisation of MTNCT are of course complex and difficult to solve. It must be hoped that the progress observed in some areas will improve its efficiency. Examples worth mentioning are the pilot

Table 8

Greek Educational Structures and Enrolments Abroad, 1981/82

Type of Structure	Number of classes (1)	%	Enrolments (1)	%
Primary:				
Non-integrated mother tongue classes	1 105	84.73	64 165	69.85
Integrated mother tongue classes	49	3.75	11 169	12.16
Preparatory classes	70	5.36	4 766	3.52
Bilingual schools	69	5.29	7 518	8.18
Greek-only schools	11	0.84	4 231	5.5
First cycle secondary:				
Non-integrated classes	93	60.00	5 373	51.57
Integrated classes	20	12.90	1 044	10.02
Bilingual schools	36	23.22	1 900	18.23
Greek-only schools	6	3.80	2 070	19.87
High schools:				
Greek-only schools	14	63.63	2 345	81.47
Bilingual schools	6	27.27	385	13.37

1. All OECD immigration countries except Australia.

Source: S. Mappa, Country Review: Greece, ECALP, 1983, p. 10.

project funded by the EEC in Berlin to produce teaching material suitable for Turkish children living in that city, or the production by the Portuguese authorities of a special textbook for IMCs to help them with the Portuguese language and culture in place of the traditional textbooks used in schools in Portugal.

Progress has also been made in Germany, France, Sweden and Switzerland in training local primary teachers to understand IMCs problems and to supervise foreign teachers responsible for MTNCT.

Further extension of MTNCT is problematical, especially if its quality is to be improved. The costs could be very high and it may be wondered whether, given the present state of public finances countries would be prepared, in the absence of convincing proof, to make a further effort in this area.

III. OUTSIDE EUROPE: SIMILARITIES AND DIFFERENCES

An overview of the solutions adopted by OECD immigration countries outside Europe -- Australia, Canada, the United States -- reveals similarities with the European countries. As in Europe, the steps taken on behalf of pupils with an inadequate mastery of the language spoken in school have not transformed the general organisation of education. Induction initiatives (special curricula and "bilingual", "bicultural" and "multicultural" curricula) have been taken on the system's margin on behalf of special underprivileged populations or those concentrated in immigrant-dominated areas. For instance, the United States 1974 Bilingual Education Act describes the populations and schools concerned as follows: "An applicant school must enrol high concentrations of children from families whose income is below poverty levels, who receive benefits from the Aid to Families with Dependent Children Programme" (39 Fed. Reg. 1966, 1974). The school populations concerned are also designated as "educationally deprived", "culturally deprived" or "disadvantaged".

This terminology reveals the welfare tradition partly underlying multicultural education. This factor is less visible in Europe, being concealed by the question of a return home, but it is quite apparent outside Europe, where the central issue is the permanent insertion of immigrants in the host country.

The main difference from the European countries lies in the fact that the introduction of these curricula is not the result of negotiations between host countries and home countries. The non-interference of home countries in the educational policies adopted for IMCs stems from the existing legal differences between IMCs in Europe and those in Canada, Australia and the United States. While in Europe these children are the guests of the host country but citizens of their countries of origin, elsewhere they are almost all full citizens of the country they live in. Because of this, MTNCT is not associated with any return home but with integration in the new country. The wide variety of expressions used to describe this tuition -- teaching of the "heritage" language in Canada, "native" language in the United States, "community" language in Australia -- reflects the existence of a different philosophical approach on the one side, but leaves little doubt on the other concerning the integration of immigrant ethnic groups.

The political context of MTNCT is therefore very different from that in Europe. But it remains to be seen why similar curricula have been introduced in such different contexts and why the results obtained in both cases sometimes look alike or on the contrary differ.

MTNC classes have been introduced everywhere with the twofold aim of facilitating transition to the dominant language (English in all three countries) and preserving the mother tongue. The degrees of emphasis placed on these two aims have never been clearly determined. In most bilingual curricula in the United States, MTNCT has been developed in line with the transition to English; in several Canadian heritage language curricular, priority is given to preserving the mother tongue.

The American Bilingual Education Act defines the intentions of bilingual curricula as being to enable children with a limited knowledge of English to increase their skill in this language so as to be able to study both in English and in their mother tongue. The Australian School Commission's 1979-81 report recommends that schools be urged to develop bilingual education for pupils who enter the education system fluently speaking only a language other than English (SC, 1978: 105).

In Canada, MTNCT is part of the strategy introduced in 1974 to develop multicultural education. As stated by the Minister of State for Multiculturalism, J. Fleming, the teaching of heritage languages is an important strategy to adopt in the fight against racist and xenophobic mentalities and behaviour (quoted in J. Cummins, 1981: 12) (the heritage language being understood as the mother tongue).

In the United States too, an abundant controversial literature has emerged on the importance of bilingual curricula for "preserving the dignity", "self-image" or "self-esteem" of the populations concerned or as a means of blending ethnic groups into the community and building a creative pluralist society (W.P. Foster, 1976).

Induction Measures

The services introduced are similar to those existing in Europe: induction classes (IC), intensive language classes (ILC), bilingual classes (BC) and catch-up classes (CC). ICs -- found especially in Canada (Crespo and Pelletier, 1983) and Australia (Mills, 1982) -- have been mainly deployed in primary education, take pupils for short periods and are in principle mixed in the sense that the pupils come from different countries. Their aim is to teach the new arrivals the official language as quickly as possible so that they will have no problem in following tuition in the normal classes.

Transitional BCs have been the main solution adopted in the United States, where the time spent in the classes has been one of the most debated topics ever since the inception of bilingual education in this country. Since there are no precise criteria for deciding when the children should go into the normal classes, this transition is not properly timed. Moreover, difficulties not only occur downstream from the BCs but also upstream, as no clear criteria exist either to determine which pupils ought to go into them.

a) <u>Teachers</u>

Teacher training and recruitment and the production of teaching material are the responsibility of the host countries. The United States Bilingual Education Act stipulates special training for teachers for bilingual education (A. Leibowitz, 1980: 31). In 1978, it was estimated that 129 000 extra teachers would be needed for this purpose (A. Leibowitz, 1980: 63). As a result of this analysis, the House of Representatives

Table 9

United States: Bilingual Class Enrolments
Title VII Programmes 1969-83

Year	Number of Programmes	Participants	Languages	Fund ($ millions)
1969/70	76	26 521	14	7.5
1970/71	131	51 918	16	21.15
1971/72	164	83 748	16	25
1972/73	217	108 816	24	35
1973/74	209	129 380	30	45
1974/75	383	236 000	34	58
1975/76	381	268 500	47	85
1976/77	400	191 718	59	98
1977/78	425	259 364	67	115
1978/79	565	302 000	70	135
1979/80	565	350 000	79	158
1981/82	493	154 000 (1)	94	..
1982/83	555	218 000 (2)	106	..

1. Excluding 143 000 refugee children.
2. Excluding 112 000 refugee children.

Sources: <u>Bilingual Education: An Unmet Need</u>, Report to Congress by the Controller General's Office, May 19, 1976.

George Blanco, "The Education Perspective", in <u>Bilingual Education : Current Perspectives</u>, Vol. 4, Center for Applied Linguistics, 1977.

<u>Guide to Title VII Programs</u>, National Clearinghouse for Bilingual Education.

<u>The condition of Bilingual Education in the Nation, 1984</u>.
U.S. Department of Education, T.H. Bell, Secretary.

decided that at least 15 per cent of the budget for each local bilingual education programme must be set aside for in-service teacher training (Bilingual Education Act, 1978).

As in Europe, teacher training for these programmes is a problem. The findings of the 1976-77 Teachers' Language Skills Survey in the United States had revealed that only 34 000 teachers in the public schools (20 per cent of the total) had the academic and linguistic qualifications to teach bilingual curricula; of these, only one-third (13 000) used a different language from English in the classroom. It was confirmed that the remaining 21 000 with bilingual qualifications only used English as a medium of instruction. In 1980-81, of the 500 000 teachers (i.e. a quarter of all teachers in the country) who had children with a limited knowledge of English in their classes, 56 000 used another language besides English and 21 000 (36 per cent) had the necessary academic qualifications to teach in BCs (US Department of Education, 1984: 17-20). The same observation was made time and time again: staff skills for teaching in BCs were inadequate. Proof of this was provided by another survey carried out by the Office of Bilingual Education and Minority Languages Affairs in 1983 on the figures supplied by 19 States: only 28 per cent of the teachers dealing with pupils who had a limited knowlege of English had the necessary qualifications (A. Uhl Chamot, 1985). Similar charges are levelled in Australia, where there is such a shortage of bilingual teachers that only very few bilingual curricula have in fact been satisfactorily introduced in primary schools extent (J. Mills, 1982: 39 and 64).

Table 10

Quebec: Estimated Induction Class Enrolment, 1970/71 to 1981/82

Year	30th September	30th June
1970/71	0	338
1971/72	382	491
1972/73	531	644
1973/74	1 103	1 445
1974/75	1 492	2 508
1975/76	2 584	3 134
1976/77	1 995	2 270
1977/78	1 776	2 271
1978/79	2 008	2 654
1979/80	2 656	3 310
1980/81	2 907	3 344
1981/82	2 127	2 559

Source: M. Crespo et G. Pelletier, "Performance scolaire, intégration sociale et 'classes d'accueil' francophones pour jeunes immigrants. Analyse diachronique d'une expérience montréalaise (1974-1983)". Paper submitted to the first Conference of the Comparative Education Society in Europe, pp. 3-4, Würzburg, Germany.

b) <u>Numbers affected</u>

Data on the development of induction services are incomplete except for the United States, where the number of bilingual programmes has grown constantly since 1970, but the number of pupils concerned has also fallen appreciably since 1980-81 (Table 9). An estimated 2.4 million 5-to-14-year-old pupils have only a limited knowledge of English. Only 10 per cent of this group are in BCs. Over half the bilingual education programmes funded by the Federal authorities are located in three States (California, New York and Texas). Ten States have no programme of this kind.

Quebec shows a similar trend: sharp rise in induction class enrolments up to 1980/81 and a drop thereafter (Table 10). Any ill-considered comparison with the United States should be avoided since in Quebec this phenomenon only concerns IMCs, i.e. pupils on their first arrival in Canada whose status is not comparable with that of most American pupils enrolled in BCs, but the analogy between the two trends needs demonstrating nevertheless.

It is not possible to forecast the future trend of induction services in the three countries considered on the basis of this information.

<u>Mother Tongue and Native Culture Tuition (MTNCT)</u>

MTNCT (still using the terminology current in Europe) either takes place in classes integrated in the education system or in extracurricular classes as in Europe: the form of organisation is the same, although the public catered for is different. However, the main difference is institutional. In the United States, Canada and Australia, MTNCT is the result of negotiations between the social groups concerned (parents' associations, teachers, etc.) and the host country, with no third party (in this particular case, the home countries) intervening to determine methods of funding and organisation, as is the case in Europe. In Ontario, for example, schools which decide to respond to parents' demands for MTNCT are made financial grants (J. Bhatnagar, A. Hamalian, 1981: 234). As in Europe, MTNC classes are provided for children with a common origin. They are therefore only found in areas which have a large concentration of groups whose main language is not English (given the special situation of these three countries, it is very difficult to use words such as "foreigners" or "immigrants" to describe these groups and even the term "ethnic group" is not quite appropriate). There are reports of MTNCT programmes being introduced for all pupils in order to prevent the segregation of ethnic groups. They concern experiments in the United States, where a group of native English-speaking pupils are learning their immigrant schoolfellows' language, but these are few and far between.

Extracurricular classes (called ethnic schools in Australia) take pupils outside official school hours. As distinct from what happens in Europe (apart from the United Kingdom), these ventures are also run by the communities themselves (i.e. their associations or other non-governmental institutions). When public finance is needed, the latter apply to their local State authorities since most of their members are full citizens of the host countries. The Australian Government, for example, has since 1981 been granting all ethnic schools A$30 per pupil, providing these schools have been in existence for two years. In Australia, and Canada (but to a smaller extent), MTNCT is almost entirely privately organised.

A good illustration of the role of private initiative in the non-European OECD countries is provided by a comparison of the educational efforts made by the Greek communities in Australia, Canada and the United States with those made in Europe. In Canada, the primary extracurricular classes set up by Greek immigrants in 1981/82 represented 99.6 per cent of all Greek educational services at that level, 95.3 per cent in the United States and roughly 90 per cent in Australia. These classes were financed by the communities themselves with the help of subsidies of about 10 per cent from the host country, while Greek Government subsidies were very small. In 1981/82, 8.44 per cent of total Greek Government subsidies for the education of children abroad went to Greek schools in Australia, while Greek schools in Germany alone took 50.66 per cent of their total. In the same year, 93 per cent of the pre-primary school teachers in Germany were recruited by Greece, while in the United States only 12 per cent of the same category of teacher had the same status. The figures for primary school teachers are even more significant: again in 1981/82, 89.3 per cent of the Greek teachers in Germany, all of those in Belgium, the Netherlands, Luxembourg and Italy, 95.8 per cent of those in Switzerland, 85.2 per cent of their number in the Nordic countries and 81.8 per cent of those in France had been appointed by and depended on the Greek authorities; on the other hand, primary teachers recruited by Greece in that year only accounted for 2.95 per cent of their total in Canada, 1.12 per cent in Australia and 4.3 per cent in the United States.

This disparity raises questions about the different socio-political status of the immigrant communities. The general impression is that those who live in non-European countries are better integrated than those living in Europe and, thanks to their economic and cultural position, are able to organise MTNCT, but also to bring pressure to bear on their host country's government in order to obtain subsidies for their efforts or, better still, as in Canada, to demand that MTNCT be provided by the State schools. Differences within the communities are of course by no means negligible and have even increased with the economic depression. The communities are not uniform in their social class composition.

IV. CONCLUSION

The criticisms levelled at MTNCT in Europe are also found elsewhere: the observation is the same. MTNCT always poses a problem. The content of teacher training always includes the same ambiguities, the teaching material raises the same problems and there is the same gap between theory and practice. Proof of this is provided by the following extract from a statement by the Director of the Centro Scuola e Cultura Italiana in Toronto at a meeting on the teaching of heritage languages in Canada:

"Finally, after years of exerting pressure on the Minister, the Heritage Languages Program was announced. Initially, there was rejoicing among the community groups because they felt that now the programs could be implemented in the proper way and the problems could be resolved. However, we soon found that the problems were just beginning. First was the fact that this 'innovative' program was a part of continuing education. Certainly it was innovative insofar as it must have been the first time that 'continuing education' was given to children at the beginning of their educational careers rather than to adults. A second disappointment was that the heritage language classes were not considered a part of the school program. Later we found out that the teachers had no official status; they weren't called teachers, they were 'instructors'." (Quoted in J. Cummins, 1981: 19).

In Australia too, where MTNCT occupies an important place in the life of the ethnic communities in Australian society, questions concerning the quality of these classes and their institutional framework have been discussed for several years now. In particular, two of the most acute problems relate to the production of suitable curricula and textbooks, and teacher training.

As a rule, MTNCT suffers because of its ambiguous position in the curriculum due to the fact that it stands as a response to social, cultural and economic problems. In many cases, MTNCT is no more than a compensatory programme for the deprived children of communities that are less well integrated in the social structure; in other cases, it is merely the result of cultural conflicts fanned by economic discrimination, the rebirth of regionalism or the rediscovery of folklore. MTNCT is therefore much more important symbolically (it compensates certain rejected communities or is even a sign of the recognition of the importance of a community) than cognitively. In these circumstances, given the ambiguity of MTNCT objectives, it is not surprising that there are no assessments of its results except in the United States where, in order to settle the important political dispute over the development of bilingual education, figures had to be collected and collated to document the conflicting positions.

Australian, Canadian and American experience demonstrates, however, that bilingual education is possible, that it is not prejudicial to the pupils' intellectual development and that it builds up personal experience and above all a community's capital of expertise, know-how and knowledge. In view of this, bilingual education (which is one of the forms of MTNCT) can be a factor of cohesion in a society and strengthen the feeling of identification with common values instead of being a weakening factor which hinders social and cultural integration (J. Cummins, 1985).

BIBLIOGRAPHY

Berque, J. (1985): Eduquer les enfants de l'immigration. Rapport préliminaire au Ministre de l'Education nationale. Ministry of Education, Centre national de documentation pédagogique, Paris, May.

Bhatnagar, J., Hamalian, A. (1981): Educational opportunity for minority groupchildren in Canada, in J. Megarry et al. (eds.). World Yearbook of Education of Minorities, London and New York.

CEC, Commission of the European Communities (1984), "Report on the Implementation of Directive 77/486/EEC on the Education of the Children of Migrant Workers", COM(84)54 Final, Brussels, 10 February.

Cummins, J. (1981): Heritage language education: issues and directions. Proceedings of a Conference organised by the Multiculturalism Directorate of the Department of the Secretary of State. Saskatoon, June 1981. Ottawa.

Cummins, J. (1985): "Theory and policy in bilingual education". Paper presented at the National Seminar on Education in Multicultural Societies, Ljubljana, October.

Crespo, M., Pelletier, G. (1983): "Performance scolaire, intégration sociale et classes d'accueil francophones pour jeunes immigrants. Analyse diachronique d'une expérience montréalaise (1974-1983)". Paper submitted to the Comparative Education Society in Europe, Würzburg.

Egger, E. (1985): "L'éducation des migrants. Evolution de 1977 à 1984. Problèmes et tendances". Standing Conference of European Ministers of Education, 14th Session, Brussels, 7th-9th May.

Foster, N.P. (1976): "Bilingual education: An educational and legal survey", in Journal of Law Education, Vol. 5, No. 2, April.

Leibowitz, A. (1980): "The Bilingual Education Act: A legislative analysis", National Clearinghouse for Bilingual Education.

Mills, J. (1982): "Bilingual education in Australian schools", in Australian Education Review, No. 18.

Ministero Affari Esteri (1983): Acts of the conference on "La riforma della normativa italiana in materia di scolarizzazione dei figli degli emigrati e suo raccordo con le strutture della scuola e della cultura italiana all'estero". Urbino, 28th-30th March 1983. Istituto Poligrafico Italiano, Rome.

Programma paragogis didacticou optico-acousticou ylikou (Programme for the production of audiovisual didactic material for the teaching of Greek to the children of Greek immigrants in Germany), Ministry of Education, Athens, 1982-1983.

S.C. 1978: <u>School Commission Report for the Triennium 1979-1981</u>. Canberra.

SOU 1974: 69, 70 about the Swedish policy as regards immigration and immigrants. Stockholm.

SOU 1983: 57, English summary from the main report "Different origins -- Partnership in Sweden, Education for linguistic and cultural diversity". Stockholm.

Uhl Chamot, A. (1985): "ESL Literature Study", in FORUM, National Clearinghouse for Bilingual Education, Rosslyn, Va., Vol. III, n° 3, June-July.

U.S. Department of Education (1984): <u>The Condition of Bilingual Education in the Nation. A Report from the Secretary of Education to the President and the Congress</u>, Washington, D.C.

Annex 1

GRAPHS ON COMPARATIVE DEVELOPMENT OF NATIONALS AND
FOREIGNERS IN SCHOOLING

PRE-SCHOOL EDUCATION

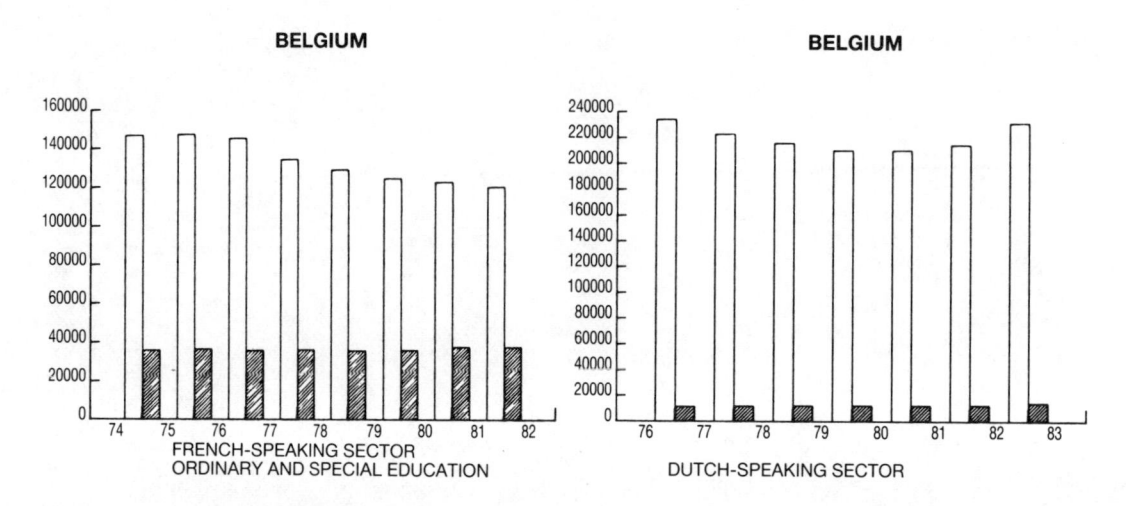

☐ NATIONALS
▨ FOREIGNERS

BELGIUM
FRENCH-SPEAKING SECTOR
ORDINARY AND SPECIAL EDUCATION

BELGIUM
DUTCH-SPEAKING SECTOR

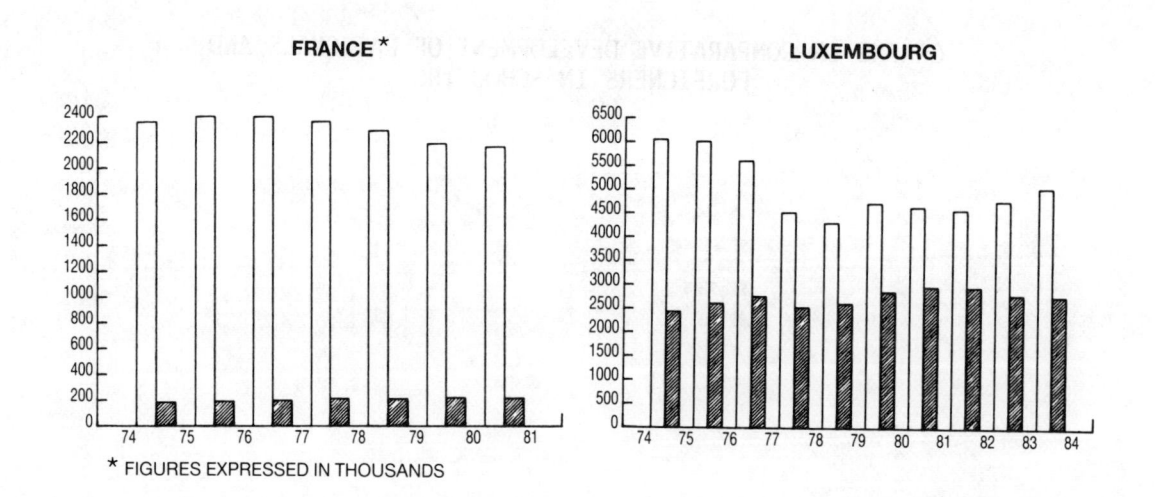

FRANCE *
* FIGURES EXPRESSED IN THOUSANDS

LUXEMBOURG

PRE-SCHOOL EDUCATION

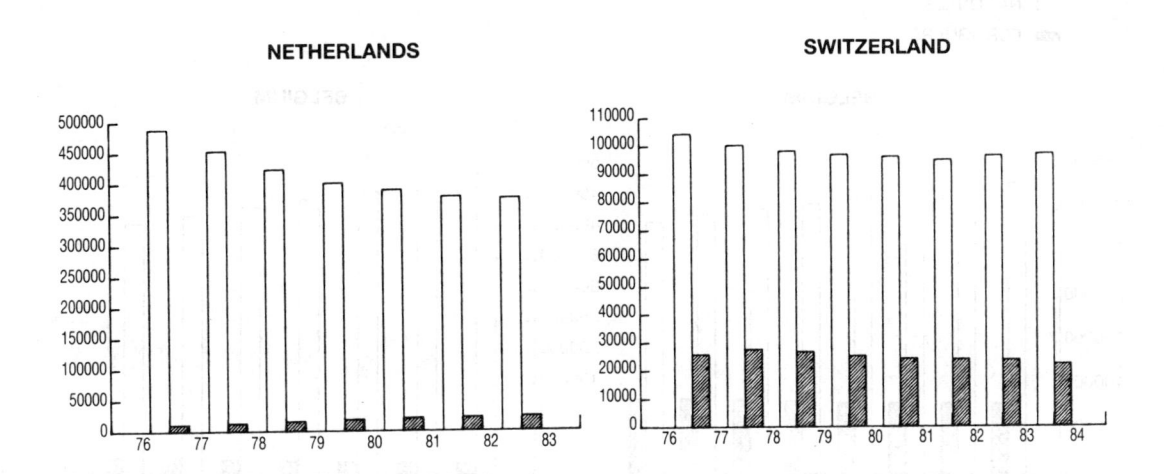

NETHERLANDS

SWITZERLAND

SWEDEN

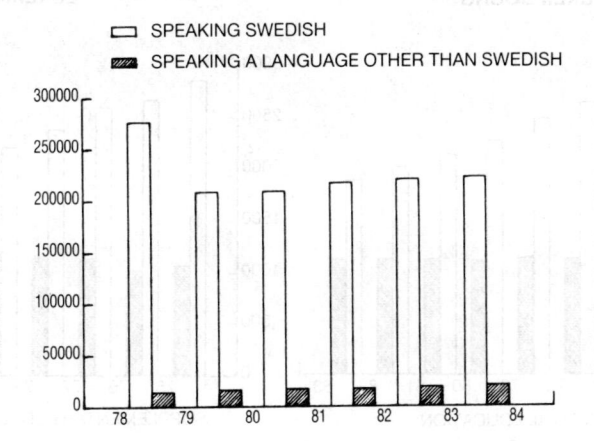

☐ SPEAKING SWEDISH
▨ SPEAKING A LANGUAGE OTHER THAN SWEDISH

PRIMARY EDUCATION

☐ NATIONALS
▨ FOREIGNERS

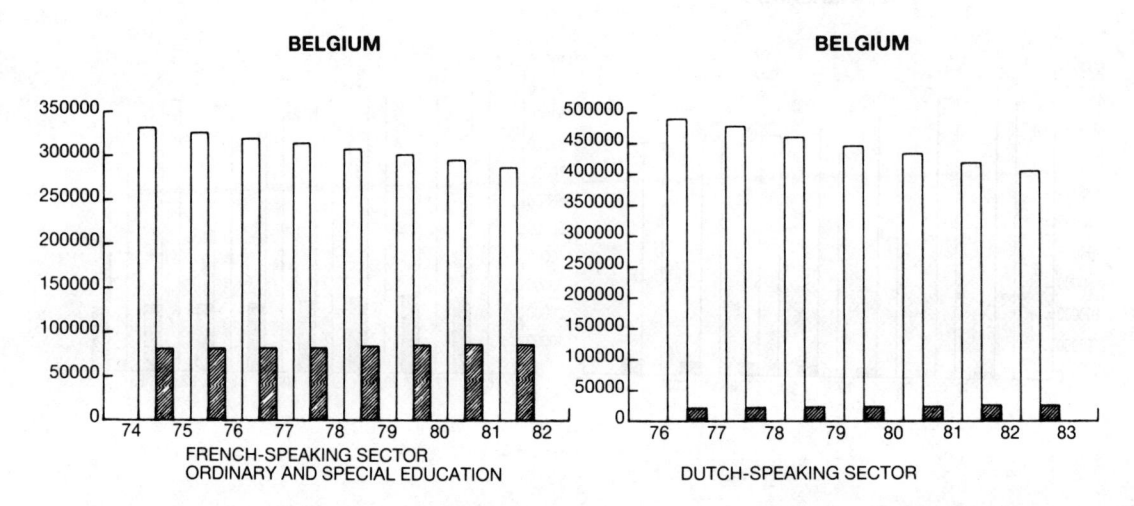

BELGIUM
FRENCH-SPEAKING SECTOR
ORDINARY AND SPECIAL EDUCATION

BELGIUM
DUTCH-SPEAKING SECTOR

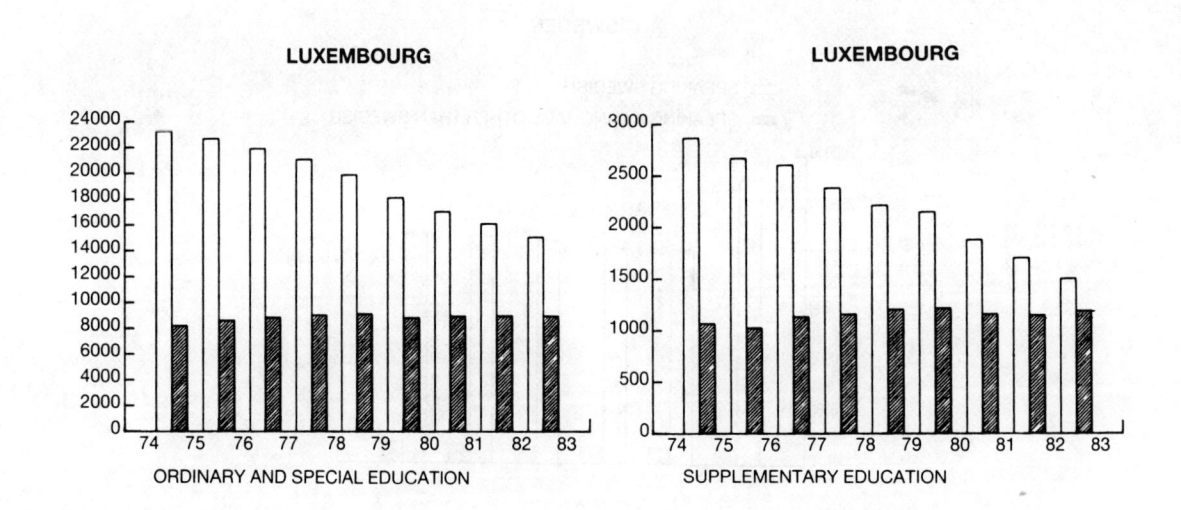

LUXEMBOURG
ORDINARY AND SPECIAL EDUCATION

LUXEMBOURG
SUPPLEMENTARY EDUCATION

PRIMARY EDUCATION

FRANCE *

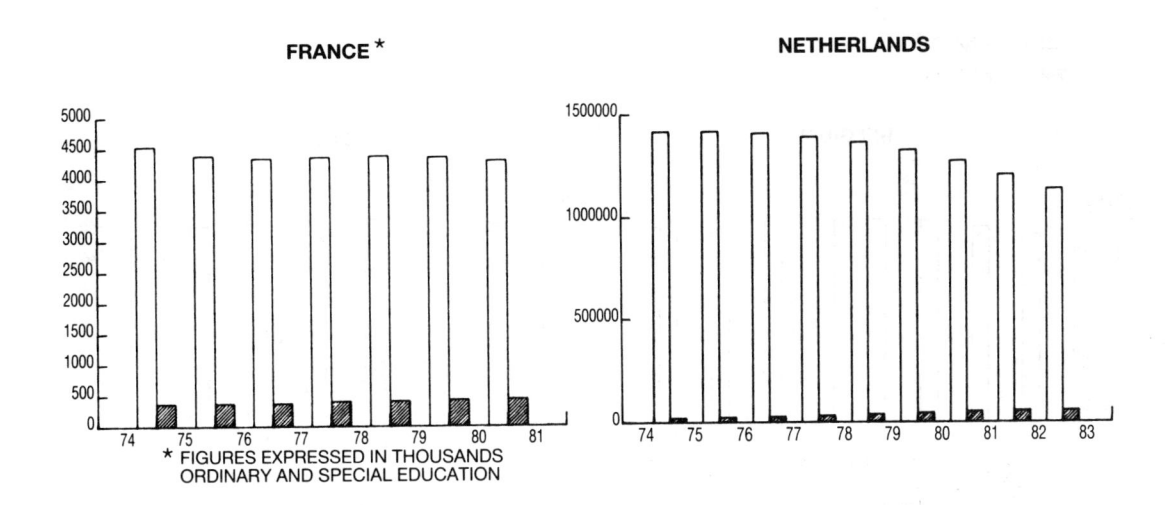

* FIGURES EXPRESSED IN THOUSANDS
ORDINARY AND SPECIAL EDUCATION

NETHERLANDS

SWITZERLAND

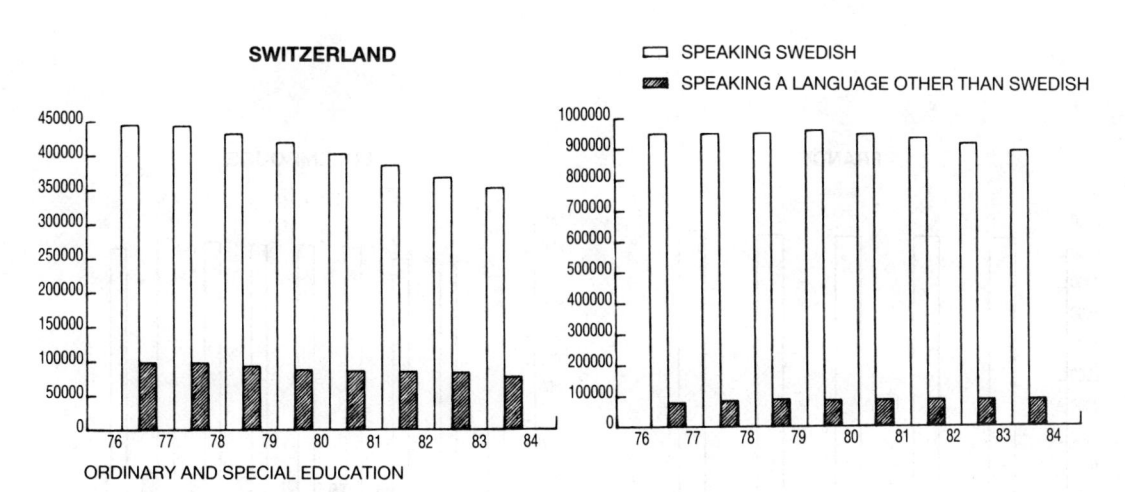

ORDINARY AND SPECIAL EDUCATION

SWEDEN

☐ SPEAKING SWEDISH
▨ SPEAKING A LANGUAGE OTHER THAN SWEDISH

291

SECONDARY EDUCATION

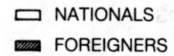

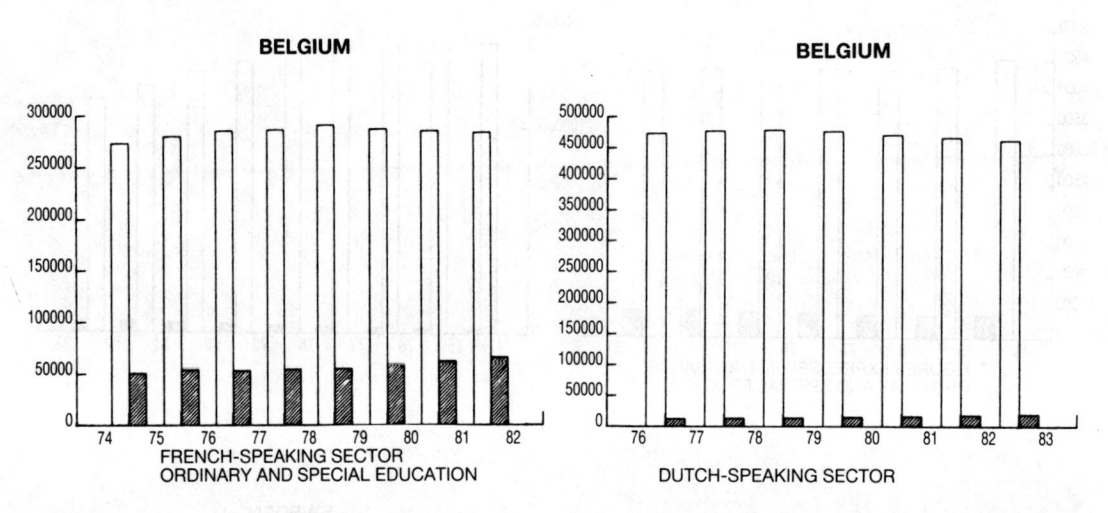

NATIONALS
FOREIGNERS

BELGIUM
FRENCH-SPEAKING SECTOR
ORDINARY AND SPECIAL EDUCATION

BELGIUM
DUTCH-SPEAKING SECTOR

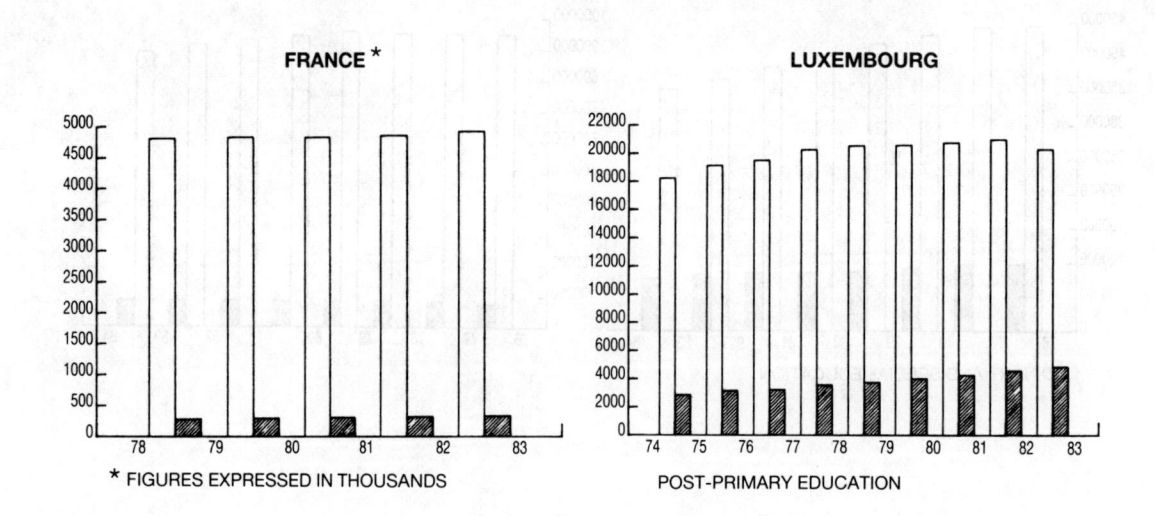

FRANCE *
* FIGURES EXPRESSED IN THOUSANDS

LUXEMBOURG
POST-PRIMARY EDUCATION

SECONDARY EDUCATION

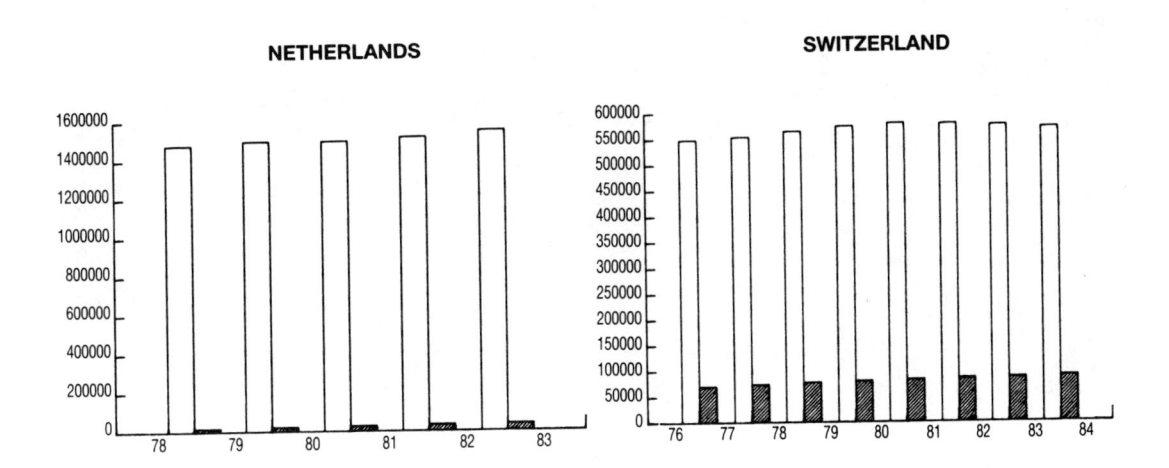

NETHERLANDS

SWITZERLAND

SWEDEN

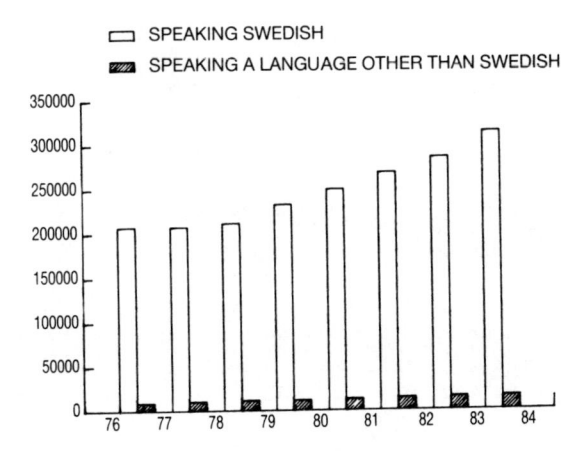

☐ SPEAKING SWEDISH
▨ SPEAKING A LANGUAGE OTHER THAN SWEDISH

Annex 2

GENERAL DATA ON FOREIGN POPULATIONS

Evolution of the foreign population in some European countries
from 1975 to 1982

	Germany (Thousands)			Belgium (Units)			France (Thousands)			Luxembourg (Units)		
	Total Population	Foreigners		Total Population	Foreigners		Total Population	Foreigners		Total Population	Foreigners	
Year	nb.	nb.	%	nb.	nb.	%	nb.	nb.	%	nb.	nb.	%
1975	61 829	4 090	6.6	9 778 200	805 400	8.2	52 600	3 442.4	6.5	357 400	88 300	24.5
1976	61 531	3 948	6.4	9 813 100	835 400	8.5	52 810	..	..	360 500	84 500	23.4
1977	61 400	3 948	6.4	9 823 302	851 601	8.7	52 973	3 518.9	6.9	361 000	84 000	23.2
1978	61 327	3 981	6.5	9 837 413	869 696	8.8	53 182	3 645.9	7.0	361 900	91 000	25.1
1979	61 359	4 144	6.7	9 841 654	876 577	8.9	53 372	3 567.8	6.9	362 300	92 100	25.3
1980	61 556	4 453	7.2	9 855 110	890 038	9.0	53 587	3 599.2	6.9	363 700	94 000	25.7
1981	61 682	4 630	7.5	9 863 374	903 736	9.2	53 838	3 636.7	7.0	365 100	95 789	26.3
1982	61 638	4 667	7.6	9 854 589	885 729	9.0	54 273	3 680.1	6.8	365 500	95 900	26.2

Sources: Germany: Statistisches Bundesamt, at 30 September of each year.
Belgium: Institut national de la Statistique, at 1st January of each year.
France: - In 1975 and 1982, INSEE, general census.
- From 1976 to 1981, INSEE, Enquête Emploi in March of each year.
Luxembourg: STATEC. Estimates, except for 1981 results of census.

Evolution of the foreign population in some European countries
from 1975 to 1982

Year	Netherlands (Thousands) Total Population nb.	Foreigners nb.	%	Sweden (Units) Total Population nb.	Foreigners nb.	%	Switzerland (Units) Total Population nb.	Foreigners nb.	%
1975	13 599.1	316.3	2.3	8 208 442	409 894	5.0	6 370 663	1 012 710	15.9
1976	13 733.6	350.3	2.6	8 236 179	418 016	5.1	6 327 192	958 599	15.2
1977	13 814.5	376.3	2.7	8 267 116	424 445	5.1	6 290 292	932 743	14.8
1978	13 897.9	399.8	2.9	8 284 437	424 188	5.1	6 286 649	898 062	14.3
1979	13 895.5	431.8	3.1	8 303 010	424 113	5.1	6 294 049	883 837	14.0
1980	14 091.0	473.4	3.4	8 317 937	421 667	5.1	6 311 705	892 807	14.1
1981	14 208.6	520.2	3.7	8 323 033	414 001	5.0	6 341 726	909 906	14.3
1982	14 285.8	537.6	3.8	8 327 484	405 475	4.9	6 384 349	925 826	14.5

Sources: Netherlands: Centraal Bureau voor de Statistiek, at 1st January of each year.
Sweden: Statistisk Arsbok, at 31st December of each year.
Switzerland: Office Fédéral de la Statistique, at 31st December of each year.

Total Population and Foreign Population by Age Group
(Most Recent Figures)
(in thousands)

Age Group	Belgium (1982) Total Population nb.	Foreigners nb.	%	Germany (1981) (a) Total Population nb.	Foreigners nb.	%	France (1982) Total Population nb.	Foreigners nb.	%	Luxembourg (1981) Total Population nb.	Foreigners nb.	%
0- 4 years	610.0	96.6	15.8	3 561.0	409.5	11.9	3 129	280	8.9	21	8.4	40.3
5- 9 years	644.2	92.9	14.4	2 604.0	326.0	12.5	3 821	341	8.9	21	8.6	40.6
10-14 years	718.3	88.6	12.3	4 638.0	360.0	7.8	4 283	327	7.6	25	8.0	32.0
15-19 years	794.5	80.5	10.1	4 268.5	218.0	5.1	4 362	278	7.6	28	7.4	26.6
Total Population	9 849.0	878.5	8.96	1 682.0 4 630.0	7.5	54 273	3 680	6.8	365	96.0	26.3

a) 0-5 years (and not 0-4 years); 6-9 years (and not 5-9 years); 15-18 years (and not 15-19 years)

Sources: Belgium: Census, 1981.
Germany: Statistisches Bundesamt, 30th September 1980
France: Census, 1982.
Luxembourg: Census, 1981.

Total Population and Foreign Population by Age Group
(Most Recent Figures)
(in thousands)

	Netherlands (1983)			Sweden (1983)			Switzerland (1983)		
Age Group	Total Population	Foreigners nb.	%	Total Population	Foreigners nb.	%	Total Population	Foreigners nb.	%
0- 4 years	883.5	68	7.7	475.0	32.5	6.8	360.0	57	15.9
5- 9 years	927.5	57	6.1	523.0	34.0	6.5	385.0	67	17.4
10-14 years	1 192.0	53	4.4	558.0	34.0	6.1	465.0	72	15.5
15-19 years	1 250.0	48	3.9	608.0	28.0	4.7	517.5	75	14.5
Total Population	14 339.5	546	3.8	8 237.5	405.5	4.9	6 384.0	926	14.5

Sources: Netherlands: Centraal Bureau voor de Statistiek, 1.1.83.
Sweden: Statistisk Arsbok, 31st December 1982.
Switzerland: Office Fédéral de la Statistique, 31.12.82.

Annex 3

ANALYSIS OF THE DATA DERIVED FROM THE THREE SAMPLES OF PUPILS USED IN THE FOREGOING STUDY IN FRANCE

Three samples (panels) were selected by SIGES at different periods to serve as the statistical basis for a more detailed observation of the educational progress of foreign schoolchildren compared with that of indigenous French children.

Much the same analysis procedure is adopted for each of the three samples: after a detailed description of the indigenous and foreign populations, broken down according to a certain number of socio-demographic and socio-economic characteristics [nationality, socio-economic category (SEC) of the head of the household, whether the mother works or not, level of education of the person responsible for the child] and "educational" characteristics (age on starting at primary school, duration of pre-school education, age on starting at secondary school), the progress of the foreign children over several years of schooling is examined by comparison with that of the indigenous children.

In the interests of a better approach to the educational observation of the indigenous and foreign populations, it seems worthwhile to review briefly the main demographic, socio-economic and socio-cultural characteristics of each of the two populations and hence to demonstrate the differences between them in each sample.

I. Analysis of the Sample of Secondary Pupils in 1972, 1973 and 1974 (referred to as the 1972-74 sample)

This survey covers 37 437 children enrolled in the first class of secondary education (sixième) in 1972, 1973 and 1974 and describes their performance at school to the end of their studies.

1. General data

    -- Total number of pupils entering sixième
        recorded in 1972, 1973 and 1974   34 437

        including: French pupils   34 941
                   Foreign pupils   2 496

        including: Foreign children born in France   1 315
                   Foreign children born abroad   1 181

There is no detailed breakdown by nationality for the foreign populations in this sample.

DIAGRAM OF THE SCHOOL SYSTEM IN FRANCE

2d long cycle 2d short cycle

General education Technical education

AGE									
18							TC		
17	SENIOR HIGH SCHOOL	TECHNICAL HIGH SCHOOL	MODERN SCHOOLS						
16	SENIOR HIGH SCHOOL	TECHNICAL HIGH SCHOOL	MODERN SCHOOLS	CES	A.2				SPECIAL EDUCATION
15	SENIOR HIGH SCHOOL		MODERN SCHOOLS	CES	A.2	A.3			
14	COMPREHENSIVE SCHOOL: 3TH GR.	TECHNICAL OPTIONS				A.3		PC	
13	COMPREHENSIVE SCHOOL: 4TH GR.	TECHNICAL OPTIONS			VC	A.3	PVC		
12	COMPREHENSIVE SCHOOL: 5TH GR.								
11	COMPREHENSIVE SCHOOL: 6TH GR.								
10	PRIMARY EDUCATION: SECOND MIDDLE LEVEL								INITIATION AND ADAPTATION COURSES
9	PRIMARY EDUCATION: FIRST MIDDLE LEVEL								
8	PRIMARY EDUCATION: SECOND ELEMENTARY LEVEL								
7	PRIMARY EDUCATION: FIRST ELEMENTARY LEVEL								
6	PRIMARY EDUCATION: FIRST GRADE								
5									
4	PRESCHOOL EDUCATION								SPECIAL SECTIONS
3									
2									

VC = Vocational certificate
A2 = Apprenticeship in 2 years
A3 = Apprenticeship in 3 years
TC = Apprenticeship in Training centre
PC = Preparatory Course
PVC = Pre-vocational Course

2. "Demographic" variables

a) Distribution of pupils according to parents' SEC

It is remarkable to note that almost three foreign pupils in four (especially where foreign children born abroad are concerned) come from a working class background, whereas only one indigenous French child in three comes from such a background (Table A).

Table A

Distribution of Pupils Enrolled in Secondary School
in 1972, 1973 and 1974 According to Nationality,
Place of Birth (Foreigners) and SEC of Head of Household

	All nb.	All %	French nb.	French %	Foreigners (All) nb.	Foreigners (All) %	Foreigners born in France nb.	Foreigners born in France %	Foreigners born abroad nb.	Foreigners born abroad %
Farmers	3 402	9.1	3 374	9.7	28	1.1	22	1.7	6	0.5
Farm workers	725	1.9	614	1.8	111	4.4	49	3.7	62	5.2
Entrepreneurs and top businessmen	681	1.8	660	1.9	21	0.8	13	0.9	8	0.7
Self-employed tradesmen and small businessmen	3 034	8.1	2 937	8.4	97	3.9	65	4.9	32	2.7
Senior management	3 541	9.5	3 455	9.9	86	3.5	37	2.8	49	4.1
Middle management	3 688	9.8	3 630	10.4	58	2.3	39	2.9	19	1.6
Clerical staff	3 693	9.9	3 607	10.3	86	3.5	50	3.8	36	3.1
Manual workers	14 523	38.8	12 771	36.6	1 752	70.2	886	67.4	866	73.3
Domestic staff	1 406	3.8	1 317	3.8	89	3.6	49	3.7	40	3.4
Other categories	851	2.3	846	2.4	5	0.2	1	0.1	4	0.3
Unemployed and various	1 893	5.1	1 730	4.9	163	6.5	104	7.9	59	4.9
Total	37 437	100.0	34 941	100.0	2 496	100.0	1 315	100.0	1 181	100.0

Source: SIGES (Service de l'Informatique de Gestion et de Statistiques du ministère de l'Education nationale).

Conversely, pupils from high-ranking and intermediate SECs are more likely to be numbered among the indigenous than the foreign populations; indeed the proportions accounted for by pupils whose father has a job in senior or middle management or is a clerical worker are 9.9, 10.4 and 10.3 per cent respectively among the former, but only 3.5, 2.3 and 3.5 per cent among the latter.

b) <u>Breakdown of pupils according to family size</u>

Here too some differences emerge between the French and foreign children: on the one hand, almost half the foreign children have at least four brothers and sisters, compared with only a quarter of the French children, and on the other hand, the average number of children is of the order of 3.2 in French families but 3.8 in the foreign families. (However, these average values bear no relation to the average number of children per woman -- an indicator more commonly found in demographic statistics -- because women having no children are also included in the calculation of this average, whereas the calculation here refers to school pupils, hence to children necessarily belonging to families with at least one child) (Table B).

Table B

Distribution of Pupils Enrolled in Secondary School in 1972, 1973 and 1974 According to Nationality and Size of Family

	All nb.	All %	French nb.	French %	Foreigners (All) nb.	Foreigners (All) %
1 child	3 036	8.1	2 916	8.4	120	4.8
2 children	9 423	25.2	9 022	25.8	401	16.1
3 children	9 221	24.6	8 777	25.1	444	17.8
4 children	5 980	15.9	5 569	15.9	411	16.5
5 children and over	9 566	25.6	8 453	24.2	1 113	44.6
Unknown	211	0.6	204	0.6	7	0.3
Total	37 437	100.0	34 941	100.0	2 496	100.0
Average number of children (1)	3.2		3.2		3.8	

1. In the calculation of the average number of children, the figure 5 has been assumed for five children and over, and no account is taken of unknowns; hence there is an underestimation of the average value, particularly among the foreigners, where the proportion with at least five children is around 50 per cent.

Source: SIGES.

3. "Educational" variables

a) Distribution of pupils according to the duration of their pre-school education (only for pupils whose father is an unskilled worker)

Whatever their nationality, the children of unskilled workers generally enjoyed a period of pre-school education lasting less than two years. But the incidence of place of birth is not without significance, to the extent that children having had pre-school education of less than one year or no pre-school education at all are much more numerous among the children born abroad than among those born in France (Table C).

Table C

Distribution of Pupils Enrolled in Secondary School in 1972, 1973 and 1974 According to Nationality, Place of Birth (Foreigners) and Duration of Pre-school Education

	All nb.	All %	French nb.	French %	Foreigners (All) nb.	Foreigners (All) %	Foreigners Born in France nb.	Foreigners Born in France %	Foreigners Born Abroad nb.	Foreigners Born Abroad %
No pre-school education	1 604	23.2	1 138	19.8	966	40.2	109	19.9	357	58.4
1 year	1 474	21.3	1 299	22.6	175	15.1	100	18.2	75	12.3
2 years	1 939	28.1	1 676	29.1	263	22.7	163	29.7	100	16.4
3 years and over	1 825	26.4	1 609	27.9	216	18.6	171	31.2	45	7.4
Duration unknown	72	1.1	33	0.6	39	3.4	5	0.9	34	5.6
Total	6 914	100.0	5 755	100.0	1 159	100.0	548	100.0	611	100.0
Average duration of pre-school education (1)	1.7		1.8		1.3		1.9		0.75	

1. In the calculation of the average duration of pre-school education, a value of 3.5 has been assumed for 3 years and over, and no account has been taken of unknowns.

Source: SIGES.

b) Distribution of pupils according to age on entering the first class of secondary education and associated streams (sixième normale or less demanding version [sixième allégée])

Twice as many foreign as French children enter the specially adapted sixième allégée option (also known as sixième de transition): of the 2 496 foreign children who entered the first class, 792 are in the less demanding stream (i.e. 31.7 per cent) whereas, of the 34 941 French pupils enrolled in the first class, only 5 979 are in that stream (17.1 per cent).

Similarly, the foreigners differ from the indigenous children in respect of age on starting the first class: slightly over 70 per cent of the foreign children were already aged at least 12 on starting the first class, as compared with 46 per cent of the indigenous children (Table D).

Table D

Distribution of Pupils Enrolled in Secondary School in 1972, 1973 and 1974 According to Nationality, Age on Intake in First Class and Stream
(6e Normale or 6e Allégée)

Age	All nb.	All %	French nb.	French %	Foreigners (All) nb.	Foreigners (All) %
All						
10 and under	1 914	5.1	1 873	5.4	41	1.6
11	17 719	47.3	17 032	48.7	687	27.5
12	15 409	41.2	14 117	40.4	1 292	51.8
13 and over	2 395	6.4	1 919	5.5	476	19.1
Total	37 437	100.0	34 941	100.0	2 496	100.0
6e normale						
10 and under	1 911	6.2	1 870	6.4	41	2.4
11	17 535	57.2	16 858	58.2	677	39.7
12	10 053	32.8	9 318	32.2	735	43.1
13 and over	1 167	3.8	916	3.2	251	14.7
Total	30 666	100.0	28 962	100.0	1 704	100.0
6e allégée						
10 and under	3	0.1	3	0.1	..	..
11	184	2.7	174	2.9	10	1.3
12	5 356	79.1	4 799	80.3	557	70.3
13 and over	1 228	18.1	1 003	16.7	225	28.4
Total	6 771	100.0	5 979	100.0	792	100.0

Source: SIGES.

c) Distribution of pupils according to previous primary schooling

Slightly more than one French pupil in two (51.1 per cent) has a normal record of primary education; this proportion drops to one in three among the foreign children (31.1 per cent). The difference has less to do with repeat years (36 per cent of the population of each category) than with alternative course options, which are followed by three times the number of children among the foreigners (especially those born outside France) compared with the indigenous children (Table E).

Table E

**Previous Primary Schooling of Pupils Enrolled in
The First Class of Secondary School in 1972, 1973, 1974**

	All		French		All Foreigners		Born in France		Born Abroad	
	nb.	%	nb.	%	nb.	%	nb.	%	nb.	%
Normal schooling	18 600	49.7	17 823	51.1	777	31.1	483	36.7	294	24.9
One repeat	13 627	36.4	12 724	36.4	903	36.2	555	42.2	348	29.5
Bypass other than CM2	1 114	2.9	1 007	2.9	107	4.3	41	3.1	66	5.6
Bypass of CM2	1 581	4.2	1 344	3.8	237	9.5	112	8.5	125	10.6
Other routes (1)	2 515	6.7	2 043	5.8	472	18.9	124	9.4	348	29.5
Total	37 437	100.0	34 941	100.0	2 496	100.0	1 315	100.0	1 181	100.0

1. Including unreconstituted or incompletely reconstituted schooling.

<u>Source</u>: SIGES, DT308.

II. The Sample of Primary School Pupils Surveyed in 1978
(referred to as the 1978 sample)

This sample, which supplies information on the demographic, socio-cultural and educational characteristics of 17 438 pupils enrolled in the first grade of primary education in the 1978/79 school year, makes it possible to examine more closely the educational results of the French and foreign pupils throughout their progress through primary education.

1. General data

```
-- Total number of pupils starting in the first
   grade primary education in 1978/79              17 438

   including:  French pupils                       16 007
               Foreign pupils                       1 431

   including:  Foreign children born in France       914 (63.9%)
               Foreign children born abroad          517 (36.1%)
```

breakdown by nationality:

-- Maghreb	666 (46.5%)
-- Portugal	414 (28.9%)
-- Other Europeans	200 (14.0%)
-- Rest of the world	151 (10.6%)

2. "Demographic" and socio-cultural variables

a) Distribution of pupils according to the SEC of the head of the household

Table F shows that the father of over one pupil in two belongs to the "Unskilled Workers" category, whereas hardly one indigenous pupil in four is in this situation, and that conversely the proportion of children of senior and middle management and clerical staff is considerably higher among the French pupils than among the foreigners. This is of crucial importance in understanding and evaluating the educational data; it does in fact show that children from disadvantaged backgrounds are less successful at school than the others.

Table F

Distribution of French and Foreign Pupils Entering CP in 1978
According to SEC of Head of Household

	French nb.	%	Foreigners nb.	%
Farmers	827	5.2	3	0.2
Farm workers	158	0.9	33	2.3
Entrepreneurs and businessmen	1 411	8.8	35	2.4
Senior management	1 536	9.6	23	1.6
Middle management	2 226	13.9	24	1.7
Clerical staff	1 847	11.6	33	2.3
Shop-floor supervisor and skilled workers	3 137	19.6	281	19.7
Unskilled workers	2 892	18.1	817	57.1
Domestic staff	543	3.4	52	3.6
Other categories	461	2.9	4	0.3
Unemployed and various	934	5.8	125	8.7
Total	15 972	100.0	1 430	100.0

Source: SIGES, document 5311: Monitored sample of primary school pupils (1978 Panel).

b) Distribution of pupils according to the level of education of the person responsible for the child

With regard to the level of education of the person responsible for the child, the pattern is similar to that for the distribution according to socio-economic categories, to the extent that the foreigners -- particularly the North Africans and the Portuguese -- are more likely to be of a primary standard and the indigenous subjects to be of a standard higher than primary (Table G).

Table G

Level of Education of Persons Responsible for the Children Entering CP in 1978, All SECs Together

	French		Foreigners		Maghreb		Portugal		Other Nat.	
	nb.	%	nb.	%	nb.	%	nb.	%	nb.	%
Primary level	5 637	35.3	675	47.2	309	46.4	230	55.6	136	38.7
Level better than primary	6 494	40.7	109	7.6	24	3.6	14	3.4	71	20.2
Illiterate	16	0.1	106	7.4						
Don't know	3 825	23.9	540	37.8						
Total	15 972	100.0	1 430	100.0	666	100.0	414	100.0	351	100.0

Sources: For the French, SIGES, document 5311.
For the foreigners, SIGES, DT309.

c) Distribution of pupils according to place of birth

Three quarters of the Portuguese children and two thirds of the North Africans were born in France, whereas over four pupils in five from countries outside Europe were born abroad (Table H).

d) Distribution of pupils according to family size

Compared with the 1972-74 sample, the differences linked to family size between French and foreign pupils increase: indeed the average number of children per family for the French pupils dropped from 3.2 in 1972-74 to 2.6 in 1978, whereas for the foreign pupils it has remained unchanged (3.8 for the two samples).

Almost a quarter of the foreign families have at least six children (40.8 per cent in the North African families), whereas the corresponding proportion of French families is barely 5 per cent. Looked at in reverse, the majority of indigenous families limit themselves to one child (16.1 per cent) or two children (41 per cent) (Table I).

Table H

Distribution of Pupils Enrolled in CP in 1978/79 According to Place of Birth

	Foreigners		Maghreb		Portugal		Other Europe		Rest of the World	
	nb.	%	nb.	%	nb.	%	nb.	%	nb.	%
Born in France	914	63.8	437	65.6	313	75.6	143	71.5	21	13.9
Born abroad	517	36.2	229	34.4	101	24.4	57	28.5	130	86.1
Total	1 431	100.0	666	100.0	414	100.0	200	100.0	151	100.0

Source: SIGES, DT309.

e) Distribution of pupils according to mother's occupational activity

Another socio-economic indicator is relevant with regard to the difference between the two populations studied: whether the mother works or not. Thus it emerges from Table J below that more than three foreign children in four have a mother who does not work, while this is only the case for slightly more than one French child in two.

Here, nationality is the crucial factor: the proportions of pupils whose mother has a job are 4.7 per cent for the North Africans, 31.4 per cent for the Portuguese, 22.5 per cent for the rest of Europe and 17.2 per cent for the rest of the world.

3. "Educational" variables

a) Distribution of pupils according to duration of pre-school education

The foreign pupils seem to have spent less time in pre-school education than the French pupils: the proportions of children having had no pre-school education or having undergone only one year of pre-school education are, respectively, 8.1 and 17.4 per cent for the foreign children, compared with 1.3 and 10.7 per cent for the French children (Table K).

One of the main explanatory factors appears to be the point at which the child became resident in France, since among the foreign pupils born in France 16.8 per cent had had no pre-school education or had had only one year, while among those born abroad the corresponding proportion jumps to 43.7 per cent.

Table I

Distribution of Pupils Enrolled in CP in 1978/79
According to Size of Family, All SECs Together

	French nb.	French %	Foreigners nb.	Foreigners %	Maghreb nb.	Maghreb %	Portugal nb.	Portugal %	Other Europe nb.	Other Europe %	Rest of the World nb.	Rest of the World %
1 child	2 562	16.1	83	5.8	10	1.5	41	9.9	22	10.9	10	6.6
2 children	6 523	41.1	281	19.6	54	8.1	131	31.6	70	35.1	26	17.2
3 children	3 612	22.7	283	19.8	96	14.4	90	21.7	56	28.1	41	27.2
4 children	1 350	8.5	225	15.7	120	18.1	56	13.5	13	6.5	36	23.8
5 children	613	3.9	148	10.3	89	13.4	24	5.8	13	6.5	22	14.6
6 children and over	740	4.6	342	23.9	272	40.8	38	9.2	21	10.5	11	7.3
Unknown	489	3.1	69	4.8	25	3.8	34	8.2	5	2.5	5	3.3
Total	15 889	100.0	1 431	100.0	666	100.0	414	100.0	200	100.0	151	100.0
Average number of children (1)		2.6		3.8		4.6		3.0		2.9		3.5

1. In the calculation of the average number of children, the figure 6 has been assumed for six children and over, and no account is taken of unknowns. Hence, there is a slight underestimation of the average values, particularly among the North Africans, where 40.8 per cent of the pupils belong to families with at least six children.

Sources: For the French, SIGES, document 5311.
For the foreigners, SIGES, DT309.

b) <u>Distribution of pupils according to age on enrolment in the first grade of primary education</u>

On average the foreign pupils, particularly those born abroad, start primary school later than the French pupils. As is shown by Table L, this phenomenon is no doubt linked to the time the child arrived in France.

III. <u>Analysis of the Sample of Secondary Pupils Surveyed in 1980</u>
(referred to as the 1980 sample)

The intention of this cohort study is to record not only the main sociological indicators but also the educational progress of 20 321 pupils from their enrolment in the first class of secondary education in 1980.

Table J

Distribution of Pupils Enrolled in CP in 1978/79 According to Mother's Occupational Activity, All SECs Together

	French nb.	%	Foreigners nb.	%	Maghreb nb.	%	Portugal nb.	%	Other Europe nb.	%	Rest of the World nb.	%
Mother works	6 883	42.9	232	16.2	31	4.7	130	31.4	45	22.5	26	17.2
Mother doesn't work	9 124	57.1	1 199	83.8	635	95.3	284	68.6	155	77.5	125	82.8
Total	16 007	100.0	1 431	100.0	666	100.0	414	100.0	200	100.0	151	100.0

Table K

Distribution of Pupils Enrolled in CP in 1978/79 According to the Duration of the Pre-school Education, All SECs Together

	French nb.	%	Foreigners nb.	%	Maghreb nb.	%	Portugal nb.	%	Other Europe nb.	%	Rest of the World nb.	%
No pre-school education	209	1.3	116	8.1	62	9.3	13	3.1	14	7.1	27	17.9
1 year	1 716	10.7	249	17.4	98	14.7	79	19.1	28	13.9	44	29.1
2 years	4 133	25.9	416	29.1	180	27.1	140	33.8	60	30.1	36	23.8
3 years	7 836	49.1	508	35.5	250	37.5	146	35.3	83	41.5	29	19.2
4 years	1 748	10.9	99	6.9	61	9.2	22	5.3	11	5.5	5	3.3
Duration unknown	330	2.1	43	3.1	15	2.2	14	3.4	4	1.9	10	6.6
Total	15 972	100.0	1 431	100.0	666	100.0	414	100.0	200	100.0	151	100.0
Average duration of pre-school education (1)	2.6		2.2		2.2		2.2		2.2		1.6	

1. In the calculation of the average duration of pre-school education, no account has been taken of unknowns.

Sources: For the French, SIGES, document 5311.
For the foreigners, SIGES, DT309.

The particular feature of this sample, compared with the 1972-74 sample, is that there is a detailed breakdown of the foreigners by nationality for most of the demographic, sociological and educational indicators.

1. <u>General data</u>

    -- Total number of pupils starting secondary school
       in 1980   20 321

       Including: French pupils   18 838
                      Foreign pupils   1 483

       including: Foreign pupils born in France 750
                      Foreign children born abroad   733

         breakdown by nationality:
                Maghreb   605
                Spain   124
                Portugal   446
                Europe, others   169
                Rest of the world   139

2. <u>"Demographic" variables</u>

    a) <u>Distribution of the pupils according to SEC of the head of the household</u>

Of the pupils of foreign nationality, 72.4 per cent belong to the "Manual Workers" category: only 3.8 per cent of them fall into the "Senior Management and Professions" category.

As is shown by Table M the distribution within the "Manual Workers" population of the North African and Portuguese pupils is fairly similar to that of the foreign pupils as a whole: a higher proportion of them than of the indigenous pupils and pupils from European countries other than Portugal come from the less favoured socio-economic backgrounds: skilled workers, unskilled workers, manual workers with no indication of skill.

Conversely, "Manual Workers" children from European countries other than Portugal show a similar distribution to that of French children belonging to the same category.

    b) <u>Distribution of pupils according to size of family</u>

The number of brothers and sisters is markedly higher among the foreign pupils than among the French children: 47.6 per cent of the former have at least four brothers and sisters compared with 14.4 per cent of the latter and, conversely, 17.8 per cent of the foreigners have no more than one brother or sister compared with 45.2 per cent of the French children (Table N).

The young North Africans are by far the most likely to belong to families of at least five children: 76.2 per cent of them have at least four brothers and sisters.

Table L

Age on Entering CP of Pupils in the 1978 Intake

	French		Foreigners		Foreigners born in France		Foreigners born abroad	
	nb.	%	nb.	%	nb.	%	nb.	%
Age less than 6	445	2.8	5	0.3	3	0.3	2	0.4
Age between 6 and 7	15 317	95.8	1 292	90.5	876	95.7	416	81.2
Age over 7	227	1.4	131	9.2	37	3.9	94	18.4
Total	15 989	100.0	1 428 (1)	100.0	916	100.0	512	100.0

1. The age on entry to CP of three pupils is not known.

Source: SIGES, DT309.

c) Distribution of pupils according to SEC of the head of the household and size of family

The data summarized in Table P show a very strong correlation among the pupils starting secondary school in 1980 between the size of their family and the SEC of the head of the household; in fact, independently of the "nationality" variable, large families are to be found in particular among skilled and unskilled workers, whereas families with one or two children remain the province of the advantaged socio-economic categories.

A significantly higher proportion of foreign children than indigenous children come from large families and from humble socio-economic backgrounds: all SECs taken together, 47.6 per cent of the foreigners have at least four brothers or sisters, whereas this is only the case for 14.5 per cent of the French children; and among the skilled tradesmen and unskilled workers the corresponding proportions are, respectively, 47.8 and 63.4 per cent for the foreigners and 21.1 and 40.5 per cent for the French children.

d) Distribution of pupils according to place of birth

There is an even distribution between the foreign pupils born in France (50.6 per cent) and those born abroad (49.7 per cent) (Table Q).

But some differences emerge when we look at the distribution by nationality: slightly over 60 per cent of the North African pupils were born

Table M

Detailed Distribution of Pupils Enrolled in the First Class of Secondary School in 1980 Belonging to the Unskilled Worker Category

	French		Foreigners		Maghreb		Spain		Portugal		Other Europe		Rest of the World	
	nb.	%	nb.	%	nb.	%	nb.	%	nb.	%	nb.	%	nb.	%
Shop-floor supervisor	904	13.7	44	4.1	13	2.9	8	9.1	13	3.4	9	10.1	1	1.4
Skilled workers	2 757	41.9	316	29.4	95	21.6	37	42.1	128	33.2	38	42.2	18	25.4
Unskilled workers	1 785	27.1	379	35.3	154	35.1	26	29.5	155	40.2	21	23.3	23	32.4
Seamen and miners	179	2.7	14	1.3	11	2.5	..	..	1	0.3	2	2.2	..	..
Labourers	220	3.4	134	12.5	74	16.9	6	6.8	34	8.8	6	6.6	14	19.7
Workers with no indication of skill	731	11.1	187	17.4	92	20.9	11	12.5	55	14.2	14	15.6	15	21.1
Workers, Total	6 576	100.0	1 074	100.0	439	100.0	88	100.0	386	100.0	90	100.0	71	100.0

Source: SIGES, DT297. Pupils of foreign nationality who entered the first class in 1980. Data taken from the Survey of pupils in the Secondary Education Panel, enrolment 1980.

Table N

Detailed Distribution of Pupils Enrolled in the First Class of Secondary School in 1980 According to Nationality and Size of Family

	French nb.	French %	Foreigners nb.	Foreigners %	Maghreb nb.	Maghreb %	Spain nb.	Spain %	Portugal nb.	Portugal %	Other Europe nb.	Other Europe %	Rest of the World nb.	Rest of the World %
1 child	2 000	10.6	62	4.2	6	0.9	7	5.6	30	6.7	11	6.5	8	5.8
2 children	6 513	34.6	202	13.6	18	2.9	24	19.4	102	22.9	42	24.8	16	11.5
3 children	5 214	27.7	279	18.8	44	7.3	42	33.9	109	24.4	51	30.2	33	23.7
4 children	2 384	12.7	234	15.8	76	12.6	23	18.5	71	15.9	36	21.3	28	20.1
5 children and over	2 727	14.4	706	47.6	461	76.2	28	22.6	134	30.1	29	17.2	54	38.9
Total	18 838	100.0	1 483	100.0	605	100.0	124	100.0	446	100.0	169	100.0	139	100.0
Average number of children (1)	2.8		3.9		4.6		3.3		3.4		3.2		3.7	

1. In the calculation of the average number of children, the figure 5 has been assumed for five children and over. Hence the underestimation of the average value, especially for the foreigners among whom the North Africans stand out in particular.

Source: SIGES, DT297.

Table P

Links Between Size of Family and SEC of Head of Household According to Nationality Among Pupils Enrolled in the First Class of Secondary School in 1980

	French										Foreigners							
	All SECs		Skilled Workers		Unskilled Workers		Labourers				All SECs		Skilled Workers		Unskilled Workers		Labourers	
	nb.	%	nb.	%	nb.	%	nb.	%			nb.	%	nb.	%	nb.	%	nb.	%
1 child	2 000	10.6	291	10.6	124	6.9	12	5.5			62	4.2	12	3.8	15	4.1	6	4.5
2 children	6 513	34.6	842	30.5	462	25.9	37	16.8			202	13.6	52	16.5	50	13.2	21	15.7
3 children	5 214	27.7	841	30.5	519	29.1	35	15.9			279	18.8	73	23.1	68	17.8	24	17.9
4 children	2 384	12.7	384	13.9	302	16.9	47	21.4			234	15.8	59	18.7	65	17.2	27	20.1
5 children and over	2 727	14.5	399	14.5	378	21.2	89	40.5			706	47.6	120	37.9	181	47.8	109	63.4
Total	8 838	100.0	2 757	100.0	1 785	100.0	220	100.0			1 483	100.0	316	100.0	379	100.0	134	100.0

in France, and the proportion is even slightly higher for the Spanish children and the Europeans other than Portuguese; on the other hand, 61 per cent of the Portuguese children were born in their country of origin, and almost all the children from the rest of the world were born abroad (94.2 per cent).

e) Distribution of pupils according to whether or not their mother works

The mothers of 20.9 per cent of the foreign pupils, compared with 42.9 per cent of the French children, have a job. But this overall rate conceals situations which vary greatly from one nationality to another: the mothers of 5.4 per cent of the North African children go out to work compared with corresponding figures of 34.4 per cent for the Portuguese children and 32.5 per cent for the Spanish children (Table R).

The majority of working mothers of foreign children fall into the "Domestic Service" category, French mothers tending to belong to other socio-economic categories (clerical and managerial staffs).

3. "Educational" variables

a) Distribution of pupils according to duration of pre-school education

The children of foreign nationality born in France should have been able to benefit from pre-school education on equal terms with their French counterparts, whereas this is not the case for those born abroad.

Overall 26.5 per cent of the foreign children had no pre-school education (compared with 8.1 per cent of the French children) and 30.4 per cent had three or more years of pre-school education (compared with 43.0 per cent of the French children).

Disregarding the "Rest of the World" category (Table S), the Portuguese children form the group of foreigners with the least pre-school education (28.5 per cent had none, and 20.6 per cent had only one year): this is explained by the fact that 60.9 per cent of the Portuguese children were born in their country of origin.

b) Distribution of pupils according to previous performance in primary education

Only 37.4 per cent of the foreign pupils underwent a normal course of primary education, whereas this is the case for 65.6 per cent of the French children (Table T).

The Spanish children and Europeans other than Portuguese show the best educational results among the foreign children (about 50 per cent achieved normal primary school performance).

c) Distribution of pupils according to age on starting in the first class of secondary education

The age on starting secondary school reflects the results achieved by the children during their primary education: 36.3 per cent of the foreign children are aged 11 or less on enrolment in the first class (compared with

Table Q

Detailed Distribution of Pupils Enrolled in the First Class of Secondary
School in 1980 According to Nationality and Place of Birth

	Foreigners		Maghreb		Spain		Portugal		Other Europe		Rest of the World	
	nb.	%	nb.	%	nb.	%	nb.	%	nb.	%	nb.	%
Born in France	750	50.6	372	61.5	85	68.5	174	39.1	111	65.7	8	5.8
Born abroad	733	49.4	233	38.5	39	31.5	272	60.9	58	34.3	131	94.2
Total	1 483	100.0	605	100.0	124	100.0	446	100.0	169	100.0	139	100.0

Source: SIGES, DT297. Pupils of foreign nationality who entered the first class in September 1980. Data taken from the Survey of pupils in the Secondary Education Panel, 1980 intake.

67.1 per cent of French children). The corresponding proportion is about 50 per cent for the Spanish children and Europeans other than Portuguese (Table U).

On the other hand, 27.1 per cent of the foreign children are aged at least 13 (8.8 per cent of French children). This proportion rises to 31.4 per cent for the North African children and 36 per cent for children from the rest of the world.

Table R

Detailed Distribution of Pupils Enrolled in the First Class of Secondary School in 1980 Belonging to the Unskilled Worker Category

	French nb.	French %	Foreigners nb.	Foreigners %	Maghreb nb.	Maghreb %	Spain nb.	Spain %	Portugal nb.	Portugal %	Other Europe nb.	Other Europe %	Rest of the World nb.	Rest of the World %
Mother works	7 173	42.9	278	20.9	29	5.4	37	32.5	144	34.4	35	22.7	33	31.1
Mother doesn't work	9 526	57.1	1 054	79.1	511	94.6	77	67.5	274	65.6	119	77.3	73	68.9
Total (1)	16 699	100.0	1 332	100.0	540	100.0	114	100.0	418	100.0	154	100.0	106	100.0
Occupation of working mother:														
Unskilled worker	771	10.7	81	29.1	4	..	6	..	53	36.8	9	..	9	..
Domestic	1 289	18.1	144	51.8	13	..	24	..	87	60.4	10	..	10	..
Other SEC	5 113	71.3	53	19.1	12	..	7	..	4	2.8	16	..	14	..
Total	7 173	100.0	278	100.0	29	..	37	..	144	100.0	35	..	33	..

1. The difference between these figures and those of the previous tables is explained by the fact that unknowns have not been taken into account.

Source: SIGES, DT297.

Table S

Detailed Distribution of Pupils Enrolled in the First Class of Secondary School in 1980 According to Nationality and Duration of Pre-school Education

	French nb.	French %	Foreigners nb.	Foreigners %	Maghreb nb.	Maghreb %	Spain nb.	Spain %	Portugal nb.	Portugal %	Other Europe nb.	Other Europe %	Rest of the World nb.	Rest of the World %
No pre-school education	1 523	8.1	393	26.5	145	23.9	17	13.7	127	28.5	26	15.4	78	56.1
1 year	3 250	17.3	251	16.9	95	15.7	11	8.9	92	20.6	34	20.1	19	13.7
2 years	4 921	26.1	285	19.2	91	15.1	32	25.8	96	21.5	51	30.2	15	10.8
3 years	6 903	36.6	402	27.1	203	33.6	48	38.7	96	21.5	45	26.6	10	7.2
4 years	1 214	6.4	49	3.3	31	5.1	9	7.2	9	2.1	-	-	-	-
Unknown	1 027	5.5	103	6.9	40	6.6	7	5.6	26	5.8	13	7.7	17	12.2
Total	18 838	100.0	1 483	100.0	605	100.0	124	100.0	446	100.0	169	100.0	139	100.0
Average duration of pre-school education (1)	2.2		1.6		1.8		2.2		1.4		1.7		0.6	

1. Unknowns have not been taken into account in the calculation of the average duration of pre-school education.

Source: SIGES, DT297.

Tableau T

Detailed Distribution of Pupils Enrolled in the First Class of Secondary School in 1980 According to Nationality and Duration of Pre-school Education

	French		Foreigners		Maghreb		Spain		Portugal		Other Europe		Rest of the World	
	nb.	%	nb.	%	nb.	%	nb.	%	nb.	%	nb.	%	nb.	%
Normal primary schooling	12 355	65.6	554	37.4	210	34.7	63	50.8	170	38.1	80	47.3	31	22.3
1 repeat year	4 526	24.1	459	30.9	205	33.9	35	28.2	157	35.2	46	27.2	16	11.5
At least 2 rep. years	1 288	6.8	186	12.5	92	15.2	15	12.1	62	13.9	14	8.3	3	2.2
Initiation class	40	0.2	52	3.5	17	2.8	4	3.2	10	2.2	3	1.8	18	12.9
At least one year of schooling abroad and other routes	629	3.3	232	15.6	81	13.4	7	5.6	47	10.5	26	15.4	72	51.8
Total	18 838	100.0	1 483	100.0	605	100.0	124	100.0	446	100.0	169	100.0	139	100.0

Source: SIGES, DT297.

Tableau U

Age on Intake to the First Class of Secondary School of Pupils in the 1980 Secondary Panel

Age	French nb.	%	Foreigners nb.	%	Maghreb nb.	%	Spain nb.	%	Portugal nb.	%	Other Europe nb.	%	Rest of the World nb.	%
10 and under	861	4.6	17	1.1	4	0.7	1	0.8	3	0.7	2	1.2	78	5.1
11	11 765	62.5	522	35.2	186	30.7	60	48.4	154	34.5	85	50.3	37	26.6
12	4 561	24.2	542	36.5	225	37.2	41	33.1	171	38.3	60	35.5	45	32.4
13 and over	1 651	8.8	402	27.1	190	31.4	22	17.7	118	26.5	22	13.1	50	35.9
Total	18 838	100.0	1 483	100.0	605	100.0	124	100.0	446	100.0	169	100.0	139	100.0

Source: SIGES, DT297.

OECD SALES AGENTS
DÉPOSITAIRES DES PUBLICATIONS DE L'OCDE

ARGENTINA - ARGENTINE
Carlos Hirsch S.R.L.,
Florida 165, 4° Piso,
(Galeria Guemes) 1333 Buenos Aires
Tel. 33.1787.2391 y 30.7122

AUSTRALIA-AUSTRALIE
D.A. Book (Aust.) Pty. Ltd.
11-13 Station Street (P.O. Box 163)
Mitcham, Vic. 3132   Tel. (03) 873 4411

AUSTRIA - AUTRICHE
OECD Publications and Information Centre,
4 Simrockstrasse,
5300 Bonn (Germany)   Tel. (0228) 21.60.45
Local Agent:
Gerold & Co., Graben 31, Wien 1 Tel. 52.22.35

BELGIUM - BELGIQUE
Jean de Lannoy, Service Publications OCDE,
avenue du Roi 202
B-1060 Bruxelles   Tel. (02) 538.51.69

CANADA
Renouf Publishing Company Ltd/
Éditions Renouf Ltée,
1294 Algoma Road, Ottawa, Ont. K1B 3W8
Tel: (613) 741-4333
Toll Free/Sans Frais:
Ontario, Quebec, Maritimes:
1-800-267-1805
Western Canada, Newfoundland:
1-800-267-1826
Stores/Magasins:
61 rue Sparks St., Ottawa, Ont. K1P 5A6
Tel: (613) 238-8985
211 rue Yonge St., Toronto, Ont. M5B 1M4
Tel: (416) 363-3171
Sales Office/Bureau des Ventes:
7575 Trans Canada Hwy, Suite 305,
St. Laurent, Quebec H4T 1V6
Tel: (514) 335-9274

DENMARK - DANEMARK
Munksgaard Export and Subscription Service
35, Nørre Søgade, DK-1370 København K
Tel. +45.1.12.85.70

FINLAND - FINLANDE
Akateeminen Kirjakauppa,
Keskuskatu 1, 00100 Helsinki 10 Tel. 0.12141

FRANCE
OCDE/OECD
Mail Orders/Commandes par correspondance :
2, rue André-Pascal,
75775 Paris Cedex 16
Tel. (1) 45.24.82.00
Bookshop/Librairie : 33, rue Octave-Feuillet
75016 Paris
Tel. (1) 45.24.81.67 or/ou (1) 45.24.81.81
Principal correspondant :
Librairie de l'Université,
12a, rue Nazareth,
13602 Aix-en-Provence   Tel. 42.26.18.08

GERMANY - ALLEMAGNE
OECD Publications and Information Centre,
4 Simrockstrasse,
5300 Bonn   Tel. (0228) 21.60.45

GREECE - GRÈCE
Librairie Kauffmann,
28, rue du Stade, 105 64 Athens Tel. 322.21.60

HONG KONG
Government Information Services,
Publications (Sales) Office,
Beaconsfield House, 4/F.,
Queen's Road Central

ICELAND - ISLANDE
Snæbjörn Jónsson & Co., h.f.,
Hafnarstræti 4 & 9,
P.O.B. 1131 – Reykjavik
Tel. 13133/14281/11936

INDIA - INDE
Oxford Book and Stationery Co.,
Scindia House, New Delhi I   Tel. 45896
17 Park St., Calcutta 700016   Tel. 240832

INDONESIA - INDONÉSIE
Pdii-Lipi, P.O. Box 3065/JKT.Jakarta
Tel. 583467

IRELAND - IRLANDE
TDC Publishers - Library Suppliers,
12 North Frederick Street, Dublin 1.
Tel. 744835-749677

ITALY - ITALIE
Libreria Commissionaria Sansoni,
Via Lamarmora 45, 50121 Firenze
Tel. 579751/584468
Via Bartolini 29, 20155 Milano Tel. 365083
Sub-depositari :
Editrice e Libreria Herder,
Piazza Montecitorio 120, 00186 Roma
Tel. 6794628
Libreria Hœpli,
Via Hœpli 5, 20121 Milano   Tel. 865446
Libreria Scientifica
Dott. Lucio de Biasio "Aeiou"
Via Meravigli 16, 20123 Milano Tel. 807679
Libreria Lattes,
Via Garibaldi 3, 10122 Torino   Tel. 519274
La diffusione delle edizioni OCSE è inoltre
assicurata dalle migliori librerie nelle città più
importanti.

JAPAN - JAPON
OECD Publications and Information Centre,
Landic Akasaka Bldg., 2-3-4 Akasaka,
Minato-ku, Tokyo 107   Tel. 586.2016

KOREA - CORÉE
Kyobo Book Centre Co. Ltd.
P.O.Box: Kwang Hwa Moon 1658,
Seoul   Tel. (REP) 730.78.91

LEBANON - LIBAN
Documenta Scientifica/Redico,
Edison Building, Bliss St.,
P.O.B. 5641, Beirut   Tel. 354429-344425

MALAYSIA - MALAISIE
University of Malaya Co-operative Bookshop
Ltd.,
P.O.Box 1127, Jalan Pantai Baru,
Kuala Lumpur   Tel. 577701/577072

NETHERLANDS - PAYS-BAS
Staatsuitgeverij
Chr. Plantijnstraat, 2 Postbus 20014
2500 EA S-Gravenhage   Tel. 070-789911
Voor bestellingen: Tel. 070-789880

NEW ZEALAND - NOUVELLE-ZÉLANDE
Government Printing Office Bookshops:
Auckland: Retail Bookshop, 25 Rutland Street,
Mail Orders, 85 Beach Road
Private Bag C.P.O.
Hamilton: Retail: Ward Street,
Mail Orders, P.O. Box 857
Wellington: Retail, Mulgrave Street, (Head
Office)
Cubacade World Trade Centre,
Mail Orders, Private Bag
Christchurch: Retail, 159 Hereford Street,
Mail Orders, Private Bag
Dunedin: Retail, Princes Street,
Mail Orders, P.O. Box 1104

NORWAY - NORVÈGE
Tanum-Karl Johan
Karl Johans gate 43, Oslo 1
PB 1177 Sentrum, 0107 Oslo 1Tel. (02) 42.93.10

PAKISTAN
Mirza Book Agency
65 Shahrah Quaid-E-Azam, Lahore 3 Tel. 66839

PORTUGAL
Livraria Portugal,
Rua do Carmo 70-74, 1117 Lisboa Codex.
Tel. 360582/3

SINGAPORE - SINGAPOUR
Information Publications Pte Ltd
Pei-Fu Industrial Building,
24 New Industrial Road No. 02-06
Singapore 1953   Tel. 2831786, 2831798

SPAIN - ESPAGNE
Mundi-Prensa Libros, S.A.,
Castelló 37, Apartado 1223, Madrid-28001
Tel. 431.33.99
Libreria Bosch, Ronda Universidad 11,
Barcelona 7   Tel. 317.53.08/317.53.58

SWEDEN - SUÈDE
AB CE Fritzes Kungl. Hovbokhandel,
Box 16356, S 103 27 STH,
Regeringsgatan 12,
DS Stockholm   Tel. (08) 23.89.00
Subscription Agency/Abonnements:
Wennergren-Williams AB,
Box 30004, S104 25 Stockholm.
Tel. (08)54.12.00

SWITZERLAND - SUISSE
OECD Publications and Information Centre,
4 Simrockstrasse,
5300 Bonn (Germany)   Tel. (0228) 21.60.45
Local Agent:
Librairie Payot,
6 rue Grenus, 1211 Genève 11
Tel. (022) 31.89.50

TAIWAN - FORMOSE
Good Faith Worldwide Int'l Co., Ltd.
9th floor, No. 118, Sec.2
Chung Hsiao E. Road
Taipei   Tel. 391.7396/391.7397

THAILAND - THAILANDE
Suksit Siam Co., Ltd.,
1715 Rama IV Rd.,
Samyam Bangkok 5   Tel. 2511630

TURKEY - TURQUIE
Kültur Yayinlari Is-Türk Ltd. Sti.
Atatürk Bulvari No: 191/Kat. 21
Kavaklidere/Ankara   Tel. 25.07.60
Dolmabahce Cad. No: 29
Besiktas/Istanbul   Tel. 160.71.88

UNITED KINGDOM - ROYAUME-UNI
H.M. Stationery Office,
Postal orders only:
P.O.B. 276, London SW8 5DT
Telephone orders: (01) 622.3316, or
Personal callers:
49 High Holborn, London WC1V 6HB
Branches at: Belfast, Birmingham,
Bristol, Edinburgh, Manchester

UNITED STATES - ÉTATS-UNIS
OECD Publications and Information Centre,
2001 L Street, N.W., Suite 700,
Washington, D.C. 20036 - 4095
Tel. (202) 785.6323

VENEZUELA
Libreria del Este,
Avda F. Miranda 52, Aptdo. 60337,
Edificio Galipan, Caracas 106
Tel. 32.23.01/33.26.04/31.58.38

YUGOSLAVIA - YOUGOSLAVIE
Jugoslovenska Knjiga, Knez Mihajlova 2,
P.O.B. 36, Beograd   Tel. 621.992

Orders and inquiries from countries where Sales Agents have not yet been appointed should be sent to:
OECD, Publications Service, Sales and Distribution Division, 2, rue André-Pascal, 75775 PARIS CEDEX 16.

Les commandes provenant de pays où l'OCDE n'a pas encore désigné de dépositaire peuvent être adressées à :
OCDE, Service des Publications. Division des Ventes et Distribution. 2. rue André-Pascal. 75775 PARIS CEDEX 16.

70595-03-1987

OECD PUBLICATIONS, 2, rue André-Pascal, 75775 PARIS CEDEX 16 - No. 43937 1987
PRINTED IN FRANCE
(96 87 02 1) ISBN 92-64-12954-5